W9-CAO-204

A12900 376263

ILLINOIS CENTRAL COLLEGE
PS3545.E8315Z517
STACKS
Hide and seek;

A12900 376263

48475

PS
3545      WEST
.E8315    Hide and seek
Z517

WITHDRAWN

Illinois Central College
Learning Resources Center

# Hide and Seek

*Other books by Jessamyn West*

The Friendly Persuasion

A Mirror for the Sky

The Witch Diggers

Cress Delahanty

Love, Death, and the Ladies' Drill Team

To See the Dream

Love Is Not What You Think

South of the Angels

A Matter of Time

Leafy Rivers

Except for Me and Thee

Crimson Ramblers of the World, Farewell

Jessamyn West

# Hide and Seek

## A Continuing Journey

ILLINOIS CENTRAL COLLEGE
LEARNING RESOURCES CENTER

Harcourt Brace Jovanovich, Inc.

New York

48475

PS
3545
E8315
Z517

Copyright © 1973 by Jessamyn West
All rights reserved. No part of this publication may be
reproduced or transmitted in any form or by any means,
electronic or mechanical, including photocopy, recording,
or any information storage and retrieval system,
without permission in writing from the publisher.
First edition

The lines from Jorge Luis Borges's poem "Limits"
are from *A Personal Anthology,* copyright © 1967 by
Grove Press, Inc., and are reprinted by permission
of Grove Press, Inc.
The lines from "Earth Dweller" by William Stafford
are from *Allegiances,* copyright © 1967 by
William Stafford, and are reprinted by permission
of Harper & Row, Publishers, Inc.

ISBN 0–15–140215–9
Library of Congress Catalog Card Number: 72–88797
Printed in the United States of America
B C D E

*For my brother*
Myron  Eldo  West
*who endured me on the earliest journeys*
*and*
*for my husband*
Harry  Maxwell  McPherson
*who kept the tradition on our continuing journeys*

# Hide and Seek

# I

I drove my husband to the Mesquite airport at ten this morning. Usually when Max is with me I don't drive. But this morning, because I wanted to remember which turns to make after he is gone, I drove. Telling means very little to me. I have to learn by doing.

At the airport the weather reports from Vegas were so bad that the pilot, who was to have flown the small Cessna there, said that if this were an emergency flight he would attempt it. Otherwise not. No emergency: Max was homeward-bound, while I stay on here for a time. Then, said the pilot, why not fly to San Francisco by way of Phoenix? It's a little out of the way, but connections could be made. Phoenix to Los Angeles by United. Los Angeles to San Francisco by a PSA commuter flight. Home to Napa by the car left in the San Francisco airport parking lot. No sweat for anybody, and the weather at Phoenix fine for flying.

While Max and the pilot canceled one set of flight plans and made new ones, I looked at the men behind the counter. They were pilots, mechanics, maybe a bookkeeper. They looked like cowboys to me because of the way they were dressed; but this is desert, not cow country. The young black man on my side of the counter, who had arrived with a tank of gas for the planes, said, "Your husband's got a nice personality. He's got what I would call a winning personality."

"You size up people in a hurry."

"I'm majoring in psychology down at Tempe."

I was quiet, listening to hear whether Max could get the new flight.

"You don't disagree with me, do you?"

"Now, you've had enough psychology to know I'm not going to say so if I do."

"Yeh," the truck driver said, "I have."

"I've agreed with you for forty years."

"You agreed with me before I was born."

"Well, I'm glad I lived long enough to tell you."

The pilot hung up the phone.

"Bruce always wanted to be a lawyer," the truck driver told me, glancing at the pilot. "He stopped flying for Pan Am so he could go back to college. Now he's gone back to flying again."

"What happened to the lawyer idea?"

"He had to give it up. Went down to Tempe, fell in love, and got married."

"He should have put his wife to work. That's the way doctors and lawyers pay for their education nowadays."

"That's the way I'm paying for mine. Hazel's teaching. But Bruce's wife got pregnant."

"You're luckier than Bruce."

"I'm carefuler. Hazel don't fail the pill, and the pill don't fail Hazel. I've got twelve more units to go on my B.S. at Tempe."

Max and Bruce came around from behind the counter and joined us.

"Would you like to fly down to Phoenix?" Bruce asked me. "No extra cost. You've hired the plane. It seats three. Maybe a little rough coming back, but not enough to bother, I think."

"Come on," Max said. "We'll be flying low enough to see everything. And air roughness doesn't bother you."

4

It doesn't; but I was eager to get the pain of parting over. I'd been saying good-bye since the day before, downhearted and sorrowful; and not liking myself because I knew that once the parting was a fact, I'd be swept with the delicious joy that solitude brings me.

It is always so: sob at Sacramento; step on the Vista Dome, and two hours later, as the train rolls upward through the Feather River Canyon, a deer on the slope above looks me straight in the eye and tears are forgotten. In the fervor of my bliss I pray for the deer's safety: "Let no bullet touch you."

Max makes these decisions for me. I can't leave. I can be left. I can be sent on my way. What is it I fear?

The four of us—the pilot, the truck driver, Max, and I—walk out onto the dusty field.

"You sure you don't want to go as far as Phoenix?" Bruce asks. "You've hired the plane."

I shake my head.

"By the time I get to Phoenix," he sings.

Max kisses me good-bye. He and Bruce climb in. The plane taxis past us.

"Wave good-bye, wave good-bye," the truck driver shouts to me reproachfully. He is waving. I wave.

Then we are left alone, the plane nothing but a dragonfly in the enormous, bleached-blue sky.

"Good-bye," I tell the young man.

I have disappointed him. He would not have neglected to wave to Hazel. He seems a lonesome fellow—big, burly, and at the same time soft.

"So long," he says shortly: a woman who does not deserve a good-bye.

I make all the proper turns, get to the bridge that crosses the river, make the short right turn there, and so to the gate, which is kept closed to keep the wild burros out. Through the gate I park on the slope behind the trailer.

The trailer is very neat and bright, filled with books and

flowers and pictures. The skull of a coyote. A mud hen's feather. It is also very empty. Which is why, I suppose, I am here.

Alone isn't the whole of the magic. That's possible in any hotel bedroom with a good lock on the door. But alone where no one is near, in a landscape that is both beautiful and frightening. Yes, a little fear is part of the attraction. Who would ever run away to a sea that couldn't drown you? You run away from danger; you run away to danger. What danger? The most attractive is the unknown. Alone in an unknown, solitary place.

Thoreau is the world's hero for living alone in a solitary place, though Thoreau's solitude has been exaggerated. There were few days when he didn't have visitors or himself walk the mile and a half that separated his woodland cabin from the village of Concord in nineteenth-century Massachusetts.

It took Henry David Thoreau twenty-eight years to get to his cabin on Walden Pond. It has taken me longer to get to mine on the Colorado. Thoreau had no good words to say for travel. "It is not worth the while," he said, "to go round the world to count the cats in Zanzibar." Yet this man who couldn't travel sat in his attic reading travel books and copying into his commonplace book page after page by those who had gone, for whatever purpose, to Zanzibar; enough quotations so that a book of 700 pages called *Thoreau as World Traveler* has been written about this stationary man.

Why couldn't he travel?

In *Walden,* Thoreau, writing of the myth of Momus and Minerva, says, "As I understand it, that was a valid objection urged by Momus against the house which Minerva made, that 'she had not made it movable.' "

Thoreau admired all people with movable houses: Indians with their wigwams; Arabs with their tents; Gypsies with their caravans. Travel was a way of living for them. The tree Thoreau really loved, was really nailed to, was a rooftree.

6

I sit alone here under a rooftree in the kind of house Thoreau recommended: one that is movable. Thoreau, ahead of his time in so much, was ahead of his time in this. What he needed, what he asked for, was a travel trailer. That was Minerva's mistake: she built a house without wheels. I call this our Walden on Wheels; and I wanted Max to paint those words on the outside of our trailer, but he refused. "You'd have two dozen people wherever we stopped asking you to explain that."

I was ready and willing to explain, but Max wasn't ready and willing to listen again to the explanation he'd already heard.

"Much travel," Thoreau said, "is apt to take the youth out of one." From ten on I certainly felt so. Wedged into the back seat of a Model T Ford or even a Franklin or a Paige, with two brothers and a sister, I felt, as he said would happen, my independence and self-respect diminish. I climbed out of the car after ninety miles' travel and a half-dozen breakdowns, old as the hills at twelve.

Papa bought his first car, a Duro, in 1910. From 1932 he had campers, travel trailers, and even one of the now-omnipresent vans. In these vehicles my parents set out for New Orleans, Quebec, Jamestown. They inspected Hyde Park, Monticello, Independence Hall. Papa fished in all the streams. Mama talked to all the people. I pitied them both from the bottom of my heart. They had run out on their home town of Yorba Linda before they knew *it*. Did they know where in those California hills the buzzards nested? Did they know varieties of cacti in the barranca? Could they name the stars overhead? Thoreau's ideal had been to travel far in Concord. My ideal was to have Papa and Mama travel far in Yorba Linda.

I wrote long, loving letters to them at every stop they made. Sad, sad old travelers, counting cats in Zanzibar.

.  .  .

7

The second sentence in *Walden* reads, "I lived alone, in the woods, a mile from any neighbor, in a house which I had built myself, on the shore of Walden Pond in Concord, Massachusetts, and earned my living by the labor of my hands only." The key word in that sentence is "alone."

Alone, alone! For those who relish it, a word sweeter than muscatel to a wino. The prohibition against drink was a sometime thing. The prohibition against solitude is forever. A Carry Nation rises in every person when he thinks he sees someone sneaking off to be alone. It is not easy to be solitary unless you are also born ruthless. Every solitary repudiates someone. Sara Teasdale, unwilling to hurt those she loved and unwilling to forego the solitude that excluded them, killed herself.

Female solitaries suffer more than their male counterparts. They were not created, as man was, for their own sake, but to be a companion to man. God made Eve because it occurred to Him after He had created Adam that it might not be good for man to be alone. Eve was then created to save man from solitude. Many women enjoy this job, full time. And there are men, no doubt, stuck with such celestially programed females who wish to God that He had not had this afterthought. For women are afterthoughts, made to prevent solitude. When they themselves hanker after what they were made to prevent, what does God, to say nothing of man, think of them? Perverse, antisocial, not outgoing, in need of a little sensitivity training? When a woman asks to be alone, not alone like Garbo, who asked only for a little privacy out of sight of her fans, but alone, alone, truly alone, separated from mother and father, husband and children, woman feels wicked, unloving, defying God and man alike. Men, in this instance (as in most), consider themselves on the side of the Lord God.

"God hath set the solitary down in families," says the Bible. God knows why; unless He—having gained more insight about human beings since the Creation than He had before, with

8

nothing but theory to instruct Him—saw the lengths to which gregariousness was going to carry them and, to counteract a stultifying and dangerous togetherness, threw a little sand into the whirring gearboxes of the communes in the form of the solitary. This has not brought the mechanism to a grinding stop; it has not even noticeably slowed things down. But, for the sand in the gearbox, particularly the solitary female grains, the effect has been abrasive.

Alone, alone, oh! We have been warned about solitary vices. Have solitary pleasures ever been adequately praised? Do many people know that they exist?

Anne Morrow Lindbergh, in *A Gift from the Sea,* urges her female readers to find some time to be alone. She would not have urged them to do so had she believed that many find pleasure in solitude. I have needed, all of my life, advice of the opposite kind. When first I read her sentences, they were as strange to me as though I had found her urging hard drinkers to extend their capacity for liquor. I was that narrow-minded, seeing all women as duplicates of myself.

I write this in, and am living in, a trailer. Since there are many varieties of trailers, I should say travel trailer, which is quite a different thing from a house trailer or a mobile home or a motor home or a camper or a van. And in each of these categories there are many subdivisions.

There are words in each generation that lack class. "Trailer" is one of these words for our generation. If you go out in the street and shout, "Trailer," you will be arrested for nothing more serious than disturbing the peace, but no one will admire you. Shout an obscenity, and you will be thought by many to be working for peace or for free speech or that you are, at the very least, a young lover. I do not know why, but this is so.

The word "trailer" raises the hackles of a variety of people. Author Wallace Stegner—traveler, camper, lover of the outdoors and of the Far West—is repulsed by these comfort-loving nomads. He saw one couple enclose an area at the side of their trailer with a white folding fence. Then he watched them sit there at twilight in their front yard, "forever," he believes, "a part of Peoria." I do not know Peoria. Perhaps it is not a good place to be forever of. Stegner, like Thoreau, is a purist. "One world at a time" is his motto. Camped in the desert, the white picket fence should be folded. But the fence is easier folded than Peoria. Fold the fence, burn it, scatter its ashes at Zabriskie Point, and Peoria will still be engraved on the hearts of those who have watched the dark come down on a Peoria back yard.

I was on Stegner's side for so long. No matter where my father's and mother's trailer was, they would, without the aid of any picket fence, be, I knew, forever a part of Yorba Linda.

My younger sister, Carmen, after taking a small trip with them, returned saying, "Now I understand where the phrase 'hell on wheels' originated." She was of Stegner's persuasion, and mine at that time.

There are those, not purists but technicians, who say, "You don't, in God's name, plan to drag one of those things behind you, do you?"

Exactly the question, I suppose, that a man on horseback 2,000 years ago asked the man who was using the newly invented wheel to pull a cart.

"You don't plan to drag *that* thing behind you, do you?" He peered down from the back of his horse with disdain.

And there are people, way beyond caring about chic—radical or wheeled—who say, "If you want to travel, why not fly or motor?"

If you don't care about seeing anything at all en route, fly. If you don't mind being unable to take in anything you do see, motor. But if you want, after the motoring is over, to live under your own rooftree and to see the wilderness you camp in, take a trailer.

# II

Solitude has always excited me.

I don't know whether this would be so if I were condemned to a prison cell or cast away on a desert island; but when the opportunity for solitude must be stolen, as for the most part it must in large families or even in small families of one husband and one wife, it is, like stolen fruits, very sweet.

Whether this pleasure in solitude is inborn or whether it came as I experienced life without it, I don't know. Did I want to be alone before anyone said to me, "Run out and play with the other children"? Certainly the pleasure in being alone is sharpest when I achieve it in spite of untoward circumstances.

What was I stealing? What am I stealing? One can't steal solitude. No one owns that. What I stole was myself from those who claimed me and who had, I myself admitted (otherwise no theft), every right to do so: parents, friends, even husband. "Steal away to Jesus," says the song. I stole away to Jessamyn, a lesser companion; but in the heart of solitude all boundaries tend to melt, and all the J.s, spiritual and sensuous, become one.

Being female and domestic, even when young, I wanted to be alone in a place of my own. I was no baby Byron or Shelley. I had no wish for the solitude of sea or mountaintop, though I liked these well enough, too. But such outdoor solitude didn't need, when I was young, to be stolen. The beaches of Laguna and Newport, of Balboa and La Jolla were still empty. The hills of Yorba Linda were inhabited only by other lovers of solitude: coyotes, rattlesnakes, buzzards. They wanted to be alone as much as I. There was no feeling of accomplishment in depriving them of my company.

The first place in which I remember being alone was not very elegant. But it was not mine and I took it and I was alone in it. And I evicted invaders. The place was a tub: a round metal wash tub of galvanized tin, which hung on a nail at the back of the "Little White House," where we lived in Southern Indiana. My grandparents lived in the "Big White House," a quarter of a mile up the road.

I was able, a big, strong four-year-old, to get the tub off its nail and to roll or drag it to a place beside the barn and out of sight of the house. There I got into it. The quarters were cramped, the view dismal: corncrib, haystack, barnyard, horse trough, horse manure. But I was alone in my own place and without a by-your-leave from anyone.

Why do these tub-sitting hours remain one of the great remembered blessings of my childhood?

You would not think that at four I had already developed a desire to return to the womb. I had had a thirty-six-hour struggle to get out of that place, with a doctor standing by ready to reduce my twelve pounds to parcels of four if my nineteen-year-old mother gave up. She didn't give up. But that experience should have made me wary of the dangers of cramped quarters.

On the other hand my reluctance to emerge may have been an expression of an innate liking for solitude; a liking intensified because I knew that I was not supposed to linger inside any longer, and because I was aware of the crowd of strangers who awaited me outside.

The tub was not forbidden to me. Sitting in a tub may have been thought an odd pastime to people unacquainted with Diogenes; it was thought odd even by Diogenes' fellow citizens.

But considering the trouble a four-year-old can get into, a mother with a tub sitter may have been considered lucky. Mama may have thought herself lucky. *I* thought myself clever: four years old and already able to get away from it all.

I had a brother of two and a half. The tub, empty, did not appeal to him. The tub with big sister in it was irresistible. He did not ask or even want my removal. All he asked was joint occupation. This I could not permit. I was not tub-crazy, but I was solitude-crazy; and you cannot share solitude. I had warned him many times, "Stay out."

One day, in spite of warnings, he stepped in. He was a plump, still-soft-boned child, and his baby fat flowed like some thick pudding into the space I did not fill there. Then it hardened like cement. Cement I might not have minded, but this cement had eyes that looked at me and a mouth that talked. It was the ruination of solitude.

"Get out," I told him.

"I can't," he said.

I didn't think he was trying very hard; and he wasn't, for when I bit him he was out in a twinkle and running toward the house, screaming, "Sister bit me, Sister bit me!"

That is not a very nice way to have started a quest for solitude in a place of my own. But it worked. No one wanted to get in that tub with me again.

# III

---◆---

When I was six my family, which now included a sister of two as well as my brother of four, left Southern Indiana for Southern California. They moved out of the horse-and-buggy age, which still persisted in Southern Indiana, into the automobile age, which was already well under way in Southern California. Papa was automobile-minded from the first, but he needed horses for ranch work; and before he could buy the Duro, he had to buy Diamond and Chinopsee.

We arrived in Whittier on May Day. My cousins were busy that evening putting May baskets filled with flowers on the porches of their friends. Hallowe'en I had heard of; not May Day. We were in a foreign country.

Our aunts and uncles and cousins were clustered on ranches round about Whittier. But land in Whittier was too expensive for a young man recently a backwoods schoolteacher. Orange groves there were already in bearing. While Papa looked for land he could afford, we lived in the house on the ranch in East Whittier that my back-East grandfather had bought as an investment.

To support his family, Papa did ranch work for his neighbors and relatives. The horses he bought to enable him to do this work were Chinopsee, a black, Indian-trained gelding, who wanted to pull the spring wagon (our only means of conveyance) at a gallop; and Diamond, a handsome dapple-gray mare.

They were a mismatched team. Diamond had a sense of duty and of fairness. The first told her that it was not seemly to pull a spring wagon with half the team proceeding at a gallop, as if an Indian still straddled him. The second told her that it was not fair for her to have to do nine-tenths of the pulling while Chinopsee, the big black playboy, showed off. When this second conviction took hold of her, Diamond refused to pull any longer. Papa called this balking, and it took him some time to discover that thrashing Diamond would not help. Diamond would not pull as long as Chinopsee cavorted. Get *him* to settle his shoulders into the collar and Diamond would do her share.

We inherited with the house on Grandpa's place a long, black hound left behind by the former renter. His name was Old Silver. Old Silver, like Don Quixote, was dark and lean, and like him was always ready to do battle. He could not have won a battle with a rat, but, lucky for him, he was as fleet in retreat as he was fierce in attack.

Mama had read somewhere of hydrogen peroxide, which was then the drug industry's newly discovered cure-all. It was known colloquially as High Life. It is a pity that it arrived before TV. Since there was visible action when it was applied, it was ideally suited for TV advertising. It boiled and fizzled and actually appeared to steam when put on a wound or a scraped knee. This, we were told, was visible proof that it gobbled up germs. Mama applied it liberally to our abrasions, and we endured stoically the peculiar feeling it gave, because of our interest in the conflict going on under our eyes.

Somewhere Mama had also heard that a little High Life applied to the skin of a dog does just that: fills him with high life. Old Silver certainly needed something—mostly sense, which no bottle ever supplies. Never one to give grudgingly, Mama anointed Old Silver with a goodly splash; it ran along his spine and from there trickled down his sloping hindquarters.

The results were beyond all expectation. Old Silver didn't

linger long enough for us to see whether there was any bubbling and fizzing or not. He himself moved like a germ in a death convulsion. He leaped small trees; he plunged through big ones. He howled like the hound of a noble family when the young laird lies dying. He seemed to enjoy an audience. First he ran the length of the ten acres on the east side of the house; then he came down the ten acres on the west side. At first we laughed till we cried. Then we just cried. This was cruelty. Old Silver would have a heart seizure and die of exhaustion as surely as if beaten to death.

He was slowing down when Papa drove in.

"What's the trouble with Old Silver?" he asked.

Mama was ashamed to tell him. I wasn't. "Mama put High Life on him."

"What in the world prompted you to do that, Grace?" Papa asked.

Mama was truthful. "I wanted to see what he would do."

"Well, now you have seen," Papa said. "What do you think of it?"

"Catch him, Eldo," Mama said. "I don't want his death on my conscience. And what are the neighbors thinking? With all this howling."

"If I'm going to catch him," Papa said, "you'd better sprinkle a little High Life on me. I don't feel up to all that running and jumping without some help."

But Papa was fresh, while Old Silver was winded, so he caught him without too much trouble. Papa wiped off the remaining traces of High Life and gave Old Silver a pan of cool milk. Except for an occasional twitch of distrust when Mama came near, he was, in an hour or so, just as he had been before the application of High Life: ready to fight.

Papa finally found land he could afford in a newly opened tract called Yorba Linda. There was no water, no house, no orange trees; nothing but rolling hills of sagebrush and cactus,

16

some of which had been cleared for barley. When he had built a house (though there was still no water), the family moved from Whittier to Yorba Linda.

Before we moved, Papa considered the problem of Old Silver. He was now even more flea-bitten, floppy-eared, punch-drunk, and filled with crazy dreams of a comeback as a fighter. He knew only two words: attack and retreat; and the connection between the two never occurred to him. With feeding he had become fatter but not smarter.

Papa thought that it might be as well for us to start in a new neighborhood with a clean slate, not be "those people with the fighting dog." There was no question of being able to find anyone who would accept Old Silver as a gift. Wherever we went, he went, to fight (and perhaps to start) our battles.

"The kindest thing," Papa said, "is to put Old Silver to sleep."

He could easily have taken Old Silver to the arroyo at the back of the ranch and put a .22 through his head. That would have been the easiest way for Papa. But Old Silver was a family dog (certainly no one claimed him as his exclusive property), and what happened to him should be decided by all of us.

"Old Silver is not a pup any longer. Sooner or later he's not going to be able to make it away from a dog he lights into, and he'll be ripped to pieces. It would be a kindness to arrange for him to go to sleep before that happens."

Papa, though the procedure was parliamentary, had already taken executive action. He had seen a druggist, who had given him chloroform, a sponge, and a canvas bag, which could be clamped over a dog's head. Put the chloroform on the sponge, the sponge in the bag, and the bag on the dog's head. The dog would then lie down and peacefully go to sleep.

"I have read about it," I told Papa. "It is called twilight sleep."

"You read too much," Papa said.

This pronouncement was not news to me, but what I had

read, or what I had understood of what I had read, made me believe that twilight sleep was a humane procedure much to be preferred to being torn apart by some big bulldog who did not understand that what Old Silver had in mind was not a fight to the death. I voted for twilight sleep.

Mama voted for peace with the new neighbors and a rest for her nerves, jangled by Old Silver's frequent deathbed scenes. Carmen and Myron were too young to understand that what was being discussed was life and death. Sleep was sleep to them.

It was the next-to-last evening in the green bungalow on Grandpa's ranch. Almost everything was packed, and nothing was left to be done but to kill the family dog. Papa went out to do it; he came back in and sat with us, waiting for sleep to take hold. It never took hold. High Life had never galvanized Old Silver as chloroform did. Papa had tied him so that he could not leap trees and crisscross orchards. What he was denied in action, Old Silver made up for in sound. The young laird had died and gone to hell, and his faithful hound had been dispatched to accompany him. The cries we heard came from hell.

"Papa, he is suffering."

Then there would come a lull. Silence. Not a sound.

"Ah," said Papa, "he has gone to sleep. Good Old Silver. Your troubles are over."

Papa was whistling before he was out of the woods. No one's troubles were over yet. Old Silver was only resting his vocal cords. No sooner had we relaxed, while our hearts softened with memories (difficult while he lived) of Silver's virtues, than the howling began again. It was far worse than the howling that followed a fight or that had accompanied whatever the sensations of High Life, uncanny as they evidently were, had been. This howling smelled death ahead. The sounds were an effort of an animal to keep death at bay. If this was to be his last fight, Old Silver intended to make it a grim one. Tied down, no shelter of back door or wagon to reach by running, Old Silver fought on alone. He had it in mind to scare death away. We sat on our chairs like mourners at a wake where the corpse keeps threshing around in the coffin.

The children, I probably the loudest, were crying.

"Save Old Silver, Papa. Please save Old Silver."

Papa, who never swore, said, "If this is sleep, I'm a hoot owl."

Mama said, "Eldo, I can't stand any more of this."

Old Silver, as if some sixth animal sense told him that inside the house the tide of death was ebbing, howled with new-found lustiness.

"Silver seems likely the only one who can," Papa said, already on his way to take the sack off Silver's head.

Old Silver, none the worse for chloroform, came to the door with Papa.

"Don't let that dog in," Mama said. "I can't look him in the eye tonight after what we tried to do."

When we left the green bungalow, its Belleflower apple tree, and its bower of Gold of Ophir roses, Old Silver was with us. Neighbors in Yorba Linda, and dogs, too, were perhaps few and far between. But on the way to Yorba Linda there were still dogs. And where there were dogs Old Silver would discover and attack them. Someplace beyond La Habra, but before we reached Brea (then called Randolph), he discovered a small, curly-haired brown dog half his size. We didn't expect a victory for Old Silver; we did anticipate rout; but we did not expect his being torn limb from limb on the day after our attempt to save him from just that. The little brown dog, with curly hair pretty enough for a ribbon, was a lion in disguise. He set his teeth in Old Silver and threw him around like a rug. While the execution was on, Old Silver didn't have enough wind to howl. Breathing was all he could manage. But finally he broke free, got under the wagon, and howled to let us know how much he was suffering. We had seen that he was bleeding. A flap of bloody skin hung down from his chest; an eye was damaged.

Papa slapped up the team. Chinopsee tried to gallop. Diamond pulled. The brown dog, having defended his territory, went back to his yard. Under the wagon Old Silver continued to tell us of his wounds.

"Is he dead, Mama? Is he dead, Mama?" I howled from the back seat of the spring wagon.

This bit of senselessness, combined with the noise Silver was making, was too much for Mama's nerves, already jangled by the execution that had miscarried and the breakup of housekeeping. She turned and gave me a sharp slap. "Nothing," she said, "that can make that much noise is dying."

In Yorba Linda Old Silver discovered the animal he believed he was born to conquer: the coyote. And the coyotes discovered in him the hound of their dreams. He pursued them deep into the foothills, baying menacingly. When the coyotes had run with him behind them as far as they cared to, they turned on Old Silver. The chase was then repeated in reverse. This time without baying, only with anguished yelps of "Help, help! I have been set upon by wild animals!" Old Silver sped for home.

"Will that dog never learn?" Mama would ask.

No, he never would; and even the coyotes soon tired of his stupidity and chased him only after a dull day's rabbit hunting.

# IV

<hr>

In Yorba Linda, as befitted a Californian, I found larger quarters in my search for solitude: a piano box instead of a tub.

We moved out to Yorba Linda at Christmas time. The rains had been early that year, and there was a good stand of barley on the hillsides that had been cleared and planted. Later, in school in Yorba Linda, we sang a song called "Barley Is King." I thought that it had been composed especially to honor the barley fields of Yorba Linda. And I still think a tall stand of blue-green barley is the lordliest of crops. Beside barley, oats are frilly, wheat blunt, rye overcomplicated, alfalfa lowly. The bearded barley is king.

We moved into the house Papa had built for his family. I don't know where he had learned carpentry, and perhaps he hadn't. We had built as the pioneers did: on the brow of a hill, where the redskins could be seen as they mounted their attack.

Wind, not savages, was the danger in Yorba Linda. Our two-story house was the first obstacle to confront the Santa Ana in its 100-mile sweep in from the Mojave Desert. Papa propped up the house with planks on the west side. On the worst nights he bedded us children down in the cement weir box (no water in it yet), and he and Mama slept on the hay in the cow shed. In time the beds in the uncarpeted upstairs bedroom marked the floors with permanent scars of their frequent east-to-west roll.

Perhaps, without knowing it, Papa's principles of construction were sound. He built as earthquake-proof houses are now built: buildings that can roll with the shocks. The wind might push, but the house could give.

Everyone knew when a Santa Ana was coming. First, the air was unusually clear and still. Then, in the east, just visible at the Pass of San Gorgonio ninety miles away, a smudge the size of a hand would appear. This was the tower of dust and sand the approaching Santa Ana was pushing before it.

The Santa Anas scared me. I waited in the night for the next gust to blow the house over. I also loved them and their force: the traveling beds, the bounding tumbleweeds, the scream and whine of the wind around—and through—our unbattened house. An unplowed land is virgin. A land without wind is dead.

It may be thought that in an unsettled stretch of rolling hills, with the nearest neighbor on a hill a quarter of a mile away, there would be solitude to spare without any need of crawling into piano boxes. There came a time when I was capable of claiming the whole landscape as my solitude, a time when I could occupy that space, fill it as fully as tub or piano box. That time was later, in my teens, when my imagination was strong enough to make the world my solitude. Now I needed a smaller container; something whose sides I could feel; something that visibly excluded.

We had a piano box because the new piano had come in it. Papa must have wondered how he would ever pay for it. There were two reasons for its purchase: first, Mama was musical; second, in the first decade of the 1900s, children who did not take music lessons were underprivileged. It was never Mama's intention to have an underprivileged child.

The acquisition of the piano and the music lessons were not

what is now called status seeking. Back East Mama had owned an organ, and when, at two, I had my picture taken, Mama stood me not in front of the organ, but in front of the bookcase.

Of this bookcase her mother wrote, soon after her daughter's marriage, "We didn't go to much expense for Grace's wedding. She didn't want it and we didn't think it advisable. I think she has a good pure husband and they are just as happy as possible for two children to be. They haven't any money but not a debt, Grace said in her letter last night. They were able to go to housekeeping at once and to take care of themselves. Grace said that they were going to have one luxury they could do without, and that was a bookcase. They ordered it from Chicago. They have a number of nice books."

The bookcase, I see in the picture, was six or eight feet high, with glass doors, of course, and almost full by the time I was two with "nice books." Neither the bookcase nor the organ was shipped to California. The books were; and Grandma was right. Most of them were nice, and most of them were no more than nice. And I read them all: *The Collected Works of E. P. Roe; A History of Yeast;* Dickens's *Bleak House* and *A Child's History of England* (the torture parts, which I still remember); Lamb's *Tales from Shakespeare;* Shakespeare himself; Wordsworth, in a leather binding so plumped up it can still be used as a pillow; *St. Elmo; Beulah; Homestead on the Hillside; The English Orphan;* Carlyle's *Heroes and Hero Worship; The Dolly Dialogue; A Life of Margaret Fox.*

The piano acquired in Yorba Linda was, I am sure, like the earlier bookcase: another luxury Grace knew "they could do without" but that "they were going to have."

The piano was a Kurtzmann. Mama said never to forget that. I still have the piano and I haven't forgotten and I still don't know what made the Kurtzmann so remarkable in her eyes. I plan to find out before I die.

Catherine Drinker Bowen writes in *Family Portrait* that she was thirty before she learned that musical talent is said to have five ingredients: "digital dexterity, sense of pitch, musical memory, sense of rhythm, and love of music." Mrs. Bowen credits herself with the last two only. Mama perhaps had the first quality and certainly the last two. But she had no musical training (except for some organ lessons as a girl). She had never heard good, let alone great, music. She had never heard an orchestra, good or bad, before the time of radio.

Before the Kurtzmann arrived, Mama played what she called a French harp, and whose proper name is, I believe, a harmonica.

Mama's "French harp" was a big one: six or seven inches long, a Hohner, of German make. It was plated with what was called German silver and decorated with scrolls like those in the *Palmer Method Writing Book* I used at school. When Mama played the French harp, the playing wasn't just an exercise of breath and lips but of her whole body, which at that time was buggy-whip slim and supple. There was no foot stomping or shoulder rocking. But she had a body, and she had a movement. Oh, yes. Perhaps it was more like a pulse. The movement took place, as I remember it, at about an inch above the straight-backed chair on which she sat when she played. She was all spirit at those times and weightless, nothing but music and a tendency to take off.

She could "tongue" the harp, a skill I don't, to this day, understand. She would also use one hand like a bird's wing, fluttering it across the harp and producing a quaver in the tune, a catch in its throat.

When Mama played the French harp, I got into a corner where my tears couldn't be seen. I sat on the floor. The carpeting was wall-to-wall, but the wall-to-wall rag rug had been hand-loomed back in Indiana and was tacked to the floor over an undercovering of straw. The coal-oil lamp on the stand table in the middle of the room didn't reach far enough into corners to light up tears.

Mama played all kinds of songs, but most were of the South

and the Civil War. Listening to her, no one would have dreamed we were Quakers: they would have thought we were a band of displaced, still-militant Rebs dreaming of the good old days back on the plantation. There were soldiers still tenting on the campgrounds, we were far from the old folks at home, and Massa was in the cold, cold ground. When Mama played "My Darling Nellie Gray," darling Nellie had truly been taken away, and no one would ever see darling Nellie again. The whole sorrow of that girl and of slavery and of human suffering was in that song when Mama played it.

She played other songs, too. Hymns. Sousa's marches. She liked whatever had feeling in it and was spirited.

She played one spirited song whose words were as strange as any I have ever heard. It was called "Few Days," and its chorus ran, "I am glad that I was born to die. Few days, few days. From grief and woe my soul shall fly, I'm on my journey home."

She sang that song ironically on days when everything went wrong: the days when the Santa Anas blew, the clothesline collapsed, the washday beans burned, on days when Myron fell into a clump of cactus, and Old Silver, defeated in battle, crawled under the house and howled for hours; when ground squirrels proved, unlike the tree squirrels of Southern Indiana, inedible in a stew. Then she sang, "Few days, few days. From grief and woe my soul shall fly, I'm on my journey home. Our camp is in the wilderness, our camp is in the wilderness, but we are going home."

The songbook said that this song was to be played *con spirito,* and thus Mama played it; as, in fact, she played every song. The day might be sad, the heart filled with tears, but the song was *con spirito.* Always. "Ships That Pass in the Night." "The Jealous Lover." "The Kidnapped Child." "The Old Rugged Cross." *Con spirito, con spirito.*

I am here in a trailer by chance; or perhaps not. Perhaps I am here by a logical chain of events leading inevitably from tub to piano box to trailer. But this *location* is surely chance.

25

This trip's destination was Brownsville on the Gulf of Mexico; not Mesquite on the Colorado. No matter how I got here, I don't want to leave. Not just yet, anyway.

It is nearing sunset now. I sit on a bed facing the river, and across the river is Arizona. I am on the California side of the river, but the Mojave Desert, through which the river runs, doesn't recognize boundary lines. What I can see in Arizona is a duplicate, insofar as I can tell, of what is all about me in California.

Upstream a wind must have been blowing all day. Coming downstream, and staying close to the left bank for some reason I don't understand, is a continuous ribbon of golden leaves: willow, cottonwood, tamarisk, sycamore. They have been moving past my window since morning. The river during that time has been a dozen colors: apricot, gray-blue—the gray of a diamondback rattler. It was, once in a while, water-colored. Now, as the sun goes down, it is molten. This liquid that moves past my windows never came down as rain or snow; it must have boiled up out of some fissure in the side of a volcano.

Upstream to the east, Iron Mountain blots the river from my sight. This mountain is neither mountain-shaped nor iron. It is dollop-shaped, a blob of something, the color of liver when liver is bloody. Perhaps it *is* the liver of a prehistoric animal, gouged out in some early fight and petrified, as trees are petrified in the desert air.

Whatever it may have been originally, each evening at this hour the shadow of Iron Mountain stains the water. The river itself is now throbbing with a rosy burning, as if there were a conflagration of red roses forty feet down (that's how deep the Colorado is here) on the river's bottom.

Each evening at this time the mud hens who went upstream in the morning return to their nightly resting place in the marshes a mile or so downstream. Their journeying upstream is controlled by temperature. On cold mornings they don't leave the warmer waters of the marsh until midmorning. Temperature has nothing to do with the homeward journey. Time triggers that. I don't know what their work upstream has been, but they are as punctual as clock punchers about quitting. The minute the shadow of Iron Mountain begins, at sunset, to lift from the river, the mud hens come into sight from upstream.

There are twenty-six of them this evening. They arrange themselves in triangles of three or four or five, and the triangles form a bigger triangle. As the mud hens pass, the rosy afterglow on the water fades; it actually doesn't appear so much to fade as to be rolled up like a red carpet—a team of twenty-six mud hens rolling up the river sheen. When the final hen has passed my window, the Colorado roses have burned themselves out. The river is as gray as a skillet behind the mud-hen team. They take the red carpet with them. They drop it finally in the marshes where they sleep. Perhaps the whole day's task of mud hens here is this sunset job. Roll up the sheen. I don't know. It is very mysterious.

A small wind blowing down through the canyon behind me sends some of the cottonwoods' few remaining gold coins into the band of passing gold. I don't suppose that this little down-blower has a name; but I do know that because it is blowing downward through the canyon from the mountains behind me it is a foehn, a fall wind, the most dangerous wind in the world for flyers. The Santa Ana is a fall wind and is listed among the world's dangerous foehns. I was elated when I found my old childhood bed rocker so honored. I wished I had known when the tumbleweeds blew about us and Papa packed his children into the weir box that we were being endangered by something world-known and scientifically classified.

Half, maybe more, of the delight of experiencing is to know *what* you are experiencing. Would falling in love be as great or as painful if you had no name for your emotions? Or knowledge that others had suffered through the same attack? Without knowledge, you might think your racing pulse and distaste for food the onset of the measles.

Without knowing, I thought the Santa Ana was a little Yorba

Linda disturbance, unknown elsewhere. I never expected to see it listed with the *"Yamo orshi,* foehn of the steep valleys of Japan," or with the *"Reshabar,* lusty and black out of the high Caucus."

I don't know why I have always been so excited by the names of the world's winds. I understand why one wants to know the names of what he loves. "A man" is not the same as "Thomas Jefferson" or "John Keats." Naming is a kind of possessing, of caressing and fondling. I suppose this is as true of winds as of human beings. If you love wind, you want the intimacy of touching your tongue to the syllables of its name: monsoon, williwau, chinook, mistral, choclater, sirocco; westerlies, line squalls, black rollers. I feel them as I write their names, I push against their strength; my cheeks burn with them, my hair streams from me!

If you live in California, as I do, and love the wind, you will of necessity have to love some pretty nasty blowers. In Southern California the Santa Ana will sandblast the paint from your car in thirty minutes. It will push a brush or forest fire ahead of it at the rate of a mile a minute. Nevertheless I love the sound and feel of these great destructive blowers. Above San Francisco, the norther, while never the equal of the Santa Ana, howls through eucalyptus windbreaks, unbroken, and with the sound of surf against rocks. It comes around the corners of houses with the heartbroken whine of a ghost shut out.

Thoreau loved what the wind *did;* if it had never blown through the telegraph wires, forming what he called his wind harp, I don't know that he would have mentioned it. He loved the earth as it was; and water did not have to flow or air move for him to appreciate it. But the air moving through the telegraph wires sent him into a real ecstasy: "The telegraph harp again. Always the same unrememberable revelation it is to me . . . I never hear it without thinking of Greece. How the Greeks harped upon the words immortal, ambrosial! They are what it says. It stings my ear with everlasting truth. It allies Concord to Athens and both to Elysium. It always intoxicates me, makes me sane, reverses my view of things. I am pledged to it. I get down the railroad till I hear that which makes all the world a lie. When the zephyr, or west wind, sweeps this wire, I rise to the height of my being."

I understand Thoreau's feeling for his harp music. I often sat in the barn in Yorba Linda and listened to barn music as the wind squeezed itself, wailing, through the cracks in the barn. But I never thought of this sound as music. I thought the sounds I heard were the voice of the wind.

People who consider themselves "real" music lovers have pitied poor Thoreau, his own chords "trembling divinely" as he listened to the wind blow through telegraph wires. The telegraph harp, they felt, was a sorry substitute for the Boston Symphony. Actually the world is not that either-or. Something blows through telegraph wires and barn cracks that can't be heard in the Pastoral Symphony or *La Mer*. Above all it is something accidental, something that Thoreau's ear (and mine) composed as it went along.

Unless Thoreau heard the wind, and especially as it blew through the telegraph wires, he hadn't much to say about it. He is, of course, a connoisseur of water: its color, its depth, its taste, its function as mirror, its transformation as ice, its use for bathing and fish breeding; but he is with water as he is with air: it doesn't have to move to please him.

Thoreau was a great one to take nature as he found it. Walden was a pond, and except when wind-whipped, it was still and unmoving. It is the nature of a pond to be quiet. Thoreau accepted that quiet. He never asked hawks to sing or whippoorwills to become predators. He didn't kick against the prick.

I would never, if I could choose, live beside a pond or a pool or a lake or a reservoir. Thoreau was never tempted at Walden's edge to shake his fist and say, "Don't just sit there.

Do something." Still waters, especially the waters of the great man-made lakes, so-called, which are really reservoirs, make me feel that way. I know the good that reservoirs do, but I don't really care to look at them. They are caged animals; a zoo where the animal is a dead river; a snake of enormous sinuosity of muscle, stripped of its rippling skin, bunched up, pegged down, movable only when man lets gravity take hold of his captive.

The river I write by was once a dangerous animal. I am living in the midst of reminders of the Colorado's strength—mountains moved by it; canyons dug by it. It has been tamed, if not killed. It can no longer move mountains and houses, kill people and animals. Instead, properly chlorinated, it will quench the thirst, fill the swimming pools, and cool the radiators of Los Angeles County's millions. Would I have Angelenos parched, their pools empty, their engines hot? No. But I don't have to admire the look of what that quenching, filling, and cooling has done to the river that flows past my window.

I don't know why the names of the great winds of the world move me so much more than the names of the great rivers. Astrologically this is wrong. My element is water, not air. Perhaps I am a true Californian in this respect. There is so much more wind than water in California that I have decided to live in the element that I possess.

All Californians *should* be river lovers. Without our rivers we would all die. As it is, our rivers are all—because we love them so much—dying. We will not let them run away from us into the sea. We cage them behind our mile-high dams. We build dams the way the Aztecs built pyramids; then we flock to them for weekend devotions, which are almost religious and *are* sacrificial. Each Saturday and Sunday, as on the steps of the pyramids, youths and maidens are sacrificed on the sacred dam waters: beheaded by outboard motors; knocked cuckoo by blows from flying water skis; drowned when stamina proves weaker than ambition. Even the no-longer-young are sacrificial victims: dead from a surfeit of beer and pizza, in six feet of intended drinking water.

Water in California has become a superhighway (the super-highway is our true sacrificial altar). It is a surface upon which a vehicle can be propelled at high speed. It has become in many ways a super-superhighway. The surface of water is not worn by travel and does not have to be repaired, so you pay no highway taxes for the gas you put in your Chris-Craft. Water is cooler than asphalt in summer and not much wetter than asphalt in winter, so as a year-round roadbed it has great advantages, to say nothing of the novelty: going fast on land is an old story to everyone in California; going fast on water is a new sensation, because the recently built dams now make it possible. The superhighways that lead us to the lakes are clogged on weekends as people with boats hasten to the super-superhighways to experience the sensation of (and perhaps become one of the sacrificial volunteers to) speed on water.

There are no laws against the explosive noises of water vehicles. Water encourages and justifies a minimum of cloth-ing. And water travel, provided you can swim and are not decapitated or mangled by flying solid objects, does have an-other distinct advantage over asphalt: it opens up in case your craft turns over.

Yesterday afternoon I saw a boat on the river that made me stare: motorless, silent; a rowboat, with two middle-aged men, fully clothed, sitting in it and using oars. They were not fish-ing. They were just ahead of the mud hens. Perhaps they were helping the hens in their job of rolling up the sheen of the westering sun? They appeared to be watching the sunset. They were out of the past. They were stranger on the river than a horse and buggy on the road.

# V

The Kurtzmann as a musical instrument (to return to Yorba Linda) was wasted on me. Here in the trailer I have two radios and a cassette player. By putting one radio in the living-room end of the trailer and one in the bedroom end, I get—I tell myself—a symphonic effect. This, to symphony goers, may sound as pathetic as Thoreau's ecstasies about his wind harp. Thoreau had three musical instruments: the wind harp of the telegraph wires; a music box, which he played at his sister Helen's funeral; and his flute. How well he played the flute I don't know, but he did master it.

This was more than I was ever able to accomplish with the Kurtzmann. I was, of course, given music lessons. Half the point of having a piano in the house was to provide the children with the means of having these lessons. A violin was bought for Myron, and I was to learn to accompany him. Was it ever the other way around, I wonder? The violin bought for Sister, and Brother instructed to sit as she stood and learn harmonies with which to accompany her solo performance? It was never the case in Yorba Linda. Brother always played the solo, and Sister was always his accompanist.

Myron and I were well paired: both equally poor musicians. Myron's teacher was a Professor Dobbin, a sad dusty-looking man, who drove a sad dusty-looking horse. Before he came into the house he always, winter or summer, carefully adjusted a fly net over his horse. I associated this care for his horse with his name, Dobbin: "We'll hitch Old Dobbin to the sleigh." Was the Professor also aware of his horsy name, and doubly kind to horses because of it?

My music teacher, Mrs. Felicia Leaman, was the Professor's opposite. No dust on her. No flies, either. *She* looked musical and was—a former singer. Now past the age for singing, she gave piano lessons. She had the female singer's big bosom and a marcelled pompadour, equally outsize and equally firm. Her color was high, her chin double. Her chin was supported by a net collar, which in turn was supported by insets of whalebone. She wore long sleeves with frills at the wrist, which swung rhythmically as her fingers, enormously arched, swept up and down the keyboard.

Professor Dobbin, at the end of the year, told Mama that Myron would never be a violinist. Mrs. Leaman had probably decided the same about me and piano playing even earlier. But she perhaps needed money more than the Professor. The story in Yorba Linda was that she had given up glorious musical opportunities in order to be near her husband, who had been imprisoned for some kind of bookkeeping irregularities. Whatever the facts were, Mrs. Leaman struggled with me for three years. The best I could do was to play the "Barcarolle" from *The Tales of Hoffman* very, very slowly and "Rock of Ages" faster than was seemly.

Toward the last, determined to teach me something, Mrs. Leaman decided to teach me the facts of life. I *couldn't* learn to play the piano, and I thought I already knew the facts of life. Mama had told them to me. I was far from thinking Mama perfect. I had a notebook filled with "things not to do as a mother" garnered solely from my observation of her mistakes with her own children. But she was a born storyteller, and her facts, though they were as fanciful as Eve's creation from Adam's rib, satisfied me. Having told me the facts, she told me never, never to talk of them with anyone else. I had the impression that she and I shared a bit of classified information, and that it would be dishonorable for me to speak of the facts she had so generously shared with me, with anyone else.

So when Mrs. Leaman, determined toward the last to teach me something, took my hand in hers and, in a voice wobbling with the mystery of it all, said, "Jessamyn, at about your age a great change comes over a girl. God in His wisdom begins to prepare her to become a mother," I was able to answer, "I know. God has already prepared me."

If Mrs. Leaman's facts-of-life talk had taken another direction, I might have listened. At that time I believed that there was a love key or a secret love word which would someday, when I was of the proper age, be given me; probably by Mama, though I thought it might possibly be found in a book. I would read; these were the books librarians kept in locked cases and wouldn't permit children to take out. With this key or word in my possession I would be able to cause boys to fall in love with me as constantly as I fell in love with them. But if all Mrs. Leaman had to tell me was what I already knew—that God planted a seed in a woman, which when she was married would be nurtured by the blood, which until she was married she had no use for, and that this seed, fed by its mother's blood, would appear at the end of nine months as a baby—there was no point in hearing all that over again.

I hadn't particularly liked the explanation the first time I heard it. A God who could make babies at all could surely have arranged some handier method. Why so many unnecessary years of monthly inconvenience and frequent stomach-ache? Why not let it all start at marriage? Why, for that matter, not hold to the rib method, which had worked so well on Adam? If God could make a full-sized woman out of a rib while Adam slept, one rib, from the same source, could easily make a half-dozen babies.

So in addition to keeping my word to Mama, I avoided conversation on a subject that didn't interest me.

"Mama," I told Mrs. Leaman, "doesn't want me to talk about such things."

Mrs. Leaman then told Mama that she felt it her duty to say that I appeared incapable of learning to play the piano.

The Kurtzmann itself was wasted on me, but the box it was shipped in wasn't. It became my house; not a playhouse, a place where I played at keeping house, but a real house where I lived. Who needs to play at keeping house when there are three younger children, and a mother never very well, to keep real house with?

Like Minerva's my house was not movable, and like Minerva I didn't care. I didn't want it to move. I wanted it just where it was: on the brow of the hill where we lived, facing east. North were the foothills, almost as well known to me as the slopes and arroyos of our own ranch. South was the sea, a blade-wide sparkle of light on the horizon. To the west and nearer at hand were the oil derricks, black as spiders' legs against the sky when the sun went down. At night we could hear the sodden thump of their pumps as the earth's insides were sucked out. There were people who said that someday the crust of Southern California, with nothing below to support it, would give way and people and cities and orchards and animals would all fall into the space where the oil had been.

I put the opening of my piano-box house to the east. I chose that view instead of foothills, oil derricks, and the distant sea. There was mystery and power out in that direction. Away in the east Mount San Gorgonio floated, on clear days, like something suspended from the sky. It could not always be seen; then, expecting to see nothing but the Santa Ana Mountains and the shallow little river that ran through its canyon, you caught sight, far beyond, of enormous, sky-blocking San Gorgonio. It was as unexpected as a ghost.

Behind San Gorgonio, deep in the Mojave Desert, was the nest where the Santa Anas were hatched. Great as it was, Mount San Gorgonio could not block them off when their time to blow came around. They poured over the dam of its mountainous walls, or through them or around them. The winds spread out in the valleys of Riverside, Pomona, and Ontario. The Santa Ana canyon thinned its share down, then shot it at Yorba Linda like an arrow. So I chose the east—where the mountains stood and the winds were hatched—as the direction my house should face.

Actually, I didn't spend much time looking out. The box was for being in, not looking out. I didn't get in there to escape work; if anyone wanted me they knew where I would be. I didn't play house there. I was a constant reader, but I never read there any more than I would read in church. I was a considerable eater, but I never ate there. I never entertained visitors there; though, since the biting episode, no one was very eager to share close quarters with me.

I got into the box to experience a feeling I had only when I was in a place of my own, alone, with no one near or threatening to be near. I do not even yet know the exact name for the feeling. It was an intense feeling of awareness and of complete peace. I might call it joy, but I could be joyful when I was with others; while box joy, tub joy, the joy of solitude, was a bliss that came only when I was alone and then only on special occasions.

At that age I did not know that I got into the box or the tub or later the room or the trailer in search of box bliss. Later I knew what I was seeking. Later the feeling included what I saw: the room and its objects—books, fire, flowers, the swinging pendulum of a clock. When the bliss came upon me or was coming upon me, I would move a chair so that the firelight could not be blocked from a brass bowl. I would replace a blue-bound book with one that was red. I would sweep the hearth if I saw that it was dusty. The room, the shell of my solitude, and its contents was a still life I had painted and was still painting. Sitting alone in that room, waiting, experiencing, I became part of the still life. The room gave me beatitude, and my beatitude filled the room.

The experience was not unlike those reported by drug takers, though nothing strange or frightening ever happened: flames never crept up the walls; wallpaper designs did not come to life with octopus tendrils; the sofa's edge never hung above an abyss. There was a high, a euphoria, a radiance that enveloped and presently ebbed. But never anything that alarmed.

In the piano box, the dream-box factory, I did not, when I was a child, usually look out. Seeing outside, when I was a child, shattered box magic. But occasionally the magic was strong enough to envelop and enhance the persons I saw moving about in the yard. They were familiar but strange; related to me but with lives of their own, of which I had heard reports only. When the mystery took hold of them (and me), they walked about like storybook figures, out of a world stranger than mine.

Seen from my piano-box opening, my mother and father, brothers and sister were both more and less than themselves: less in that they were part of my dreaming; more in that, though they were part of my dreaming, the dream enlarged and enhanced them. I saw them not as the flat figures of one summer's evening and relatives of mine to boot, but as characters, persons with the experience of their known past and even of their imagined future enveloping them.

William Stafford says it all in "Earth Dweller":

> *It was all the clods at once become*
> *precious; it was the barn, and the shed,*
> *and the windmill, my hands, the crack*
> *Arlie made in the axe handle: oh, let me stay*
> *here humbly, forgotten, to rejoice in it all; . . .*
> *The world speaks everything to us.*
> *It is our only friend.*

The earth was adorned on such occasions with more than barns and sheds and cracks in the ax handle; they and people and animals were revealed to me in this beautiful, piercing, sweet-to-the-point-of-sickness awareness.

# VI

———◆◆———

There is no movable furniture in a trailer. No one was thinking of a "cabin in the clearing" when he called the living quarters of a trailer a cabin. He was thinking of a ship. If there is an instrument that measures oscillation (and I am sure there is), a trailer never experiences anything like a line squall, let alone a hurricane. But winds blow trailers over, and there is a constant jolt and sway as the big land cruisers make the legal limit of fifty-five miles down a highway less than water-smooth.

The beds in the bedroom are attached to floor and walls, as is the chest of drawers between the two beds. There are lockers over and under the beds and over the chest of drawers. Windows occupy the space between the overhead lockers and the beds; above the chest are three windows. The bedroom is, in fact, built like the observation car of a train, with beds to recline on instead of chairs. There are heavy curtains to shut out the view—or the viewer, if you want privacy.

Between the bedroom and the second room, which is combination living room-dining room-kitchen, there is a hall. Out of the hall opens, on one side, a bathroom, with shower, tub, and toilet. On the other side is a clothes closet and, next to it, a floor-to-ceiling stack of drawers.

The kitchen has the usual equipment: stove, double sink, refrigerator, freezer, cupboards. The kitchen is not very large, and this suits me. I have no desire to spend much time there.

The front end of the trailer, which is the dining-living room, has the same arrangement of windows as the bedroom at the back. A table, which can be extended to seat six, is hinged to the wall. On each side of the table is what trailer makers call a divan; actually a three-quarter-length sofa, a love seat.

The trailer floor is covered with vinyl in a cream-and-brown pattern. On the vinyl are what rug makers call—I don't know why—area rugs. There is one each in bedroom, hall, and bath; two in the kitchen-living room. They were designed by someone remembering the patterns and colors of hardwood leaves on the floor of an October forest. The beds have fitted covers of old gold in a brocade pattern. The little sofas are upholstered in the same material. The curtains are of a lighter gold material, lined to keep out light and sound. The cushions on bed and sofa are of deerskin, suede side out; all taffy-colored, from the shades of the first dark boil-up of the molasses to the butternut of the final pulling.

This (not including the rugs or pillows) is more or less the standard equipment for a trailer the size of ours. But this is only the pre-fab siding from the Irishman's shanty with which Thoreau built his cabin. There is no real rooftree in a trailer, until you yourself have raised it. And it is this, your own rooftree, that makes you like *it* over your head instead of a motel's ceiling when you travel.

When motels were motor courts, their furnishings weren't always aesthetically pleasing, but they were not then the result of market analysis or consumer polls. They were what the motor-court builder had on hand when he finished building the four rooms under the cottonwoods that he advertised as "Cottonwood Court: Beauty Rest Mattresses—Vented Heaters—Sleep off the Highway."

The heaters and the mattresses were the only new equipment the trailer-court owner bought. The rest came out of his attic or the spare bedroom, which wasn't often used, or it was what had been donated by relatives. There was a braided rug on the Congoleum in front of the bed, made of authentic old shirts, aprons, and Norfolk jackets, which had been cut into strips by aunts and grandmas, then braided and sewn together by them. When you put your feet on that rug, you put your feet on family history. The quilts and comforters had been Grandma's. The slat-backed rocker by the vented heater was Aunt Dessie's. Aunt Dessie had rocked seven children in it and "had never sent a child to bed hungry or with dirty feet." Mrs. Decker, wife of Mr. Decker, who owned the court, told you this. The washstand, complete with a compartment for a chamber pot (but with chamber pot missing), had been the Deckers' own when they started housekeeping. They had been proud of it. They still were. It was curly maple. Mrs. Decker had put a wicker fern stand, frayed, but with a flourishing Boston fern in it, beside the rocker to add a "homey touch" to the room, and to remind you to stop at Cottonwood Court on your return trip.

It may not have been your idea of home, but everything in the room had been part of someone's idea of home, and you could smell love and pride around every frayed edge.

The modern motel room represents someone's idea of a way to make money. (Not that that was absent from Mr. Decker's mind.) Today's motel room comes off an assembly line. To feel at ease in it, you need to have come off an assembly line yourself. It is explained to you by a porter as one explains a mechanism. Living in it is a matter of pushing buttons. You feel that, like an astronaut, you should have had some months' training in a mock-up before stepping into it. You are surprised to find that normal gravity prevails. Almost nothing else that is normal does.

How could this overnight storage space for humans be humanized? I don't know that it could, or that most people would want it to be. First of all, you'd need a saw, with which you could perhaps separate the elephantine, omnipresent, wood-grained, plastic object designed to hold suitcases, TV, and radio; and to serve also as desk, dresser, and dressing table. It is the washstand of a past day, bigger but less commodious: no commode—you have to trek off to the bathroom for that.

And when you get to the bathroom, you'll be frustrated. To give the appearance of germlessness, drinking glasses have been popped into plastic bags. Never try, if really thirsty, to get a glass out of its envelope. These plastic bags are more durable than sarcophagi. Simply drink from the little basin the plastic covering forms inside the glass. Infinitely faster. Probably cleaner, too.

Toilet bowls are also protected by a plastic strip to assure you that you are the first one there since the last one: a kind of technological maidenhead. This had best be removed.

No one who builds a motel has any idea that anyone in a bed will be interested in the view outside. No motel bed ever faces a window. This may be well calculated, since the view outside is ordinarily a spur of the Southern Pacific track unused except for shunting purposes at 3 A.M., an eight-lane highway, or the rear view of a Safeway Store and its ramp for unloading produce. These are noisy rather than sightly views. Still, if I have to hear something, I like to see what I'm hearing.

This leaves hotels (skipping hobo jungles and backpackers, who ask only for a dry, level spot for their sleeping bags) for overnight travelers. Hotels are fine but are found only in cities.

A furnished trailer, like the old-time auto court, is someone's idea of home, though it may not be yours. This one, given the limitations of space, though it is larger than you might think—twenty-three feet by eight feet (the cabin at Walden was fifteen feet by ten feet)—is mine.

In the alcoves on each side of the dining table are books: twenty-three on the left, twenty-eight on the right. I have just counted them. They are at hand when you sit or recline on the mini-sofas. They are bound in various colors. They are as bright as the flowers or lamps here at the living-room end of the trailer.

41

In the bedroom the door has been taken off one of the overhead lockers so that the thirty-four books there are visible and easy to reach. The books are both old and new, known and unknown, some called great a century ago, and some still waiting to be called. Thoreau, of course. Hazlitt and Belloc and Sir Thomas Browne, Christy Brown, Eudora Welty, William Stafford, Josephine Johnson. Slater's *The Pursuit of Loneliness*. Slater would pity me from the bottom of his heart: deplore tub, piano box, *and* trailer; he would get me out of here and into a commune as quickly as possible, get Thoreau out of Walden and into Brook Farm. Was Thoreau never lonely? Certainly. Where do you think writing like his comes from? Camaraderie?

There are pictures on the walls, good and bad, framed and unframed, originals and reproductions. The bad pictures are the originals, painted by Papa in the last half of his eighties. They are all landscapes. It pleases me to carry the landscapes he painted and was proud of through landscapes he traversed so many years ago. Sometimes I think we pass the very hill he put on canvas and that now hangs in the trailer.

"Hill, meet your picture," I say. "Picture, this is how you looked when younger." Papa, our lives are still intertwined.

There is a cat by Hiuan Tsung on the wall above my head. Another cat carved in wood by an Italian known only to God rests on the chest of drawers. There are two O'Keeffe-white coyote skulls. Real, I mean—not painted—and, by God, coyote, I *think*. I picked them up in the canyon in back of where I am living; skulls carved from, or at least made from, the mice and ground squirrels and baby quail eaten by the two coyotes.

There is the leg bone, complete with hoof, of a wild burro. It also came from the canyon of coyote skulls. It is as heavy as lead. That burro ate barbed wire and beer cans. It is a fine weapon, the ideal weapon for the perfect crime. A blow on the head with that, and the coroner's report will be "Death by a kick from a burro."

There are live flowers as well as these dead relics. At this time of year, January, and in the desert, the flowers I have gathered are greasewood, which is now in bloom; black-eyed Susans; tamarisk; the white, starlike blossoms of the gourd vine; and wild tobacco's yellow honeysucklelike trumpets.

Thoreau went to Walden for economy's sake. What he wanted to save was not money but his life; the hours of his life, that is, for of such are lives made. He did not want to waste a single hour "creeping down the road of life . . . pushing a barn seventy five feet by forty. . . ."

Thoreau was not much tempted by barn pushing. But there are women who do like to keep house; and if they live in a house, factitious cares like window washing and rug shaking and bouquet replenishing will constantly tempt them. I am one of these women. Sweep, mop, shake rugs, make beds, dust. I can even get a little rhythm into dishwashing. It is a housework dance, and if you have danced it well, you will also, when you finish, have painted a picture: the still life that, when the candles are lit, will cause the picture in the eye of its maker and solitary beholder to blossom into a luminous universe, its tendrils extending into every vein of his body.

This is a bliss that barn pushers do not, I think, experience. But it is a bliss even so, which I would achieve as economically as possible. Two rooms, shining, give me as much satisfaction as nine. These two, my Walden on Wheels, can be taken care of and leave me time for other blisses and lives.

There is, of course, a stove—another barn to push—and it can be a temptation for women with a weakness in that direction. The stove in this trailer has four burners—three medium and one large—and what is called a Vue-Magic oven. This, in the language Thoreau used, means that the oven has a light in it.

The stove does not much tempt me. When I was young, I thought that there was enough time in life for marble cakes and hermits and pigs in blankets. I have begun to doubt it. I make time (this is impossible! What I do is take time) for dusting and scrubbing and gathering flowers. I do this because I live in my eyes and because bending and twisting—what is called big muscle work—exhilarates me. Finger work, which is what cooking requires, I do not care for. To feed a hungry family, yes, but not for pleasure. Julia Child, who puts as much bounce into cooking as is possible while staying in reasonable contact with floor and stove, is still pretty much of a wrist-down operator.

The house cleaner is, compared with the cook, selfish. The cook cooks for others, to give them pleasure. I don't clean house, "put a room to rights," to please others. I do it for myself. It does for my soul what prayer does for others. And it takes so much less faith. House ordering is my prayer, and when I have finished, my prayer is answered. And bending, stooping, scrubbing, purifies my body as prayer doesn't. When it comes to religion, I am by nature a Shaker, not a Quaker.

I do not understand why there are so many more books about cooking than about housekeeping. Is taste more primary than what is visual and tactile? Do the recipes appeal to the technologist in a technological age? The alchemist? Is the recipe a formula? Do you combine this and that, apply heat, and chemistry takes over? There are no formulas for housekeeping. Housekeeping is half interior decorating. And interior decorating is half art. A pinch of this and a gram of that and the oven set at 375 degrees (400 degrees in elevations of more than 5,000 feet). We are impressed by such instructions, but art is not achieved by formula. Any fool with a strong back can scrub a floor, but is cooking a science? We can't all be fanatics and produce bombs, but we can all be recipe readers and produce *pâtés* and soufflés and *pots de crème*. That's what the recipe writers tell us, anyway.

The woman who makes a house say welcome *may* do so for the pleasure of family and friends. She does not, however, expect her still life, though it may be slightly askew at the end of the day, to be totally destroyed. But that's what happens to the pot roast and the blackbottom pie. That's what they were made for: total destruction. That's why I say the cook is less selfish than the parlormaid. What does the cook have to show for her work? Memories of praise and of sighs of repletion? But she can't live on in her work. She can't be a lark in her own pie and enjoy the scenery after the baking is done. To say nothing of the eating.

Mama was a cook. She cooked because she wanted to give others pleasure; she did it in spite of overwork and poor health. She did it in spite of makeshift materials and a lack of funds to buy better. She sat on her high-legged stool and banged out pies, cakes, puddings, pot roasts, and dishes nameless till she put them together and named them.

Anyone who can boil water can, I suppose, boil a bean. But to boil navy beans with salt pork so that the beans are tender but intact while the water they have been cooked in has become creamy and thick is not a trick everyone can bring off.

We were all mad for Mama's beans; even once when, by mistake, she cooked a box of the 1910 version of the pill with the beans. She didn't know what she had done until the minute she tasted the beans; then she knew that something extra—and unsuitable—had been added.

Mama always baked corn bread to go with beans; two big pans of it. The rough texture of corn bread complemented the soft smoothness of the beans. New onions and radishes, if they were in season—and in California they usually were—accompanied them.

The dessert, with beans, was chocolate pudding; not rich with eggs or cream, but very black and sweet. Mama's chocolate pudding was served with what she called dip: whole milk enriched with a little cream, flavored with vanilla and nutmeg, and sweetened with sugar. Dip came to the table in a big pitcher. You could make fine washes and ravines in a helping of chocolate pudding by a sudden flash flood of dip.

Mama cooked dishes I have never eaten elsewhere. "Tomato

gravy," for instance, which was, I suppose, the equivalent of a tomato bisque but which we ate on slices of bread. We had gravy made of everything and served with everything, and at every meal—breakfast, dinner, and supper. No meat was ever fried without a gravy being made with the fat it had been cooked in: bacon gravy, liver gravy, ham gravy, pork-chop gravy, chicken gravy, rabbit gravy. We did not ever have, as I remember, fish gravy.

We did have a strange fish dish, however. Salmon was ten cents a can then; three for twenty-five on bargain days. Mama combined diced cooked potatoes and salmon—two or three cans, I suppose—and made what was technically a fish hash, a kind of limp version of fish and chips. With fish hash the dessert was an enormous bowl of "ambrosia." Ambrosia was chopped navel oranges and English walnuts combined with sugar and left to stand for a couple of hours in the cooler.

"Enormous" was Mama's standard unit of measurement for everything. Since there was no possible way of knowing exactly how much anyone wanted, and since telling anyone, "There isn't any more," was out of the question, Mama always made too much of everything. She believed in excess. How can you tell whether or not you have had enough until you've had a little too much?

She wanted a pen with a thick barrel and a big swinging point, one capable of making large, loopy tails on her ys and gs, and exclamation points that really exclaimed. She began many a letter with, "This is Dad's pen, and how he can put up with such a little finicky namby-pamby point is beyond me. I'm going to hunt up my own pen." That would be some job; and the reason she was using Papa's pen in the first place was that hers was lost. It wasn't that she never put anything away in the same place twice; she never put anything away once. After I had been home for a visit she would write, "Everything was put away so nice by you—and lost—while you were here. It will take me a little while to dig things out. I know, petty, you can't help putting things away. I won't try to change you, but I don't 'spect you can change me either."

I wasn't trying to change her. I was trying to give her what I thought would be the pleasure of orderliness. Orderliness wasn't a pleasure to her. I don't to this day know exactly what orderliness *was* to her; perhaps it seemed a prelude to lifelessness.

She wanted to say of her cup, as the Psalmist did of his: "My cup runneth over." Literally, she wanted a big cup, and she wanted it *full*. There was nothing she disdained more than some cautious pourer who gave her a cup three-fourths full. "Fill it up," she would say. And she did as she would be done by with others. After Mama filled them, their cups ran over. "Have some more. Have damn near all of it," the hillbilly said. Mama didn't hold with that language, but that was her spirit.

She made sloppy joes, though without the slop, forty years before they were invented. She cooked a piece of boiling beef tenderly, put it through the coarse blade of a meat grinder, seasoned it, moistened it with its own juices and a touch of homemade mayonnaise, then made sandwiches—shoeboxes full of them—for the everlasting Sunday and holiday automobile trips of my youth.

She made for these occasions what she called traveling pies: pies with a crust heavier than usual and a thicker filling. A quarter of a pie of this kind could be held in the hand and eaten without dripping or crumbling. Sour-cream raisin pies made fine traveling pies. Mama decorated the tops of her pies the way medieval scribes decorated their manuscripts: vines and tendrils and blossoms running all over the open spaces. She crimped the top and bottom crusts together with a scalloped edge as thick and fancy as the embattlement of a castle. I could never learn the art of that fluting which she accomplished with such a quick and birdlike flutter of her hands. A pie whose edges I had tried to flute looked like the playground of beavers. Something unusual had surely been going on there; but to what purpose, who could say?

Mama made her own mincemeat, and this truly was none-such. When Mama minced meat, she minced *meat*. There were fruit and spices in her mincemeat pies, but basically they were meat. You could sail around the world with nothing but a sufficient supply of those pies and never get scurvy or suffer from a protein deficiency.

Mama made plum puddings, a dozen or more at a time, which she steamed in one-pound Hills Brothers coffee cans punctured to admit steam. She made fig newtons, each one about twelve by eighteen inches in size: actually two layers of pastry with fig jam spread between the layers. The black figs came from our own trees, and Mama peeled them by the dish-panful. She was fair-skinned, and the white milk of the fig skins made her hands raw; but she couldn't resist making fig newtons, fig jam, even pickled figs when fig time came around. She made guava jelly: fine-flavored, beautiful to look at, but it felt in the mouth like a spoonful of skinned snakes.

No child need cry for candy when Mama was near. She had a sweet tooth herself and would stir up a batch of candy at the drop of a hat: divinity fudge, which she called heavenly hash (for this she needed Papa's help to pour the hot syrup over the beaten egg whites); penuche; sorghum-molasses taffy; fudge (which became Carmen's department, as gravy was mine); candied orange peel; sugared English walnuts.

Mama's cooking was a blend of Southern Indiana, which was Kentucky, and Southern California, which still has some Mexican overtones. When I first ate peas served without a cream sauce, I thought I might as well have been eating them raw; and I wasn't sure I wasn't. Green beans cooked without bacon and some new potatoes to thicken the broth were about as sapid as stewed alfalfa to me.

When Mama cooked red kidney beans, combining them with meat and chilies and tomatoes to make chili con carne, she was cooking Southern California, not Southern Indiana. She made a salad of wilted lettuce, which was Southern Indiana; but she also sliced big beefsteak tomatoes and drizzled a little olive oil and vinegar over them, which was the West, not the East. She stewed old hens and topped them with dumplings so light they threatened, when the lid was lifted, to float toward the ceiling like big summer clouds. She made dumplings with everything: beans, stewed blackberries, old hens.

If I asked my brothers and sister, "Which of all the dishes Mama cooked do you remember best?" the vote would go, I think, for tamale pie. Not one of these present-day potluck (or "pitch-in," as they say in Southern Indiana) tamale pies, which is a kind of corn meal flavored with tomatoes and chili powder and hamburger, but the real right thing: a tamale in everything but corn husks. Mama would no more have thought of using hamburger in a tamale pie than in a mince pie. The meat was boiling beef, cooked and cut into small pieces. Into the meat broth went yellow corn meal. Into the mush that resulted when the corn meal was cooked went meat, tomatoes, whole-kernel corn, olives, chilies, chili powder, and what other seasonings Mama's tasting told her was needed.

This combination was baked in the bottom half of a turkey roaster, and the result was a cubic foot or more of food of a quality that can happen perhaps only when one is young. The top of the pie had browned while in the oven, and this brown crust was dotted with nickel-sized blowholes through which the chili-colored juices had oozed.

A tamale pie was the dish, still warm, that most often awaited homecoming children who, arriving late at night, were hungry. There it was on top of the stove, big enough to serve a threshing crew, but no more than enough for two or three tamale-crazy young people.

A tamale pie is nothing that can be thrown together without effort. The meat had cooked all afternoon; the other ingredients had been put together at suppertime; the pie baked while supper was eaten. And all this was done by a tired woman on a three-legged stool, a cloth more often than not tied around her aching head to keep it from bursting.

That is why I say the cook is more loving than the parlor-maid. No child recalls the beauty of a welcoming room as vividly as he recalls the satisfaction of a waiting dish of warm food. "The way to a man's heart is through his stomach," not through his eyes. It is the same with children. There have been many records left of Mother's groaning board; very few of her shining, well-kept house. But I lived in my eyes as well as my stomach, and Mama knew this. Orderliness was beyond her, but when I came home she tried to fill my eyes, too.

Once when black-eyed Susans, growing wild, were blooming in a nearby muddy field and we had no flowers of our own to pick, she put on Papa's boots and picked an armload for a centerpiece to greet my homecoming. I remember those daisies better, even, than the tamale pie.

A man who spent forty-four of his forty-six years with his knees under his mother's table must have appreciated her food. Yet Thoreau never mentions what he ate there. Was there flannel hash? Codfish cakes? Indian pudding? Thoreau never says. Mother Nature produced the food he liked, and in some ways he was more of a grazer or browser than a diner. He ate uncooked acorns and found them savory.

Once Thoreau gathered a bucketful of acorns and took them home to cook. One taste of stewed acorns convinced him that acorns were better nibbled as he walked than cooked in the kitchen.

Thoreau was a wild-apple connoisseur, and he knew which tree produced the best fruit. "There is a wild apple on the hill which has to me a peculiarly pleasant bitter tang, not perceived till it is three quarters tasted. It remains on the tongue. As you cut it, it smells exactly like a squash-bug. [Not a *squashed* bug.] I like its very acerbity. It is a sort of triumph to eat and like it, an ovation. What is sour in the house, a bracing walk makes sweet. Let your condiments be in the condition of your senses."

God knows what diseases Thoreau would have found in the senses of a family that relished tamale pies, foot-long fig newtons, and traveling pies.

We did eat and relish cactus apples and elderberries, and we tried ground squirrels and jack rabbits. But for them our palates were too diseased, or our walks not bracing enough.

# *VII*

———◦•◦———

Late each afternoon I take a walk in the canyon that runs at right angles to the river. I go with a two-year-old Pekingese whose name is Spry. Years ago when I lay bedfast with tuberculosis, my mother bought me a Pekingese. A cat, Samantha, had been given me (the first pet I ever owned), but Max did not like cats. My mother's idea was to provide me with an animal small enough to scamper about my room but which would not disgust Max. As it turned out, the Pekingese disgusted us both. I thought a Pekingese was an old lady's lap dog, and, bedfast, I had enough old-lady symptoms already without adding lap dogs to them.

Thirty years later, I saw a litter of Pekingese pups in a pet-store window and wondered, "Did Mother know best?" She did. A Pekingese is not a lap lover, old lady's lap or anyone else's. The German short hair, the collie, the Doberman, the German shepherd—we've owned them all—they will curl up, insofar as they can accommodate their curl to your lap, for endless hours. Not the Pekingese. It endures a little fondling, then it is off and away.

Why is it that a boy and his dog is a sight that gladdens the heart, while an old lady and *her* dog are at least pitiful, if not comic, to contemplate? The old lady needs the dog more than the boy; perhaps that is the reason calendars are decorated with boys and dogs, not with old ladies and dogs. We don't care to see pictures of that kind of need. The dog represents the beginning of the boy's emotional experience, but represents the withering of the old lady's: men, children, grandchildren, all gone; nothing left but her poor little lap dog. Most of us don't care to be reminded of that stage of our lives. Spry and I will never appear on a calendar. We are reminders: few days, few days.

The canyon I walk in is a little, minor, nameless canyon, so narrow that I can, in places, touch both of its perpendicular walls at the same time. This canyon is actually the track left by those desert killers the flash floods. I have never seen an animal in this canyon, never heard a bird. I have seen the tracks and droppings of the wild burros. It is here I found my burro leg. Formerly domesticated animals who have gone wild are more exciting to me than wild animals caged. A tiger or a llama can pick up the trick, however painful, of living in a cage; but for a domesticated animal to readapt itself to life in the wild is a more mysterious process. I would far rather see a herd of wild little Pekingese climbing the canyon walls than the wildest baboon in the world behind bars.

The only human relic I have found in the canyon is a weathered, well-worn cotton glove for the left hand. Left-handed as I am, this seems to me to be a sign of some kind; but a sign, like many others, that I can't interpret.

The canyon, in spite of, or because of, the left-handed glove and the foreleg (if it is) of the burro, is a world aeons away from my trailer under the cottonwood trees. My stomach contracts when I enter it. Spry, usually venturesome, quartering far ahead of me, walks into the canyon behind me. What sign has he been given?

I walk into the canyon in the subdued dazzle of desert sunshine at four o'clock. Inside, I look up and am able to see the moon already shining. It is frightening to have left sunshine behind and to have chosen darkness. The canyon is narrow, but I am not claustrophobic. It is what surrounds this narrow canyon and the manner in which it was made that frightens me.

I know what gouged out this crack through the mountains. The canyon is a wash. The Grand Canyon is simply a wash on a larger scale. Both were made by water. The Grand Canyon has had the point of that great plowshare the Colorado itself constantly furrowing it deeper. My nameless canyon, the canyon of my daily fright, has had only the inconstant, though never ceasing, action of flash floods. The flash flood, unlike the Colorado, has no iron-bound contract to reach the sea; it does not plod on night and day, day in and day out. The flash flood is a more spontaneous worker. One downpour, one cloudburst, another bit of excavating completed, and it stops for a time. The tools with which the work has been done litter the canyon floor: boulders, stones, rock slabs, pebbles, gravel, sand. All colors. Every size. Heavy and round to smash. Sharp to cut. Rough to abrade. It is more than a little sadistic. The flash flood uses the materials of the mountain to cut itself through the mountain. What would you think of a surgeon whose cutting tools were his patient's incisors? Thus mountain is used to operate on mountain.

The mountains of this desert are not mountain-shaped, as we ordinarily think of mountains. The desert is antianthropomorphic. It shapes itself to please itself, not man. Man's blueprint for a mountain would be a pyramid. Desert doesn't know this or, knowing, doesn't care. The only characteristic desert mountains share with other mountains is altitude: they're higher than the land about them.

The mountains through which my narrow, frightening canyon runs are claw-shaped, table-shaped, finger-shaped. One mountain is named Finger Mountain. The mountains that rear up perpendicularly to form the walls of my canyon are mushroom-shaped, old-fortress-shaped, boat-keel-shaped. They are the shape of false teeth fashioned by an inexperienced dentist for a creature with an inhuman mouth. Some of the moun-

54

tains run in ranges. Some do not run at all, but squat. Some rest apart from other mountains in big lumps, apparently dropped from containers conveying materials intended for more impressive structures elsewhere. Some rise like the sharp old nipples of flabby breasts; nipples still upright above what books on mountaineering call detritus, the technical name for the mountain's own eroded and sliding body.

A book could be written, probably has been written, about the colors of desert mountains. This canyon contains most of these colors. They are the colors of gems: coral, topaz, bloodstone, moonstone, black coral, jade. I know more about animals than I do gems. These mountains look animal-colored to me. They are the colors of mice, lions, gophers, mules, lizards, dragonflies, rats. One is the color of a dead rat; dead about two weeks, intact, but already gone a little green.

They are the colors of horses: claybank, blood bay, sorrel, roan, palomino, chestnut, dapple-gray.

They are cow-colored: Jersey, Holstein, Hereford, Black Angus. They are especially the color of the paste-colored French cow the Charolais. And some are like Brahmans.

But for the most part they are rodent-colored, every kind of rodent, winter to summer, whiskers to tail. Many of the rodents have been clawed: are streaked with their own blood or smeared with the colors of their own last dinner.

The canyon-eye view of a mountain is a peculiar one. You do not look down on it or up to it; you enter it.

The first mountain the canyon enters is not a mountain at all—as mountains are generally judged. It is bowel-shaped, mule-colored, chocolate-iced, and encrusted with white pebbles, like almonds in a confectioner's roll of fudge. Mules, guts, and fudge are perhaps unsuitable objects to describe the beauties of nature. I am not now talking about a beauty of nature. I am not sure I am even talking about nature. This strange excretion (to reverse my figure) seems outside nature. A monstrosity made by a monster.

Beyond the monstrosity is something that is at least mountain-high and, as mountains go here, mountain-colored: an earth-stained Jersey. It moves upward, narrowing as it gets higher in a series of terraces. The three uppermost terraces appear to be half-ruined fortresses rather than the top of a mountain. The terraces are darkened by what looks like streaks of smoke. Is this a mountain? Or a deserted habitation? Who lived here, built their fires here, pushed the boulders I have been clambering over to the floor of the canyon below?

This is fantasy. Water moved those boulders, not people. But even as I clamber over, squeeze through, and stumble across them, I have the feeling that from the battlements above I am watched.

The shape and color of the canyon tightens my chest. The thought of the streams that did the shaping makes my heart thump. Flash floods are not called flash for nothing. They happen in a flash. This is January, the rainy season. It has been raining north of here in the country that drains southward into the Colorado.

If that sudden wall of water that is the prow of a flash flood appeared some yards away, could I make it up the almost perpendicular walls to the handhold of an outthrust tamarisk bush I see above me? Would Spry follow? Could I make it carrying his fourteen pounds of muscle and wriggle? Would I abandon Spry? Watch him pounded to fur amidst the boulders?

Death by flash flood is more cruel and punishing than death in ordinary drownings, though no drowning can be ordinary to the person experiencing it. The drowning each man suffers is extraordinary to him. He will never experience another. The sea is always waiting to swallow you. Oxygen was as scarce in Thoreau's calm pond as in more turbulent waters, but the pond and the sea (except in the tidal wave that some Californians believe will come) stay in their places. They don't pursue you. The flash flood roars down a dry canyon to swallow you: you and your little dog; the burros and coyotes and snakes and

56

lizards can scramble to safety. It has to be a calculated catastrophe, intended for you. An hour earlier the wash was stone, sand, mesquite—all sparkling in the sun. An hour later it will sparkle again. Meanwhile you and your little dog have died— have been sacrificed? By whom? For what? The monster who made the monstrous mountain?

Death by flash flood has a quality of punishment that other drownings lack. Ponds and rivers swallow you up: glub, glub, glub. Three times, they say, and you are one with the old bottles, the dead fish, the retreads that didn't hold up. No hard feelings. You entered the water, you sank. Sorry about that, sister. The flash flood may not *drown* you at all. It may crack your skull on a mule-colored rock. Cave in your chest against a boulder that's been waiting for you for 10,000 years. The flash flood plays with you the way a cat does with a mouse. It may toss you high, dry, and safe into the arms of a salt cedar. It may kill you before a drop of water gets into your lungs. Leave you finally unrecognizable except to an anatomist. "Somebody had a good time with her before he finished her off." Anonymous, finally, as other bones in the desert you love.

I went the farthest into the canyon I ever have this afternoon, figuring every step of the way which rock to climb, which bush to lunge for in case I heard the growling hiss of the flood feeling its way toward me.

# VIII

There was no light in my cabin to welcome me. Lights gleamed a quarter of a mile away in the one occupied cabin below this stretch of the river on whose rim I am perched. A widow of eighty, a Mrs. McCurdy, and her son, a man in his fifties, live in this—shanty, I suppose Thoreau would have called it. The roof is of corrugated iron. The floor is cement. The walls appear to be of plywood.

Max, before he left, took me down there. "These are your only neighbors," he said. "I don't want to leave you until you have met them."

The house consists of one room, which is bedroom, kitchen, sitting room, and studio; for Mrs. McCurdy, at the age of sixty-six, became a painter. There are more objects in that one room than many a mansion contains. I hope before I leave to go down there, pen and pad in hand, to make a list of what is visible. The mind, my mind at least, cannot hold them all.

It does not matter much what the walls are made of. They are, be they cardboard or Beaverboard or plywood, held together tighter than a wasps' nest with the glue of photographic memorabilia: pictures of old movie stars, of family groups, of advertisements new and cute in their day—"Old Dutch Chases Dirt"; "The Diamond Dust Twins Will Make Your Home a Gem"—Christmas cards, Christmas exhortations, "Paul and Virginia," a string of pansies with kitten faces, "Horses Running Before a Storm." These were on the walls. Next came innumerable objects on the surfaces of tables, dresser, bureau. It is at this point that pen, paper, and adding machine are needed.

Mrs. McCurdy is very short; a troll, brown and square, made in a forge, sturdy as metal and more rustproof. She came to the river when she was sixty-five, with her husband, an invalid who died here. Someone gave her, to take her mind off her bereavement, a kit of materials, which, if properly used, would result in an oil painting: numbered paints to be applied to numbered areas on a picture already outlined on canvas. Mrs. McCurdy mastered the art of painting by numbers in short order. She then decided that it would be far more fun to put colors of her own choosing on pictures she outlined herself. So she became, at sixty-six, a painter. At seventy she bought a motorcycle in order to travel the length of the river, for she was a landscape painter. After a lifetime of skimping she is now, at eighty, well known and well to do. She is no Grandma Moses dealing in the minutiae of nostalgia: painting without perspective, her daisies the size of dinner plates; her horses, the size of mice. Mrs. McCurdy paints landscapes in the same monstrous way they were originally designed here: brutal, gloomy, and threatening.

The first time I talked to her I made a terrible mistake. Admiring her pictures, recognizing her talent, I said, "What a pity you couldn't have gone to an art school as a young woman."

It was as if someone, after reading a story of mine, had said, "What a pity you never had any training in creative writing."

Mrs. McCurdy said, "Thank God I didn't. Those fellows who went to art school! Look at their pictures. You can see every brush stroke they made. Look at a picture of mine. Not a brush stroke visible."

It was God's truth. Her pictures appeared to have fallen onto canvas with the totality of a flash flood. No inchy-pinchy business of one stroke after another. They were like stories without words. A page full of print and no pausing to pick up the meaning piecemeal. An eyeful of meaning at a glance. Your eyes might be a little bloodshot after the viewing, but you knew you had experienced something.

Mrs. McCurdy's pictures sold like hot cakes. I don't know whether people liked the pictures so much, or they felt that by buying one they were buying a piece of the artist. Lily (I was soon calling her that) has sold her motorcycle and bought a Scout. She piles her canvases into this and goes down the road to where she hits the main highway running between Los Angeles and Las Vegas. Then she sets up shop beside the road. Mainly she sells to gamblers, homeward-bound, with nothing to show for their weekend but time and money wasted. A picture of Lily's makes them feel that their trip has not been useless. They have discovered this genius.

Lily is a shrewd bargainer. She was a businesswoman for three times as long as she has been an artist. She charges what she feels the market will bear, what she feels the customer needs to pay for his lost weekend to cleanse his conscience. He usually needs to pay a good deal, Lily feels.

She could move out of her—there is no accurate name for it—cabin, hut, shanty, igloo, hogan, shack, nest, a hundred times over. She has no intention of doing so. There is an element of superstition in it. "I found my life here," she says; she owes some loyalty to what she has found. She loves her life. She says so with the brush strokes that do not show. Her past life is attached to the walls of her house when she goes inside. She has made a cyclorama of her past and can live in her victories and defeats as do Southern towns with like constructions commemorating the War Between the States. The life she is living now she paints.

Her son lives, or at least sleeps, in a little lean-to porch, which is tacked onto the front of the cabin. There are two cots there. Son sleeps on one; the dog, the dog's puppies, and the cats sleep on the other. I believe that whoever goes to bed first chooses whichever cot appeals to him.

Lily calls her son Son, except for one or two slips when she referred to him as "my husband." I think they were slips, though Son's position is certainly ambiguous. At first I couldn't call him Son; but since no one else calls him Theodore, I finally came to it.

Son does no observable work except to feed the animals. He has made the feeding a trained-animal performance. Circuses do not do better, though their animals are larger. Dogs, pups, cats, line up on a series of boxes and wait there patiently for their rations.

The mother dog is a beautiful curly-haired mixture of many breeds. She has been trained to kiss Son. "Kiss me, Blackie," Son says, and Blackie comes at once to Son and presses her muzzle against his mouth. No sooner has she curled up in her former position than Son says again, "Kiss me, Blackie," and the poor bitch rears herself up to repeat the performance. This goes on perhaps a dozen times; the dog always obedient, the man always inexorable. Lily says nothing. I say nothing. The man is Lily's son, and the dog is Son's bitch. Why the performance, I do not know, though I have developed some guesses.

What Son had done earlier in life I have not yet found out, either. He has had several wives, several children, and presumably held several jobs. He says he is "looking after Mother." Mother didn't say *that,* but she dotes on Son: "He is so clean, so neat, so fastidious." She picked up a tract by one of the radio preachers and put it in my hand. "Son cried like a baby when he read that."

I like a man who can cry. My father cried. My brother Rusty cries. And that tract, only for reasons other than Son's, might have moved me to tears.

Son has a car, but he never leaves their place, which is small. The river flows by. His dog kisses him. Mother praises him. Fish? Swim? Sweep up the golden cottonwood leaves? Never. Is he without a driver's license? Is there a warrant out for his arrest? Is there something else?

Mother says, "He is so sweet. He just follows me around like a little child. He never says a bad word in my presence."

When I first saw Son I thought, What a beautiful, pitiful face. I am not sure that I would use either of these words now. I'm not good at judging faces (and I'm not sure that anyone is). Is Churchill's the face you would have expected to save Britain? Or Jefferson's the face you would have expected to order the exploration of the Northwest? Occasionally a man and his face match. Keats looked like Keats. Dr. Johnson looked like Dr. Johnson. Thoreau looked a good deal like Thoreau. Does Son look like Son?

Amongst Lily's gallery of photographs was one I didn't recognize. "Who do you think that is?" Son asked. I didn't know and said so. "Most people think it's Alan Ladd." "Is it?" "No, it's me."

Twenty-five years ago Son may have looked like Alan Ladd. Not now. Forty years ago someone told me that I looked like Blanche Sweet, that square-jawed Swede with ropes of blond hair wrapped around her head. I've forgotten much that I've been told, but that I remember. But I don't expect anyone now to see me in an old picture of Blanche Sweet. That, perhaps, is the pitifulness I saw in Son's face: the longing, never lost, to be Alan Ladd; the ability, never developed, to understand that the days of that possibility have passed.

I walked quietly and quickly past the McCurdys' lighted cabin. Those two interest me. Son has a secret in his violet Alan Ladd eyes. Will he tell me sometime? All of Lily's secrets are on canvas. She hasn't Son's need to confide.

Tonight I have the high of escape. I wanted to get to the trailer with it intact. I didn't stop at the McCurdys'. I couldn't say to them, "I barely escaped a flash flood." If I say it, it's a lie. But in my mind, it is a fact. I got home safely with the fact: I made the trip, I risked it, I escaped the flood. How lucky can you get?

# IX

———⋅⋅———

The trailer is perched two feet from the edge of the bank of the Colorado. The river flows six feet below. The curtains are not drawn, and my lights are reflected like goldfish on the crests of the ripples.

When I was young I knew two rivers, and I'm not sure which was more real to me: the one I had never seen or the one near at hand in which I sometimes swam.

The river I had never seen was the Wabash. Mama played and sang of it: "Through the sycamores the candlelight is gleaming on the banks of the Wabash far away." Grandpa and Grandma's white house was far from the banks of the Wabash, but when Mama sang, I saw *it,* beneath the sycamores, lighted by coal oil, not candles.

Sometimes it was summer, and lightning bugs flitted around the chinaberry tree and I could smell Grandma's cinnamon roses and dooryard lilacs and flags. Sometimes it was winter, and snowflakes, curled like goose down, floated about the house. Winter or summer, I imagined myself standing outside the house, but not excluded or lonesome. Inside I could see the fire on the sitting-room hearth, and I could smell the wood smoke. And when I was tired of looking inside, I looked down at the unknown river, the river Mama sang about, the "Wabash far away." It was a big river, thick and slow, but it never stopped moving. On its banks lived those we had loved and left behind us: the poor benighted Hoosiers.

The river I knew was the Santa Ana. I thought about it less often when I was a child than I did the Wabash. There is no need to think about what you possess. There never was a river more suited to children than the Santa Ana. Winter was another story. Then, at the time of heavy winter rains, the Santa Ana (this was before it had been molested by man) could rise up and take out bridges, drown cows, and flood the towns of Anaheim, Placentia, and Yorba.

In summer you had to lie down in the river and roll over if you wanted to get wet all over. The water was crystal clear, and it flowed over sand that was sometimes gold, sometimes silver. Beer cans, tires, and plastic containers had not yet been invented. Summer, the sand, the water, children in old overalls and castoff dresses. The Santa Ana had one thing in common with the Wabash: sycamore trees grew on its bank. The river's waters were dappled by the shade of the big sycamore leaves; the mottled tree trunks appeared to reflect the dappled waters.

The minute Papa and Mama arrived in California they began traveling. They had never read Thoreau. They didn't know he had written: "What need to travel? There are no sierras equal to the clouds in the sunset sky. Are these not substantial enough?" No, said Papa and Mama, they are not substantial enough. We want the Sierras.

They didn't get the Sierras at once. They traveled in the beginning by nonmechanized horsepower: Diamond and Chinopsee hitched to surrey or spring wagon. We went to the Santa Ana in the spring wagon.

All Californians travel toward water: toward the sea; once toward the rivers; now toward the rivers impounded and called lakes; toward snow, which is frozen water. And even when Californians head toward the desert, they do so more to marvel at the presence of swimming pools and fountains than to play in the sand.

Papa and Mama were no exception. They went to the "Santa

Ana," which was the river. They went to Newport Beach, which was the sea. They set out with four children, traveling pies, shoeboxes of beef sandwiches, and foot-and-a-half fig newtons. Sometimes, not often, they traveled on Sunday. Occasionally they stayed overnight. They always took a trip on the Fourth of July, on Memorial Day, on Labor Day; they made excursions during spring vacation; on Christmas they drove to Big Bear or Baldy or Mount Lowe to see the snow.

The three big children rode on the backless, springless seat of the spring wagon. If we got tired we could lie down on the wagon floor and take a nap. Papa, Mama, and the new baby, Merle, who had been given a fancy name like all of us, rode on the front seat, which had a back and springs. Merle was to be Mama's last chance to produce what she had always wanted: an Indian-nosed, black-haired, bronze-faced baby like the man she had married. With Merle she missed totally: he had red hair, blue eyes, a big pug nose, and fair, freckled skin. He was never called anything but Rusty.

When we got to the water we swam. In the shallow, golden Santa Ana we were handled like princelings of a rich realm by the warm, gentle water. Sometimes a current would lift my dress to the waist, and, bloomerless (bloomers held too much water to wear swimming), I saw with pleasure my white minnow-shaped body, dappled with the shadows of sycamore leaves.

We were not princelings on the beach. There we were buffeted and pounded and scared. I, at least, was scared. We slept on the beach, and I could feel the earth tremble as the great waves struck the shore. Mama, who couldn't swim a stroke, who wasn't even a firm-footed wader, scared me as much at the beach as tidal waves did at home.

She got the blues; she got homesick. She came to see me once on a Friday afternoon after I was married, planning to spend the weekend. She read Elizabeth Maddox Roberts's *The Time of Man* through in a couple of hours, then she got in the car and started the seventy-mile trip home. "I am homesick for Eldo," she said.

She groaned and called upon her Heavenly Father when she was in pain. When she was in the hospital you could hear her corridors away. She was every nurse's least favorite patient. She managed to kick one nurse as she lay in bed, attached to nameless and numberless tubes. She didn't care for their baby talk. She wanted things faster and hotter and bigger than they gave them to her. "Isn't she deft?" she said to me of a nurse bumbling around her bed. "Did she say I was daft?" the nurse asked me suspiciously. The nurse's intuitions were right. Mama hadn't said it, but that was what she meant.

But she was physically brave. She drove faster than Papa. She refused one whole afternoon to speak to me and Carmen when, leaving the Grand Canyon, we headed back by the safe southern route of Arizona instead of striking north through Utah, where truck drivers had warned us of blizzards ahead.

When her doctor told her, "You have a lump in your breast that will bear watching," she answered, "We won't watch it. We'll take it out." She made the date, told no one but Papa, and in three days was rid of a malignant tumor that was spreading faster than any doctor could watch it. She lived another seventeen years after that, with never a word of fear about its recurrence, and with nothing but laughter when her hurried clapping on of a simulated breast resulted in lopsidedness. She called herself an Amazon, after those ladies of legend who cut off their right breasts so that their accuracy in drawing a bowstring would be unimpeded.

This was all in years to come. At the beach Papa, who could swim, went out a modest distance and swam in, powered by an incoming wave. Mama, with sunbonnet tied firmly under her chin and skirts modestly hoisted, waded out to take the dare of each wave personally. "Dare," in the lingo of Southern Indiana, was "banter." She "bantered" each wave to get her. The sea was an old hand at the game, and she wasn't. The undertow

66

48475

of a wave, seaward flowing, knocked her down; off her feet, she could not leap to hold her head above the frothing crest of the incoming wave.

I did what ostriches are said to do. I buried my face in the sand so that I would not see what was going to happen next: either Mama swept seaward or thumped down, lifeless as kelp, at our feet. And what I felt as I knelt with eyes hidden was rage. I was as ready to pound her and strangle her as the waves. The wicked, stupid, selfish, thoughtless woman.

"Open your eyes, Jessamyn," she said.

And there she was, standing by my side, drenched from her sunbonnet to the toes of her black lisle stockings. I opened my eyes and hit her: a blow not calculated to hurt (it was on full, wet skirts and below the knees), but to let her know how I felt. And that she was never to do that again.

She wouldn't let Papa punish me. "I know how she feels. It's the reason I whip Merle when he runs away and comes back safe. I don't want to kiss him to death."

So long as the travel was by spring wagon behind Diamond and Chinopsee I did not try to escape. But when the automobiles came, when the trips were longer, and the four in the back seat were larger, and when, I suppose, as Mrs. Leaman had warned me, God was preparing me to be a woman, then I wanted more room and more quiet for the job.

# X

—•—

Thoreau planned a book on Indians, and though most of his items on Indians are contained in his unpublished Indian notebooks, *Walden* and the journals are filled with his observations and reflections on Indians. The red man seemed to him to have somehow escaped the contaminations that plagued the white man. An Indian was only a little less noble than a tree or a pond. The index to his journals lists more headings under "Indian" than under "Ice," though not many more. He has four times as much to say about Indians as about poets, and ten times as much to say about them as about the moon. He knew that historians, in his day, had neglected them, that their lore was too little appreciated. Yet Thoreau had about as little contact with Indians as I have.

For all of its Spanish name—Mesquite—the town where I shop is an Indian town. It is surrounded by their fields and filled with their Pontiacs. The men stand in the sun outside the bars, leaning against the wall and gossiping. Indian men get fat in a seemly manner: no potbellies. The entire torso, beginning at the Adam's apple and reaching to the hipbones, thickens and broadens. "When to the age of forty they come, men run to belly, women to bum," the old saw says. Not so with these Indian men. The fat begins at the shoulders, and the belly protrudes no farther than the chest.

When they see me and Spry coming up the street they call

out, "Hello, Woolly." "Woolly" is, I take it, their name for Spry, though I am a little frizzy-headed myself. I keep a close watch on Spry. I read too many stories when young of the Indian liking for roast dog. Under his wool Spry is obviously a fat little morsel. In my mind I have saved him from too many flash floods to lose him now as a Saturday-evening feast for Mojaves.

I would like to talk to these men. I would like to lean against the side of the building and drink a bottle of Schlitz with them. I do not think of them as noble, as Thoreau did. I think that they, and Mexicans, are handsome: men, women, and children. If architects preach now—and they do—that buildings should be of a color that blends with the earth, then Indians and Mexicans are architecturally sounder than Anglo-Saxons.

If the drinkers were women, not men, I would feel freer to join them; freer but not as interested. As it is, I cannot do it. I'm not sure that Thoreau, free man that he was, could do it if the drinkers were Indian ladies. This is not a matter of color but of sex. And the men themselves quite likely would not care to have me join them.

We do usually exchange a few words, beginning with some discussion of Spry. Yesterday I was wearing a string of "beads" carved by a Pima Indian. The necklace is made up of five strands, each strand consisting of alternate bears and birds. The birds and bears are separated by minute shell circles. The color range is from gray to rose. I would rather own this than diamonds. As we exchanged remarks about Spry, one Indian lifted a strand of the necklace.

"This is Indian," he said.

"Pima," I told him.

"Where did you get it?"

"At the South West Museum in Palm Desert."

"Once we all wore them."

"Not the Mojaves," another drinker told him.

"If we caught a Pima we did. Now—" He gestured at the row beside him. The gesture said, "Now we drink beer."

Now they drink beer, and white money buys what once Indians made or won in battle.


My father had Indian blood. I knew this, though in the early 1900s it was something to keep quiet about. But I never truly *saw* Papa's Indian blood until, sitting in my piano box one late afternoon, I watched him, then Superintendent of the Yorba Linda Water Company, drive into the yard with Julian, his Mexican helper, on the wagon seat beside him. Papa was *darker* than Julian. Julian had some Castilian delicacy about him that Papa lacked. When Papa first came to California, someone seeing him asked, "Who is that greaser?"

Back East, Papa had an Indian grandmother. When his mother, squaw once removed, came to visit us in the Little White House, she put a fishing rod over her shoulder in the afternoon instead of settling down with the other ladies for a couple of hours of quilt piecing or rag braiding. She brought home fish for supper, too. A successful fisherman showed her Indian blood even more than one who had fished and failed.

It was this part-Indian mother Papa looked like. Inside my piano box, in the haze of my solitary observing and knowing, I could see her face in his. She, with a war bonnet and her black hair braided instead of knotted, could have been a great Comanche chief. There was a tenderness about the mouth that might have been a handicap for a chief. But the bronze brow, the implacable cheekbones, the strong prow of the nose, the big broad shoulders, would have constituted chief equipment in any tribe. In my fanciful vision, I saw my paternal grandmother as all Indian and all chief.

She married a man shorter than she was. Not wispy at all, but thick rather than rangy, with a big round jaw and a red walrus mustache. He was a reader, a hoper, and also a renter. To the thrifty Quakers of Southern Indiana (and in Southern Indiana you had to be thrifty to survive) there were only two things worse than renting: drinking and fornicating. (Dancing and card playing led to these other evils.) Grandpa West did not drink or fornicate. He was a pious United Brethren, baptized while there was still ice on Graham Creek. But economically he was loose. He didn't own land of his own. He rented, and was constantly convinced that he could rent a more productive farm for less money—somewhere else. So my grandfather was a mover, too. A renter *and* a mover.

If my father ever had inclinations in these directions, and Papa probably did, for he came from a family that hoped easily and despaired quickly, my mother put an end to them. An aunt, after an unfortunate confession at a revival, had come home and cut her throat; a cousin brought an end to a family quarrel by walking out into the woods and throwing a hangman's noose from a convenient sycamore limb. Papa knew that if he wanted to rent and move, he would have to do so without Mama. And as for suicide, that was a cowardly kind of murder, and Mama had no intention of living even with a would-be murderer. Mama was timid (when alone she sat up all night with the lamp burning), nervous, and small. But there were certain things she would never permit. Renting, moving, and suicide were very near the top of her list. At the very top, perhaps, was the death of a child of hers. That she would not for a moment countenance.

Why did the Renter, the Reading Renter, want his big Indian chief? She could throw a 100-pound sack of wheat across her shoulder and walk off with it as easily as another woman could shoulder a baby. Papa knew the duty a son owed his mother. But he had missed in his mother something he craved. "I can never remember her hand touching me, except on my backside, with me lying across her lap."

Why did the Indian chief want the man with the red walrus mustache? Moving on was perhaps in her blood, even more than in his. Her people had been accustomed to strike camp. She didn't judge him by Quaker standards.

Once, on a visit to the Little White House, she found Papa

(Mama was big with child) on the back porch doing the churning. She took the dasher from her son's hands before she had hat or coat off. "Men do not do housework," she told her daughter-in-law. Well, that was what *she* thought. The Renter perhaps never did any. But for her son there was always plenty of housework to do.

This woman who could not fondle a child perhaps enjoyed being fondled by a man. She gave the Renter four towering black-haired sons and a fifth no less large, with red hair; and finally a daughter, gentle and soft, doe-eyed, with the Renter's disposition.

Grandma West, before she married, was a Clark; the descendant, so legend had it, of the older of the two famous brothers, the one who, sometime before he became the hero of Vincennes, had had a blanket wife. Perhaps his only wife. He never, with preacher and legal papers, married another.

Papa was a reader and dreamer like the Renter, but his frame and his color were all Comanche; not a great towering chief like his mother—the Renter's blood had softened him a little—but a brave all the same. He toed in. His teeth didn't overlap like a white man's. When he died at ninety, though never a thin stringy man, his belly was still as flat as a board. A farmer in Indiana (schoolteacher, too), a rancher in California, he didn't have a drop of agricultural blood in his veins. He was never a man to hang over a fence admiring the hay crop. Barley was never king to him, no matter what he sang. He was a reasonable man, and having planted orange trees, knew that they had to be tended. So he tended them. "I think I was born lazy," he said. "I never saw the day when I wouldn't rather read and fish than plow." If so, he married the wrong woman for a career of that kind.

Those gone, those newly met—the imagination plays about them. Alone in my trailer, I think about Mama. She, who was riding in trailers thirty years before I stepped into one, would laugh to see me now so trailer-happy.

She was not a pretty woman. She evidently didn't have to be. She had beaux galore and kept Papa, as a young man, in a jealous frenzy, breaking parasols over the heads of other admirers and tearing up the pictures she had snapped with them at county fairs. Plain girls are more likely to incite these outbursts than beauties. They can then say to themselves, "I may not be beautiful, but I am certainly adored." The beauty looks in her mirror and knows that she is adorable. No one needs have a tantrum to prove it to her.

I often thought Mama downright ugly. I don't know whether or not she was. As an adolescent I had a quicker eye, I fear, for ugliness than for beauty. On shopping trips to Los Angeles I saw faces so gross, so cruel, so vindictive, so unloving, my own heart withered. Postures so humped. Gaits so awkward. Bodies so bloated. I could not believe that the people I saw on Main and Mission really looked as I saw them. If beauty is in the eye of the beholder, perhaps ugliness is there also. Was there something in me that caused me to hunt out and find ugliness? I didn't want to think so. I decided instead that people are not themselves on city streets: there—spending money, trying to save money, bone-tired, lost half the time, jostled by strangers, cheated by merchants, money gone God knows where—the face on the street is the mask, made up of all these feelings, that covers the true face. The true face can be seen only in a home. That very night around a supper table, these same forbidding, frightening, disgusting faces would, through the grace of their families, become, if not beautiful, then at least human and loving. So I told my accusing heart; but my reasoning mind told me that this ugliness, these faces of selfishness and hatred, would sit down at the table that night and, because of long acquaintance, be unnoticed.

Except on special occasions of "dressing up" or "going out," Mama did not think that she had a visible exterior. She herself lost awareness of that exterior. When lit up like a bonfire with compassion, gaiety, excitement, anger, she was unaware of straggling hair, uneven hemlines, or the old napkin she had

73

grabbed to use as a handkerchief. She was what she felt. She was the light and not the lamp.

Only once I think I saw Mama as she appeared most often to others. I came into the room where women were laughing and Mama was talking. The woman I saw talking was a stranger to me, a stranger with big, blazing blue-green eyes, a large red mouth, and a haystack pile of chestnut hair. I stood in the kitchen door like a rock; like a seeing-eye rock. So this was Mama. This was the woman other people saw.

Most often I saw the lamp and not the light. I saw ugliness in my mother's face. She was often in pain, easily exasperated, quick to anger, impatient, unfair. The lines from her nose to her mouth would deepen; her mouth would grow hard. I would say to myself, "Mama, I hate you." But then I would hate myself, for what is worse than a mother hater? Especially one who can't be steadfast in his hating and is finished with it in thirty minutes. And how could I hate Mama longer? She knew me and cared for me as no one else could. Papa was a kind and reasonable man. There are occasions that demand more. Mama knew that.

Back East, as a first-grader walking home through the snow, I saw, crouching by a log at the bottom of a snow-filled ravine, a black bear waiting to eat me. I sloshed hip-deep through wet snow in a two-mile detour to avoid being eaten, and arrived home wet and crying to tell my bear story.

Papa explained to me patiently that all the bears in Indiana had long since been killed. I knew better. All but one. That one I had just seen.

Mama understood that all the reasoning in the world would not put an end to this not unreasonable conviction that *one* bear in the general killing had been missed.

"Take her and show her, Eldo."

Eldo did. The bear was a twisted stump, with just enough of its black bark visible above the snow to make it look—even Papa had to admit—like a bear. After that, what I had once felt with my own hand to be a stump I could no longer imagine as a bear.

I was left-handed in an age when a left-hander had that hand tied behind his back by his teacher when he started school. Papa did not think this unreasonable. He was orderly. There was no left-handedness in *his* family. Even the Renter was right-handed. Mama was not orderly. Nor would she have an unnatural order imposed upon me. I went to school with a note: "This child was born left-handed. Do not try to change her." They didn't try.

When I graduated from the eighth grade it was, for some reason, important to me to have a graduation dress with lace on it. Mama was no dressmaker. She could sew, of course. She had to. But the best dress she ever owned, Papa, seeing her struggling to fit a pattern to material, had made for her: satin lapels, slit skirt with accordion-pleated inset, and all. Whatever was patterned, diagramed, blueprinted, Papa could make. He taught himself and us to play chess from reading the *Encyclopaedia Britannica*. A pattern drove Mama wild. Given directions, she lost her head. Recipes ended up her own—and improved.

But my graduation dress, Mama made without help. She used a pattern and achieved, in my opinion, a dream of loveliness. It had Chantilly-lace (imitation, Mama told me) sleeves and bodice to the point where the smocking of the high waistline began. The material was white voile. I was twelve years old, figureless but with a slim waist and broad shoulders, so that the close smocking at the waist and the fullness of the imitation Chantilly lace gave me an imitation figure. Not that I cared one way or the other. I can't remember thinking about figures until the next year in high school when I saw in the rest-room mirror that the line of my sweater had been interrupted by a couple of bumps. My feeling was about that of a woman who sees her smooth calves suddenly disfigured with varicose veins. If my stomach bulged, I could suck it in or ask

Mama for a Ferris waist. But the only way to cope with breasts seemed to be to get bigger and bigger sweaters.

In my white voile, lace-sleeved, smock-waisted dress, unaware as yet of figure problems, I was absolutely content. The graduates, twelve of us, sat in a semicircle of kitchen chairs on the stage of the school auditorium (and manual-training room), hidden from the audience by a green baize curtain. When the curtain was pulled, a great sigh of pleasure went up from the audience. I was, I thought, a vision of delight when first I burst upon their sight. All eyes, I thought, were on my beautiful dress. I looked at Mama down in the audience with pride. It was her handiwork that had made them gasp.

Did Mama look at me with pride? I don't know. She may have been as disappointed in my looks as I was in hers. One day after gazing at me for some time, she said, "You have a mouth like your Dad's, and I always thought his mouth was so sweet." Where did that leave me? I wasn't sure.

She wrote to her mother in the East: "Myron is good and Jessamyn is good, I guess. But she is never still a minute, body or tongue."

She said, "Jessamyn, never forget that handsome is as handsome does." I haven't forgotten it, but I have never for a minute believed it. Handsome is one thing, and doing is another. The twain sometimes meet, but that is pure coincidence, and when it does, it is usually a hardship for all concerned.

Once before a party she told me, "Jessamyn, you have very pretty eyes." She tried to build me up. She had two beautiful children: her first-born son and her second daughter. They did more for me than Mama's praise. I was of *that* family. I was born a moon, a fine reflector. I was Carmen's sister, and her beauty lit me up. Carmen knew quite well that people see exteriors, and she kept hers in good order. The boys who swarmed around her were a promise to me that someday the same thing would happen to me. When the key was given me. When I learned the word. Were we not of the same blood?

I now think that I was a plain girl, but when I was young, I didn't know it. I never said, as other girls did, "I hate my nose," "I hate the color of my hair," "I hate my legs," "I hate my teeth," "I hate my eyebrows." I didn't hate any part of me, though breasts seemed, when they appeared, an unneeded excrescence. My nose and teeth were straight. My hair was long and, when I bothered to wash it, shining. I knew that longer eyelashes and fewer freckles would be helpful. But the truth was I, too, thought I was transparent. My body was transportation, good transportation; I was a fast runner. I could kick higher than most boys. But I didn't live in kicking and running. I lived in what I felt, and there was too much of that to leave much space for worrying about looks.

Papa, as President of the School Board, had the job the night I graduated of handing out our diplomas: rolls of paper tied with white satin ribbon. It was a job Papa had looked forward to. But in mid-June, with California fruits ripe and inviting, Papa had eaten too many. He had the summer complaint. He would never be able to survive, sitting up there on the stage for two hours of recitations, songs, and a final speech—bound to be long-winded—from the County Superintendent of Schools, without having at some time to make a run for it.

"Nothing for it, Grace," he said, "but to give up the job and let Mr. Jepoon hand out the diplomas himself."

Boiled milk and strong tea hadn't helped, but Mama never gave up easily. She intended to see her husband hand out those diplomas himself. If the practical didn't help, she would try the imaginative.

We were in the midst of a hot spell, which comes sometimes when a summer Santa Ana too weary to really blow contents itself with spilling torrid desert air over the seaward valleys. In such weather Papa often got very bad nosebleeds.

"Eldo," Mama said, "there is no reason why you can't have one of your nosebleeds Friday night."

"I don't know that I can manage a nosebleed on order," Papa said. "And even if I could, I don't see that a nosebleed plus the trots would put me in any better shape for handing out diplomas."

"I don't intend you to have a real nosebleed," Mama said, "but just to pretend that you have one."

Papa began to get the picture.

"I don't like the idea any too well. Up there on the stage with twelve young people, one of them my own daughter, acting out a lie . . ."

"Do you want to hand out the diplomas?"

"Of course I do. You know that."

"Are you willing to say, 'Please excuse me, I've got a hurry call to the bathroom'?"

Papa wouldn't even answer a foolish question like that.

"Well, then, you take a couple of handkerchiefs with you. When you get a call, clap a handkerchief to your nose and hurry out. Come back with your face and hair a little wet. Put the handkerchief to your nose once in a while as if you're fearful of a setback. Everybody knows you get nosebleeds."

Nobody had to tell Papa how to act with a nosebleed. He was experienced there. A little beet juice on one handkerchief he wouldn't hear to, however.

"Enough's enough," he said.

One man's enough is another's privation. It was a good thing Papa was the one pretending to have a nosebleed. Mama, a born actress, didn't get onto any kind of a stage often and couldn't resist, when she saw her act was succeeding, adding to it. If she had been the one pretending to have the nosebleed, there would have been beet juice to spare. And if the response to that had been good, it would have occurred to her how much the audience would enjoy being let in on the secret of what those sudden off-stage gallops were *really* for. She would have created a scenario as she went along for her audience's pleasure. They would have laughed their heads off, nudging each other and saying, "Those nosebleeds are just a pretense. The summer complaint is what really ails her."

This bit of spontaneous acting, and overacting, would have come easily to her. But she could not have done what Papa did: preside in cold blood at a formal meeting. This would have given her the nervous jimjams. What we call structured was for her destroyed. "They will organize it," said the Devil of Christianity, and stopped worrying. Christmas was organized, and Mama ignored it. Mother's Day was organized, and she despised it. Thanksgiving was organized, but cooking up feasts seemed too natural a pleasure to her to be hurt by a set date. Besides, the dates used to vary, which took off some of the structural curse. Perhaps she was Quaker to the bone: each day and moment too sacramental for labels. Birthdays? Yes, for the old. She pitied old people, because she knew where she was headed. But for the young? Forget it. Wedding anniversaries? Hardly. Who wanted to be reminded of that ludicrous occasion? (She had had a toothache and a shivaree of horse fiddles and shotguns that had gone on until her mother, a woman as purposeful as the Renter was vague, went out onto the upstairs balcony and said, "That'll be about enough for tonight. Save something for the infare tomorrow.")

Mama didn't go to my college graduation. She and Papa were on a camping trip. She never went to hear any of my school debates. "One word more about Independence for the Philippines," she said at the supper table, "and you can go eat alone in the kitchen."

At a party given by high-school girls for their mothers in the school gymnasium, she took it into her head to grab the rope used for climbing exercises in the gym, which was tied back for the evening onto the balcony that overhung the gym floor; then, loosened rope in hand, she swung out over the heads of all, a female Tarzan. Edgar Rice Burroughs should have seen this Jane!

79

She who would not let her children say "belly," let alone "butt" or "snot" or "puke" or "ass," would, with fast, older girl friends of mine (they were all older), joke about marriage: saying, in my hearing (though she didn't know it), "It's nothing but dishes and douches, dishes and douches." What this meant, I had no idea; and the dictionary, as usual, was no help.

And this rope-swinging nosebleed-faker and anniversary ignorer was a slender, prayerful, pious, migrainous Quaker lady. If I was, for mothers (and I was), the Ideal School Girl— which meant that I got good grades, wasn't giving anyone boy trouble (much to my sorrow), and didn't seem to care much what I wore—Mama was the School Girl's Ideal Mother. Boy, did they wish they had a rope-swinging, piano-walloping, ta-male-pie-baking mother like mine! And a good part of the time I *wished* they had mine. In any crisis—black bears, Chantilly lace—she was *there*. She would always be there. I knew that. But there was an awful lot of living one had to get through between the lace and the bears.

The mother I really longed for at this time, though I didn't understand this until much later, was my back-East maternal Grandma, the one who could put shivareers to rout. She had been, for the first six years of my life, my real mother, while Mama was busy having babies and being a bride (she got over the toothache) to the husband she adored. "The children of lovers are orphans." Grandma Milhous had taught me how to make biscuits and to recite, "When God sorts out the weather and sends rain, why, rain's my choice." (It isn't, whoever does the sorting.)

"I don't want anything in life but Jessamyn," she wrote my mother. God, whoever sorts the weather, doesn't encourage putting all your eggs into one basket. By the time I was nine Grandma was dead.

So, without knowing it, I was Grandma's girl. I wanted a mother just like the girl that dear old Grandpa married. I wanted a short, plump, gray-haired, structured-to-the-bone mama, with a deep interest in Independence for the Philippines. I was not only asking a new moon to be full; I was asking a moon that waxed and waned to be constant.

At Walden, Thoreau put all of his furniture outside when he cleaned his cabin. He makes no mention of furniture moving when he lived in Concord in his mother's house. She probably set her foot down at the idea of putting the furniture out on the sidewalk. Thoreau did say once that furniture drove him crazy. But my opinion is that his mother's reply to that was, "It's time for you to take your walk, Henry."

In Yorba Linda I, too, set everything outside except the Kurtzmann, the stoves, the beds, and the dressers when I cleaned house; out onto the lawn (by this time there was a lawn), where it could get an airing as the house got a cleaning. Mama didn't care. She was untidy but clean, and what I was doing was cleaning.

Papa cared. He believed in cleanliness, too, but thought it could be achieved in some less spectacular fashion. A front yard full of furniture looked untidy to him.

He would come home from work and stop in front of the stacked furniture.

"People will think you are crazy."

"I don't care what people think."

"I care," he said.

"What's crazy about being thorough?"

"Now, don't bandy words with me."

Mama enjoyed bandying words. In fact, there was scarcely anything she enjoyed more. She made up words from scratch, by combining words, by turning them upside down, by running them backward. She built word palaces. Structures came out of her mouth like Steinberg pictures: wobbly, made of material fabricated on the spot, and no more useful than a poem. The bandying might start, if Mama was doing it, on the subject of furniture in the front yard. It wasn't likely to stop there.

Papa didn't forget what had started a conversation or where he expected it to go. He was a word lover, too; but his words were all prefabricated, straight out of Webster's Unabridged (which had come as a bonus with the *Encyclopaedia Britannica*). Words like "sapid" and "pinguid" and "cachinnating." "This is very sapid," Papa would say to his hostess, unnerving her for the rest of the meal. Papa would no more have made up a word than he would have created Frankenstein's monster. He reasoned that a man who hadn't mastered the current supply shouldn't add to it.

When Mama talked, the listener lived at the point of Joyce's pen. Like Joyce she used words that didn't exist—but her meanings were clearer than Webster or the *Britannica* ever managed. Mostly she was funny. This doesn't mean that she wasn't often mad as a wet hen, or dying with grief, or swollen with pride (not of herself but of the Milhous family). She could not be solemn and literal even on that serious subject. The world was a wilderness, few days, few days. She knew that. Oh, how she knew it. She grieved. She slapped mustard plasters onto her throbbing head. And was funny. My God, my God! She gave Him all the praise, but He had given her the ability, the compulsion, to pull a word or a happening askew, to show the world to us as it was, slantwise and si-goglin. She had, for normal family intercourse, a form of domestic glossolalia—a gift much esteemed nowadays—though she would have a fit of her soft, hearty, big-mouthed laughter at the idea that God was putting crazy words in her mouth the better to reveal God to man. But maybe He was. Maybe she underestimated Him.

Papa was the one who used words to make poems. Poems as we knew them then went clickety-click, with a wham-bang of rhyme at the end of each line. Poems (then) were reasonable structures: so many feet to the line; so many lines to the stanza; an idea (not too strange) that was concluded in the last stanza; and the whole made memorable with rhyme and rhythm.

*For of all sad words of tongue or pen,*
*The saddest are these: "It might have been!"*

A lot of truth in that; and since it was written by a New Englander, "been" and "pen" may have been an acceptable rhyme. Assonance certainly wasn't intended.

Papa wrote poems like that. He sent them back East to the *Banner Plain-Dealer*—poems praising California (he didn't know that Thoreau had said that those who went to California were 3,000 miles nearer hell). The *Banner Plain-Dealer*, not knowing it either, printed them. Papa took pride in their acceptance, but he never saved a one. The fun was in the making.

Papa made verses to put on place cards when Mama had the Eastern Star ladies to lunch (Waldorf salad, fried chicken, gravy, mashed potatoes, creamed peas, maple-raisin cake, and floating island pudding). Could Mama have written a verse if she tried? She never, to my knowledge, tried. I think she knew that what she felt about the Eastern Star ladies and Waldorf salad and our camp in the wilderness couldn't be crimped into lines of equal length, every other line ending in words that sounded alike.

Papa made verses. Mama came very near to talking poems. Papa and I both knew that. I hoped to heaven Mama would do her poem talking at home. It was entertaining, but it lacked decorum. Other mothers didn't ride on the nib of Joyce's pen. I don't think Papa cared. He was in love with Grace; crazy-talking Grace.

They met in their word pleasure in long evenings of anagrams. Papa was very good. Mama was better. She didn't have to play possum with him, which she did with me when I played with them and was beaten by both. She would let a finger by chance drop upon a letter, which would permit me to take one of her words. She would hum a song whose title just happened to contain a word that I, if I had my wits about me, could make with the letters I had.

Papa thought this babying took the fun out of the game for

me. It did. I was belittled by it. But Mama was more sensitive than Papa to the pains of losers. Perhaps because she was more set on winning than he, she knew better what losers suffered. Papa had a little of that easygoing Renter blood in him. It was just a game, wasn't it?

They played anagrams on more or less equal terms. But they couldn't read together; not a letter, not the *Weekly Star* or even, with complete Christian harmony, the Sunday-school lesson. Mama was finished with a page before Papa was well started. I have tried to account for this difference in speed. In any IQ test Papa would, I'm sure, have left Mama far behind. But Papa read the words, while Mama read the meaning. Mama read what the writer wanted to say, which needed perhaps considerably fewer words than he had used in the saying. She read perhaps what she needed to get out of the reading. But she never, in the times I have heard Papa challenge her, failed to give him enough of the gist of what she had read to satisfy him.

They differed in another reading trait. If Papa read what he thought was true or witty or timely, he wanted to read it aloud to a listener. He insisted, in fact, on reading it aloud. This, I suppose, was the teacher in him. We enjoyed discussion. I could talk with him about Independence for the Philippines or the meaning of Browning's "My Last Duchess" all evening long. But not with Mama. She didn't want to discuss. She wanted to *be*. And people who enjoy reading aloud have no idea how painful their slow performance can be for a fast reader. It is comparable to forcing a music lover to listen to a fifteen-minute composition drawn out note by slow note to over three-quarters of an hour. Such listening pulls the brain apart, waiting for the laggard to arrive at a destination where you have been waiting for days—it seems.

Mama was careful of other people's feelings. But once in a while she would say, in the midst of Papa's reading on some subject that wouldn't have interested her even if she had read it herself, "Eldo, you are casting your pearls before swine." Occasionally this made Papa huffy enough to stop. Usually he kept right on casting.

I wasn't Mama, though. I was a twelve-year-old girl and couldn't tell Papa what or what not to do. He was the one who told me. "Don't bandy words with me," he said. So I didn't. I kept the furniture off the lawn.

But my bedroom was at the back of the house, and it had double casement windows. Through these windows I still, bandying or no bandying, continued to lower all the movable furniture when I cleaned my room.

My dearest possession was a desk. I didn't spend much time at it, but I knew what desks were for. People sat at desks and wrote. They cast up their accounts there. They wrote their checks there. They filed their correspondence in the desk's pigeonholes. I didn't have any correspondence to file, so I borrowed old letters to give my desk a used look. I kept it open, with a bottle of ink, a pen, and a notebook on the green felt of the hinged lid, so that if an idea struck me in passing I could jot it down.

Where did the desk come from? Why did *I* get it? I got it probably because I clamored for it. It came from Japan. It was the color and more or less the size of a young giraffe: it was tall, thin, wobbly, with spotted bamboo legs. It would never be noticed in a forest except when it refused to run.

By unhappy chance Papa came home for lunch one noon by the back way just as I was carefully lowering the desk.

"Drop that," he called.

I knew he didn't really mean it. It was his anger at the sight of a desk wriggling out of a bedroom window that spoke. If I had answered, "Papa, if I drop it, it will break into a thousand pieces," he would have said, "Well, pull it back in, then."

I don't suppose I really loved my desk as much as Abraham loved Isaac. But I loved it. And I dropped it, not because my father's word was law, but because I wanted to put him in the wrong. Abraham would have slit Isaac's throat because he loved God. I dropped my desk—and it splintered into a thousand pieces, as I knew it would—to demonstrate to all what a cruel and spiteful father I had. Abraham wasn't like that.

Mama rushed to the back door, where she could see the carnage. "Oh, Jessabee," she cried, "you've dropped your desk."

"Papa told me to do it."

"Eldo, you surely never told her to smash her desk?"

"I told her to drop it."

"Why? She was only cleaning house."

"I told her not to clean house that way."

"You ought to be thankful you have a daughter who likes to clean house."

"I'd be more thankful if I had one who obeyed."

But he was sorry. He marched into the house and ate his lunch without another word. That night he gathered up the pieces of my ruined desk, took them to the barn, and tried by lantern light to fit them together again. They wouldn't fit. The poor giraffe was dead.

Such is the irony of fate that now, with a place of my own, a cabin in the wilderness, I do not own one piece of movable furniture.

# XI

———•••———

Papa and Mama lived at the right time and were in the right place and of the right age to ride the crest of the wave of the future in 1910. That wave was transportation by means of the horsepower developed by an internal combustion machine. They were in their twenties. They had grown up in the backwoods of Southern Indiana. Their only means of travel had been behind the rump of a buggy horse; a twenty-mile journey was a real expedition. Their honeymoon was a fifteen-mile trip to Clifty Falls, where a small creek, the Muscatatuck, dropped 100 feet or more over some minor limestone ledges. Here they were in California, a state that had much that Indiana did not possess; and what Indiana did have, California had in forms bigger, older, and brighter than Indiana.

The ocean itself was a novelty. Think of it! Across that water lay China!

There were mountains in California, the highest in the United States. On some the snow never melted; on others there were peaks partially covered with snow, villains with their switchblades showing.

The lowest spot in the United States was in California, as well as the highest; the saltiest water; the tallest tree; the oldest tree; the strangest tree; the hottest desert; the least rainfall; the only volcano. There were animals they had never seen: mountain lions, coyotes, road runners, jack rabbits, ground squirrels, rattlesnakes, gophers, centipedes, tarantulas, trap-door spiders, condors, sea lions.

There were fruits and vegetables they had never tasted: loquats, pomelos, pomegranates, kumquats, kid-glove oranges, unprocessed olives, black figs, artichokes, chili peppers, cauli-flower, boysenberries, alligator pears.

California! What a place to find yourself in while still young and with a means of travel the world had never known before: a mechanical car! Think of it! A horseless buggy! You climbed into it, and without horses, oxen, mules—it went. Incredible! It would have been a miracle in the hills of Southern Indiana, with nothing more to see than Clifty Falls and the fort at Old Vincennes. But in California! Going to the moon is undoubt-edly a miracle, but what have you got when you get there? And their mode of travel when they get there is what? A mechanical car. In California they had something to see, and Papa and Mama proposed, equipped with *their* car, to see all of it—fast.

The automobile didn't mean much to us children. I think Papa and Mama soon took it for granted themselves. We talk a lot about technique and its products, how our lives are changed by these products, and how men of the past would marvel at our accomplishments. But bring Pepys, a worldly man, back to earth, he who was "with child with curiosity to see any new thing," and rockets and Hovercrafts and frozen foods and electrical can openers would not impress him half as much as the disappearance of religion from our lives. In the seventeenth century the name of God was in every man's mouth. Religion is no longer a burning issue in politics. A few men still kill each other in God's name; but the fires that killed the martyrs have all died down. How we travel and at what rate is a fact Pepys could absorb in a day, but he might never get used to the absence of God in our lives. He might need to carry with him, as the astronauts do, some device to provide him with the atmosphere of his own world, the religious world of the seventeenth-century England he had left behind him.

Papa's first car was a Duro. It had acetylene headlights, which were lighted with a match and were housed in brass containers about the size and shape of spittoons. The car itself was red, topless, and doorless. Its horn was a rubber bulb the size of a pastry bag. When squeezed twice rapidly, it went "honk-honk" mildly. Mama didn't think it authoritative enough. She carried in her lap a Klaxon horn, which she sounded on curves at approaching cars and in open country simply to celebrate our escape from danger. It was authoritative. There is no telling how often she saved our lives by Klaxoning, nor how often she barely escaped driving Papa up the side of a mountain with a sudden unexpected blast.

We went in the Duro prepared for breakdowns. We all had books. A soft ball. Mama carried mending. But I remember her most often working on her word lists. She kept in notebooks—actually the long narrow books children used in those days for their spelling lesson—people's unusual names: names she found in newspapers, read on mailboxes, or was told by her friends. I've heard her greeted with, "Grace, I've got a name for you that you'll never believe." Papa enjoyed words, but a word wasn't enhanced for him by being the odd name of a preacher over in Buena Park. Mama enjoyed the combination of words and people.

She had her lists of unsorted names: Smoocher and Lead and Pussy and Smack. When the Duro broke down, she organized her lists. She had lists taken from reports of marriage licenses. A Mr. Lyon married a Miss Lamb. She didn't joke with us children about it, but I'm sure she giggled with Papa about the Lyon and the Lamb lying down together. There were such strange coincidences in the matter of the union of names in marriages that it was difficult not to believe that the couples were game players in real life as Mama was on paper. Mr. Money married Miss Banks. Of course. Where else would he go? Joy married Bliss. Head married Foot. Singer married Organ. A Mr. Rufus King married a Miss Ivy Throne.

That *Ivy* bothered Mama all of her life. She thought it surely must have been a misprint for Ivory. How was an *Ivy* Throne going to support a King?

At breakdown time she went through her lists, putting names as yet unclassified under the headings where they belonged. Foods were together; professions, household objects, animals, acts (like Ryder, Smoocher, Tatler). God-awful names. Mama didn't call them that, of course. But there were names she would never have consented to bear. "I would go to law before I would have a name like that." She did not consider Phillpot a nice name. Or Souse. Or Bumstead. She considered the Misses Hogg of Texas spiritless not to have changed their names. She liked the names in her and Papa's family. West she thought poetic, and suited to a man with Indian blood. Clark was the English pronunciation of Clerk; and a clerk in the beginning was a man who used his head and his pen, both items she respected. Her own name, Milhous, was prosaic enough, but there was nothing ridiculous about being named for so useful a building. McManaman, her mother's name, was Irish and its meaning unknown, but it wasn't a laughable or vulgar name.

While Mama worked on her word lists and I read, Myron stayed close to Papa, handing him tools like an apprentice surgeon. Carmen took a nap. Rusty ran about getting into mischief, unless, as often, he was tied with a long rope to the spoke of a wheel. He might scream, but at least he wouldn't get run over.

Pretty soon Papa would crawl out from under, yell, "All aboard!" and we'd be off to wherever we had been headed in the first place: San Gabriel Mission, Pio Pico's Palace, Mount Lowe, Seal Beach, Mount Rubidoux. Sometimes the breakdown lasted for so long that wherever it had happened was accepted as the place we were going. The journey was to breakdown and back.

After the Duro, which I think didn't last long, came a

series of Fords: Model Ts, Model As, touring cars, and finally sedans. When I bought my first car, a convertible, Papa was grieved. "Cloth tops," said he, "are a step backwards. We've advanced beyond that. Get a sedan. Get something that will shut out the weather." But convertibles were fashionable, and I liked the idea of letting the weather in. Papa was shamefaced about my convertible before his friends. "It's a quirk she has," he said, as if I had reverted to a horse and buggy. He associated a convertible, I think, with the first new Ford he owned. He had driven it, top down, in summer weather to San Diego and had arrived with a family whose faces were as swollen and glazed as candy apples. *He* didn't sunburn, but his family of towheads and redheads did. The purpose of the trip was to visit the San Diego Exposition. All I can remember of that Exposition, which must surely have had a wonder or two, even though it was playing second fiddle to San Francisco, was the pain of my swollen face and the pain of my hand firmly clasped by Mama, who never once let go while we were in the Exposition's halls. There was a chain of command. Mama held my hand in a vise; I held Rusty's. I was twelve years old, of a juicy age, Mama had read, for white-slave dealers in South America. We were down near the border, and if there was one thing Mama had no intention of my ending up as, it was a young white slave. Any white-slave dealer who, after a look at my pumpkin-sized, tomato-colored face, had regarded me as useful merchandise would have been a fringe operator at best and a difficult man to work for. I am glad now that Mama never loosened her hold. Poor Rusty, burned even worse than I, two years old and of no commercial value to anyone, unless he had lived in the Ireland of Dean Swift's modest proposal, suffered as lower links in a chain of command always do: the recipient of the amassed pain of those above him.

After the Fords came all kinds of cars: Franklins, Reos, Paiges, Graham-Paiges, Durants, Chevrolets, a Packard, a Maxwell, a Dodge. The Paige was the transition car between the touring car and the sedan, and in its time it was a wonder. The Paige was actually a sedan not yet completely firmed up.

The Paige was the last car in which I ever took a prolonged trip with my family. I had begun to escape long before its purchase, when I was seventeen. When I was eleven or twelve, I was considered old enough to be left alone when the family went on all-day trips. Mama felt sorry for me. The wheel never turned under her that didn't give her pleasure. She waved until the last, pitying me, thinking of the sights they were going to see and that I would miss. I don't know the name for what I felt as the dust of the Ford or the Franklin died away, leaving the air as clear as if my family had never passed through it. At first some sorrow, then some misgiving: would I truly be missing great sights? And the great funny squeals of excitement from Rusty, never again to be heard in this world? It might be so. But when I came inside and closed the door, that savage, trembling excitement of being alone, alone in an empty house, once again possessed me.

Has a person arriving ever given me the pleasure of a person leaving? A door opening, the joy of a door closing? These are terrible questions to be asking yourself at twelve. If the answer is no, does it mean that you don't love your own mother and father, brothers and sister? I was unable then to give myself as satisfactory an answer as I can now. I had so much more family so much more often than I had solitude that solitude was the rarity, the jewel. Reverse the situation: be alone six days of the week, then let the door open, and the people who enter may be as exciting as solitude.

Though I am not sure. Solitude, like a drug, can be addictive. The more you have it, the more you want it. Solitude is an unending colloquy between you and yourself and such persons as inhabit your memory or are called forth by your imagination. It is painful to have this colloquy interrupted by the voices of real people. "Be still, be still," you want to say to them. "I can't hear what's being said." In the heart of solitude, when barriers between yourself and the world melt, your body becomes, as Thoreau said, "the organ and channel of a melody, as a flute is of the music that is breathed through it."

The door opens. "Oh, you're alone. I was afraid I might be interrupting a conversation."

"A conversation? You *are* interrupting a communion!"

I had two reasons for not wanting to travel. The first was that I wanted to be alone, and there is no place where you are less alone than when wedged four deep into an auto seat built to hold three at the most. The second reason was that I had my doubts about travel itself. "Many a weed here stands for more of life to me than the big trees of California. . . ." And my family was undoubtedly headed for big trees, while I had not yet digested volunteer oats and tumbleweeds.

All young people reach a point where travel with their family is a chore if not a pain in the neck. This was not my feeling. It wasn't that I didn't want to travel with them. I didn't want to travel with anybody: not with Teddy Roosevelt up the Amazon or with Geraldine Farrar on a concert tour.

# XII

———◆———

When Papa and Mama left for a camping trip of several days, they sometimes solved the problem of what to do with their reluctant traveler by leaving me with Mama's father, Grandpa Milhous. He was now a widower, and they believed (or hoped) that I would be company for him and help with his housework. The housekeeping after life with an undomestic whirlwind like Mama was easy. Cooking for a man who said that he had never eaten a better meal than a well-cooked sweet potato and a well-sliced uncooked beefsteak tomato was a snap. I was company for him to the extent that I was an audience for his music and stories. These did not break into my solitude. They did not ask for a response. The music was a concert that didn't need applause; the stories were a book that required no comment. That is the way I think Grandpa wanted it.

Grandpa Milhous was a small man—neat, sandy-haired, and light-complexioned, with a somewhat shamefaced smile. He thought a good man of his age should not be inclined to levity, yet the stories he told were pretty funny. It worried him that a man of his upbringing should be so prankish.

He later married a very peculiar second wife—a prankish act, indeed—a spinster of fifty-odd. She had no hair and wore a wig in the days before wigs were chic. The wig was shaped like a thatched beehive of the Old Country, straw-colored and pretty unstable. It might, if worn with herringbone knickers and boots, get by today; but Loll had no boots and no knickers. She also had no eyebrows. Of other things she had more than enough. She was a true miser.

She washed the waxed papers in which oleomargarine was wrapped, hung them on the line to dry, then stored them in crackling piles like the pelts of some old deer slayer. On Monday mornings she made enough toast to last through the week. The oven heat that would toast two slices of bread would toast fourteen just as easily. A room was filled with old newspapers containing items she had not had time to read on the day the paper arrived. She turned off (there is a faucet that does this) the water that flows into the holding tank of a toilet. She did this to cut down on irresponsible flushing, which wasted water when there was no real and crying need for flushing. Washing wore out clothes, so mostly she hung them on the line and aired them.

She lived into her nineties. There is nothing like a diet of week-old toast and an engrossing hobby to prolong life.

Loll was certainly a change from Grandpa's first wife, who was a perfect grandmother. I think she may have been less than perfect as wife and mother.

Grandpa Milhous was thirty when he married Mary Frances McManaman, who was almost thirty herself. Mary Frances was called Dollie by her own people, because she was doll-like: very small, with pink cheeks, round blue eyes, and black hair, which lay in flat curves of black satin against her forehead and cheeks, like the hair painted on the head of a china doll. The Quaker family she married into (Dollie, like my own father, was a United Brethren before she became a Quaker by "conviction") felt that "Dollie" was too frivolous and worldly a name for a Quaker matron; particularly a Quaker matron who was going to be a daughter-in-law of theirs. So they changed her name. For the rest of her life Mary Frances Milhous was Dollie to the McManamans and Mollie to her in-laws.

The Milhous family were great hands for name changing. A son with the sound Biblical name of Ezra married a girl whose name was Lima. "Lima! She had as well be called Montevideo. Or Lima Bean!" So *her* name was changed to Dorothy.

The Milhouses got their comeuppance in name changing when a Milhous daughter whose name was Hannah married a man named Francis Anthony Nixon. "Hannah!" exclaimed the Nixons. "Can't you just hear people calling her Hanner?" So they changed *her* name to Mildred.

Jess Milhous soon discovered, if he had not known it before, that this small-boned, pink-cheeked girl he had married was not only no doll, she was downright manly—if the attributes of energy, ambition, and clear thinking should any longer be attributed solely to men.

In a day when young people were marrying even earlier than they do today, why did Jess and Dollie wait so long?

Jess was a young man of little self-confidence. He was the second son of a Quaker minister who had already borne a son who was genial and confident from birth. The second child, of necessity, plays second fiddle. This task is more onerous when the first fiddle turns out to be a virtuoso and would have been first no matter what his position in the birthing program. Jess's own mother, the Quaker minister, said that Jess had been given a "queer turn" because her husband, Joshua, had taken to chewing tobacco while she was carrying Jess. There is no telling what a female Quaker minister in 1855 considered a "queer turn." But Jess Milhous was undoubtedly a shy, stand-offish young man, with the sense of humor a young and uncomely sibling has to develop. Such a one has the choice of being funny or tragic. Given a little will power and some pleasure in words, he chooses to be comic. Only the beauties choose to be Byronic and tragic.

Jess, except that his hair was sandy-red instead of brown, looked a good deal like Thoreau. Both were on the small side: Thoreau, five feet seven; Jess, five feet nine or so. Both had big noses and large gray-blue eyes. But where a man makes himself, in the expression of his mouth, Thoreau did a better job. His large, sweet, smiling mouth contradicts every sharp word he ever said. That nose, that brow, may have written the castigating words, but his mouth wrote, "I love my life. I warm toward all nature."

Jess may have loved his life, but he could not say the castigating words about what was not lovable; the effort of holding them back twisted his mouth a little. You can't think one way and speak another without the mouth becoming a little warped.

Nevertheless I think Grandpa Milhous and Thoreau shared five characteristics. Both were men of probity. Both loved nature; and, more surprisingly, both loved music: Thoreau his telegraph harp and music box, Grandpa his accordion and his Gramophone, with its morning-glory horn. Both relished odd people and anecdotes about them. But above all, both were idealistic about love, and no hand with the ladies (the two may go together). Jess then made the mistake, I think, of marrying an equally idealistic young woman, and one who had been hurt by the actions of her brothers and sisters.

Mary Frances McManaman was one of a brood of lusty young Irishers. A sister-in-law told Doll McManaman that she had had her second child alone in a sod house in Kansas while Doll's brother was out tomcatting. Her first child, a little girl of two years, her only companion in the ordeal, had said, "Mama, Mama, there's a kitten in bed with us."

Doll was up to a physical ordeal of that kind, but she never intended to go through with it while the kitten's father was off drinking with a saloon girl. She never had to. She had waited through days of schoolteaching and disapproval of her own high-stepping brothers and sisters for someone like Jess: a man who had never tasted and would never taste alcohol in his life; a slow, quiet Quaker, good, though a little touched, perhaps, by his tobacco-chewing father.

What Jess was waiting for I don't know. A girl with Doll's

principles, perhaps. Perhaps simply a pretty girl who would have him. More likely a pretty girl who let him know she would have him. Should Jess have remained a bachelor? Would he have been happier? Perhaps. But a wife who was a cross between Emerson's Aunt Mary and Teddy Roosevelt charging San Juan Hill was a powerful mixture for that quiet man, though a perfect grandmother for a certain kind of child.

Mama adored her father, quite likely because he was so much more easygoing than her mother. To my mind he had some less-than-adorable traits. But Mama was loyal to her men: her father, her husband, even her brother. This did not apply to her father-in-law. Still, however much she might deplore the traits that made her father-in-law the man he was, she never failed to make it clear that the Renter's son, *our* father and *her* husband, was pure gold—almost entirely Clark—and that the Clarks, in spite of their Indian blood and suicidal tendencies, were handsome, hard-working, property-owning Christian people.

Mama had ways of accounting for her children's merits and shortcomings. The Wests and McManamans provided the shortcomings. (The McManaman shortcomings, while *wrong,* weren't totally unappealing.) If we were without fault, we were wholly Milhous. My brother Myron, except that he had the Clark olive skin and handsome bone structure, was almost wholly Milhous. The Milhouses believed, and with reason, that handsome was as handsome did. As a result they tried harder, even when handsome, which wasn't often.

I was McManaman-Milhous; not enough scallawag to be a charismatic McManaman; not enough piety to qualify as a complete Milhous. But I was entirely on her side of the house, and we got on each other's nerves much the same as close distaff relatives can. Sometimes she said that she felt she had in me a second mother—which is one mother too many. "Mama," she said of her mother, Doll, "would come into the house, which was just beginning to be comfortably warm, throw open all the windows to the cold air, and say, 'Oh, what a beautiful balmy day.' You do the same." How much of what we consider choice has been decided for us in the womb by matters of body temperature, blood pressure, and pulse rate? The cold-blooded snake may charm the warm-blooded bird, but if the bird is smart, she'll run, or, better still, fly.

My sister, Carmen, was a Clark in looks; a McManaman in her ability to attract and be attracted by the opposite sex. But since she was the second girl and accustomed to a big sister who could do the housework, she had developed a lazy streak, which was, of course, according to Mama, pure West.

Rusty, the baby, was hard to assay. Some pure Milhous gold; a lot of McManaman drive and charm, which made up for the lack of Clark beauty; and the whole streaked through with occasional smudges of West dross.

Papa, it now seems to me, was pure angel to put up with this kind of nonsense. He couldn't have done so except that he knew that for him and with him Mama would have walked away barefoot from all of her exemplary kinfolk.

The McManamans weren't all exemplary, and they posed her a problem. She was too honest and too touchy to pretend that they were. The truth was that she preferred sins of commission to sins of omission. The McManamans were rather large-scale committers for their era and area. They drank, they played cards, they chased women; they were, someone said, Odd Fellows first and United Brethren second. The great-aunt by marriage, the one who had had a kitten in bed, said to me once, "Jessamyn, perhaps I shouldn't say this to you. You're a Mac, and so is your mother. But there's a hard streak in the Macs. They'll get what they want, no matter how much it hurts someone else." (She had a tough streak herself to have endured a husband who, when she told me this, was in his seventies and living with a twenty-year-old waitress.)

Mama's only brother, a Mac to the bone, invited Papa in

the first year of Papa's marriage to accompany him to a nearby railroad town, where two girls succumbing as usual to Mac charm were giving it away. When her brother died, Mama eulogized him to me thus: "He didn't have a debt in the world, all of his property was clear, his word was his bond."

This affronted me. This was a banker's report on a customer. Why not mention his real wit and generosity and the affection he generated? But perhaps a brother capable of a proposal of the kind he had made her husband, economically sound though it was, could be praised only on economic grounds.

Perhaps the Mac blood boiled more fiercely in Mama's veins than I ever realized. Possibly she idolized her father and his people in an attempt to avoid Mac pitfalls. She praised her father as Christian. Sometimes he seemed to me less Christian than chicken.

It was not only that any form of bragging or boastfulness was repulsive to him; it was especially repulsive if well founded. If you have a light, his advice was, put it under a half-dozen bushels.

If the apple crop is good, do you plan a trip to Philadelphia? Keep quiet about your plans. The crop may fail, and the neighbors will then have cause to wag their heads and say, "Oh, yes, he was all set for Philadelphia. But the worms got to the apples before he did." Keep quiet about the apples and Philadelphia. If the crop is good and you do go, let the neighbors be the ones to say, "I hear you just got back from Philadelphia." At this you can nod with a shamefaced smile, and any further information about Philadelphia will have to be pumped from you in driblets. In this way you get the reputation for being a modest, closemouthed fellow, which was the kind of fellow to be in a backwoods Quaker community in the 1880s. Grandpa wanted—who doesn't?—to be known for something. He chose the possible—to be what he could: cautious, closemouthed, a man who never said a bad word about anyone.

Mama never ceased trying to make a Milhous of herself. An

Irishwoman (with a Welsh streak) through and through, she never ceased trying to be thoroughly Quaker: something that has been declared to be a contradiction in terms.

Jess Milhous undoubtedly gave his only daughter much love. But he also gave her a set of maiming inhibitions. She was advised by him to follow his example: never to take a chance, never to stick her neck out, never to make a fool of herself, never to give herself away. She was made to stay in the eighth grade for two years after graduation. Was she prepared to say that she had mastered every subject taught there? No, not with her father asking the question she wasn't. She was made to apologize to a boy for waving to him before he waved to her. Did she want to grow up forward, a boy chaser? No, she didn't. She was made to go upstairs to bed after reading those two dreadful words "bucking bronco" out loud. Did she want to be vulgar? No, that was not her ambition.

The sexual self-consciousness that her father passed on to her and that her mother (knowing the blood that ran in her daughter's veins) no doubt added to, the daughter lost in bed with a loving man. But though she herself had been freed, she preached the straight doctrine as she had been taught it to *her* daughters.

Dollie and Jess were undoubtedly less lucky, in bed and out, than Grace and Eldo. Dollie was a McManaman determined (like Mama) to be a Milhous (except in some matters in which she considered Jess clearly wrong). She probably *was* a Milhous in bed, but once she got out in public she became 100 per cent McManaman. She saw no virtue in hiding *her* light under a bushel. She was superintendent of the Sunday school (a job usually held by a man); correspondent for the *Banner Plain-Dealer;* a speaker on temperance; and, as an ex-schoolteacher, a leader in school affairs. She kept me, out in California, bombarded with clippings; with magazines that carried articles and stories appropriate to my age; with books: *Anne of Green Gables, The Thrall of Lief the Lucky;* with poems I was instructed to memorize and deliver. She had let Mama, when Mama was a girl, enter elocution contests (which she won). She primed her for spelling bees (in which Mama was less fortunate). She made for both of us dresses not calculated to keep us out of the public eye.

Grandpa did not approve of a number of his wife's activities, particularly the Sunday-school superintendent's job. He did not believe in speaking up on any occasion, and least of all, as a Quaker, on a religious occasion. And the Sunday-school superintendent had to speak up. But Grandpa knew well enough that to stop a McManaman from doing what he had his heart set on doing, someone would *have* to speak up. And this Grandpa could not do, not to his Doll.

Mama held it against her mother that she spoke sharply to Jess. "I don't think Papa ever entered the door without Mama's saying, 'Jess, did you remember to wipe your feet?' "

"Well, had he remembered?" I would ask.

"Not always. Not very often, I guess."

Jess, the silent man who played it close to the chest, who had no intention of giving himself away or making a fool of himself, was yet willing to keep a hired man away from his work for an hour while the two of them leaned against the railing in a fence corner, gabbing. Grandma didn't approve of this, either. "Jess's requirements for a hired man," she said, "are a glib tongue and a hearty laugh. I choose my hired girls for the amount of work they can turn out." And with Grandma buzzing away at their side they turned out a great deal.

You could make a fool of yourself in Sunday school, or at a meeting of the Ministry and Oversight Committee, or even at a pie supper. But who could make a fool of himself standing in the corner of a rail fence talking to his hired man? There comparisons were not being made. There Grandpa felt safe, his "queer turn" forgotten. So there Grandpa stood, talking.

Grandpa had the grain, tiny as a mustard seed, of an artist

in him—very tiny and completely crushed by his era, his place in the sibling order, his religion, and finally his wife. Mama responded to this spark of creativeness in her father, and she resented her mother when she quenched it.

Grandpa was a storyteller: to hired men, to children, to those with whom he couldn't lose face. He didn't blurt out his stories. He didn't, as Mama did, turn the day's happenings into stories so that we, knowing that nothing unusual had happened, were short with her because she put suspense into stories that didn't merit it. "Tell us what happened," we urged, impatient with so much nutcracking for so little kernel.

Grandpa's stories were set pieces. He had thought them through in his mind before he told them. They were not about the day's happenings. Their suspense was an organic part of the story; the tension of will he-won't he was not added to snare the listener, like a rabbit into a box trap. The not knowing, the suspense, the tension, was what the story was all about. It was what the hero had endured. It was not what the listener had to endure. It was what the listener craved. The hero was most often Grandpa himself, but he was a very modern non-hero: a small man for whom things did not go right. The hero was the boy who believed that all Johnny Rebs were ferocious men, devils in everything but horns and tails. When the small boy hero encountered a Johnny Reb in the woods, the listener, who now believed with the small boy that all Rebs were black-hearted, waited for the boy to have his head lopped off by the Reb's saber. But while he waited he saw, as the boy did, that this Confederate was a thin, starved boy, feverishly hunting wild blackberries and greedily eating them. And while the listener had waited in fear with the boy, he had also had his eyes opened to a truth: people are not so very different. Confederates were like other men: young and old; cruel and kind; well fed and starved.

Grandpa's stories were all like this. They were often funny; he (or the hero) usually came out the little end of the horn, and the listener, at least if he was a child, learned that there was more than one way of looking at the world.

Since Grandpa's stories were formal—he, the narrator; I, the audience—no conversation about them was expected. I might say if my curiosity got the better of me, "Did you ever see the Reb again, Grandpa?" But this was not expected or even wanted. The story ended where Grandpa ended it.

Grandpa's stories, because they were rounded, well shaped, the sharp edges cut off, slipped through the mind more easily than Mama's. Grandpa's stories were finished before he gave them to you. There was nothing more to be done with them. He had done it all. He had made it all. Modern ready-mix packagers have discovered that the consumer enjoys most the mix to which he has to add something. But down to the last appropriate word Grandpa's stories, when they ended, were finished. He had a point, and he had made it. There was nothing the consumer could add. He was, with an entirely different subject matter, a kind of O. Henry. He liked surprise endings. The noise in the strange house that had alarmed him had been caused by his own dog, broken loose and dragging his chain behind him upstairs to his master's bedroom.

Mama was a Chekhov at that point where Chekhov makes a note of what he wants to write, then wonders. Mama did not make notes. She told us. Something she had seen or heard and had wondered about. "I liked to hear Mama's wedding ring clink against the glasses as she washed them." Why? "The old man who had never had a wife had a pretend-wife to whom he talked when he thought no one could hear him." Did you hear him? "When his wife was sick, Henry Little always got in bed with her and stayed there until she was well." Did you see them?

Grandpa's imagination had had sixty-five years to work on his stories when he told them to me, aged eleven or twelve. There was nothing much more he or I could do to them. He told me one or two after supper. While I washed the supper dishes, he sat at the cleared table, draped with its soft, back-

East tablecloth of red or blue checks. There was no hot water in that California bungalow, and the water for dishwashing was heated on a Florence kerosene three-burner stove. There was a wood stove, but it was used only in winter; and in winter, because of school and because the long automobile trips were taken in summer, I didn't visit Grandpa. The Florence kerosene stove, as the summer twilight thickened, put splashes of golden light on the brown floorboards. It also, whatever the time of day, hummed. Perhaps not as wildly or beautifully as the telegraph harp, but certainly more melodiously than anything you'd expect from a kerosene stove. It didn't stick to one note, or even one rhythm. Its tune was mostly domestic, but it could rise to a soft, high, piercing wail of Gaelic sorrow, then subside to lower, lulling, cradle cadences.

And there was the smell of kerosene, dear to anyone whose first experience of light has been accompanied by that smell. What bareness to have experienced, from the beginning, light without smell.

So there we were in the kitchen at summertime, the door open onto the Valencia groves and the big red barn, which still housed horses as well as the Hupmobile. Grandpa and I: he who needed company, and I who craved solitude. I wasn't much company for him, nor he as much solitude for me as I thought I wanted. But quite likely we could neither have endured more.

After the dishes were washed, the table set for breakfast, and the stove turned off, Grandpa played his accordion. I don't remember his songs as I remember Mama's. I heard hers more often, of course. But he played with none of Mama's emotional bravura, and his music was out of a more distant past than hers —quiet, sorrowful little pieces, as finished as his stories, and with all of the same finality and symmetry of things over and done with. What came out of Mama's harmonica was her living breath, and for as long as she lived and breathed this planning and dreaming went on.

Grandpa never asked me if I wanted to hear him play his

accordion. But the Gramophone was a more formal matter, and he issued an invitation to hear it as though he were suggesting a Chautauqua tent concert by the Piney Woods Singers.

"Would you like to hear the Gramophone before you go to bed, Grace?"

Grandpa often called me Grace, and I was old enough to understand that Grace was who he wanted me to be—or even momentarily thought I was. I always said I would like to hear the Gramophone, though the answer was only half truthful. I often waited for the evening to end so that I could climb the stairs to my own room.

The Gramophone, like the organ back East, was kept in the parlor. We went through the dining room and sitting room to reach the parlor. I wondered if Grandpa remembered, as I did, the day when Grandma's casket had rested on trestles in the bay window at the end of the parlor. She had died in mid-February, and the parlor had been heavy that day with the scent of Chinese lilies, then at the height of their blooming. There was no Gramophone then; nor even a music box of the kind Thoreau had played at the parlor funeral of his sister Helen. And if there had been, Quaker propriety (his own) would never have permitted Grandpa to play it. A bell had been given in memory of his mother, the Quaker minister, to the Quaker Meetinghouse down the road. It was still crated. It could not be hung until after the death of those elderly Quakers who believed that bell ringing was not conducive to godliness.

Grandpa's records, in any case, were not suitable for a funeral, though probably just right for a widower needing to fill the emptiness caused by the departure of a wife like Doll Milhous. They were less music than vaudeville turns: some singing and a lot of patter; "The Three Little Blackberries"— three little black boys happy, as 1915 liked to believe, as only little black boys could be. Grandpa would have been surprised to learn that this happiness was the result of "soul," which in his experience was a Quaker possession.

"The Preacher and the Bear" was a story in song of a bear who got a preacher up a tree. From that position the preacher prayed, addressing himself half the time to God, half the time to the bear. He obviously felt that the bear could do more for him than God. This situation should not have been as funny as it was to Grandpa. The preacher's plight and prayers kept Grandpa laughing continuously, though silently. The bridge of his big nose wrinkled; tears of mirth, I thought, dampened his cheeks.

He was a sad man, so he told funny stories and listened to funny songs. He believed in purity and married a pure girl; he himself was pure, but he couldn't remember to wipe his feet. It takes more than purity to make a bed happy or keep a house clean. Grandma was an impatient woman, and Grandpa was a slow, musing man. No man ever knows the woman he missed by being so laggardly he wasn't there before her impatience took hold of her. There Grandma was, the lamp lit, the fire laid, a rosebud in her jabot, and Grandpa out, slow-spinning a story she could have disposed of (and ruined) in two short sentences. She could anticipate him seven ways to breakfast and from July to eternity, and by the time he got home with his unwiped feet, the rosebud had faded, and the jabot itself had lost its flutter.

Mama, I think, never failed her father; nor was he conscious of any failure with her. He must have known that she loved him more than she loved her mother. I was named for him, though at Doll's insistence (she was the planner) and with Mama's own fancy additions. I don't believe these additions cut any ice with Grandpa. Certainly they didn't with me.

When the cylinders chosen for the night's concert had been played, Grandpa, ready for bed, ended the evening.

"I hope you have a good night's rest, Grace."

I slept in the upstairs bedroom. The windows faced south, toward the Pacific. On clear days you could see Catalina, a gnarled brown forefinger on the far side of the silver streak that was the sea. Just across the La Habra Valley, four or five miles away, were the Coyote Hills, topped by oil tanks that held the petroleum whose removal from underground was going to cause California to cave in someday. I stood at the window in full possession of the solitude for which I had refused the trip with my parents.

There was not the same excitement in being alone with Grandpa as there was in being alone at home. Grandpa now wanted to be alone, too. This unoccupied room, the rounded foothills, the summer evening's rosy haze—all these Grandpa gave me freely.

I thought of Papa and Mama and the "tids," as Carmen called us, sitting by a campfire in Yosemite, or under the big trees in Sequoia, or maybe camped for the night by Mono Lake. I was lonesome for them. What was I doing here in the house of a dead woman, companion to an old man who didn't even remember my name half the time? Grandpa had his memories. What did I have?

I had solitude. I had loneliness. I had the suspicion that I had perhaps made a poor, possibly a crazy, choice. But lonely as I was, and with complete knowledge of the jollity and of the good fried biscuits being eaten around the campfire in Yosemite or Sequoia, I yet would not have joined my family if I could. I knew what I was missing. I also knew what I was waiting for, though I could not name it. A presence dwelt in the growing darkness, the blurring of the oil tanks, the throbbing silence of the house; in the memory of the trestled coffin, the scent of lilies, the murmuring oilstove, and Grandpa's sad toe-tapping tunes learned so long ago. This presence would soon manifest itself and envelop me. I could not name it. It could not speak. But I had to be alone and to wait for it.

# XIII

When I first awakened this morning I couldn't believe my eyes. Outside my window was a wall of pure gold; my window was filled with blazing, shimmering, pulsating gold. I blinked, I rubbed my eyes, I stared, before I understood that what I was seeing was simply sunrise on a bleached hill not far from the trailer.

In the night I saw a comet, or what I thought was a comet, though it was not tailed like Halley's. It was more like a ripe peach splashed and trickling. I had to show it to someone, so I lifted Spry up for a look. He saw something—bird or animal—and barked. But the comet was wasted on him.

The joy of this place—apart from my living the life of a desert father here—is that I live on the Colorado, not the Ohio or the Hudson or any river east of the Mississippi. It is a river of the West, flowing through desert land, bearing a Spanish name, harnessed but not tamed. The Rio Grande, the Snake, the Eel: rivers of the West that have moved mountains and not yet been sucked dry by man. The wild Indian rivers, fighting for their lives and condemned like the Sioux and Comanche and Apache to live in the reservation of a reservoir. Contradictory rivers, great volume without visible rainfall; suckled on snow tits, milk fiercer than that which fed Rome's founders; moving seaward in spite of barriers; mirroring buttes and saw-tooth ranges and canyon walls; nourishing mesquite and sage and cottonwood and salt cedar. No mill-town rivers, with girls at the looms; no flatboat road-steads bringing in the settlers with town plats already in their pockets. The rivers of the West were the settler's enemy. They did not carry him to where he wanted to go; they barred the way. They thundered at him with their own flash floods. They have been conquered now, and man moves on to the moon.

I'm not the greatest woman in the world for going, but when it comes to stopping, I am hard to beat. Once in a while I can make a change of the mud I stick in, but I am at least a periodic stick-in-the-mud.

Max and I started this trip with Brownsville, Texas, as our destination. The route we chose was fairly roundabout: Napa, California, to Newberg, Oregon. Newberg to Boise, Idaho. Boise to Reno, Nevada. Reno through the Owens Valley to Death Valley. From Death Valley the next stop was to be Phoenix, Arizona. But the Colorado got in the way. We stopped here, and we asked ourselves, "What does Brownsville, Texas, have that the Colorado doesn't have here?" The answer to that was easy. The ocean and a temperature that stays pretty close to 80 degrees all winter long. The temperature isn't a constant 80 degrees here, but there are few days when it isn't at least 70 degrees. The Colorado isn't the Gulf of Mexico. But are there mud hens on the Gulf? Red mountains reflected like bloodstains in the water? Wild burros? Canyons as narrow as the eye of a needle? So here we stuck; and I so deeply that even when Max's work called him home I stayed on, to taste the solitude and the strangeness more deeply.

Lily McCurdy understands my attachment to this spot. It has held her here for fifteen years. But even she feels that I needn't restrict myself to one canyon for my walks.

"Try the third one down," she advises. "It's a lot wider than that dinky little wash you walk in every afternoon. When I had my motorcycle I could ride up that wash clear to the rimrocks."

I know that she is right about exploring other canyons. But I haven't half seen my own dinky little wash, with its strange walls and mounds and turrets. I may not explore many canyons here, but I plan to be well traveled in this one. I already know several things about my wash. Its trees are not treelike. The flowers blooming there now form a carpet rather than a garden. Its animals are invisible, though I see their tracks and droppings, and in the night I hear their voices. The wind that blows here can move rocks. The water of this dry wash can kill you. I never forget that. Its colors are unearthly.

A nonpainter does not have enough names for the colors he sees in the desert. This is perhaps a sign that the nonpainter shouldn't try to portray colors with words.

Writers who have been color-crazy have never been the best writers. Such writers are perhaps painters with no talent for painting. They try to do with the pen what they were never able to accomplish with a brush. More has been written of blue than of any other color. John Addington Symonds has a whole book called *In the Key of Blue*. Rachel Annand Taylor, in her *Life of Leonardo da Vinci,* says that green has always been the favorite color of homosexuals; green was Da Vinci's favorite. However, Symonds, a homosexual, says, "Green, I think, is the poorest of all." He is speaking of those colors whose various shades can best be conveyed in writing. "I have been especially attracted to the qualities of blue," Symonds writes, then proceeds with a chapter of prose and poems to show what he can do with blue.

Lafcadio Hearn is also a blue man. "Being the seeming color of the ghost of our planet, of the breath of the life of the world, blue is likewise the color apprehended of the enormity of the day and the abyss of night. So the sensation of it makes appeal to the ideas of Altitude, of Vastness, and of Profundity . . . blue is the tint of distance and of vagueness. Blue is the color of Vanishing and Apparition. Peak and vale, bay and promontory turn blue as we leave them . . . in the volume of feeling awakened in us be the sensation of blue, there should be something of the emotion associated with the experience of change, with countless ancestral sorrows of parting."

People no longer say, "I am blue," as they once did. Mama would begin a letter, "I am so blue this morning." (She often wrote a paragraph or two of a letter before it came to her that she was writing, not conversing. Then she would insert without explanation, "Monday, 7:30 A.M. By the fire in the dining room. Dear Jessamyn.")

"Blue jewels, blue eyes, blue flowers," Hearn writes, "delight us; but in these, color accompanies either transparency or visible softness. It is perhaps because of the incongruity between hard opacity and blue that the sight of a book in sky blue binding is unendurable. I can imagine nothing more atrocious."

The sky itself in the desert has neither of Hearn's two requirements for a pleasing blue: "transparency and visible softness." I came home early yesterday from my canyon walk and found the trailer overly warm. I opened the skylight in the living room, and when I did so, a square of hard blue sky hit me in the face with the force of a blue-bound book dropped from 10,000 feet. Atrocious.

The river, which is a hundred colors as the day passes, was blue as the sky yesterday evening: a seaward-moving sapphire, a gem-plated blue highway for motorists without wheels.

I don't want the moon any more than Thoreau wanted California, but if it hadn't existed, Americans would have had to invent it. To go fast, to go far, noisily if possible, seems to be in our blood. We are the children of generations who have done nothing but move on. Leave England, leave Germany, leave Italy, leave Spain. Get to a seaport. Cross the Atlantic. Cross the continent. Such a people *had* to go to the moon.

Somewhere upstream a wind was blowing yesterday. A few weeds passed gulfward as I sat watching. A desert river is very different from a river that passes through forests. That river carries whole trees, the wreckage of boats, timbers from God-knows-what flood-torn buildings. A desert river is lucky to have picked up a foundered tumbleweed, a bit of mesquite. Once only, though I know that there are many fish in its forty-foot depths (I have never seen one), I heard the plash of a fish leaping clear of, then falling back into, the water.

It continues to be strange to hear but not see animals. There *is* a road runner who is not afraid to make himself visible. He steps across the lane between my trailer and the McCurdy cabin. The road runner is a proud bird. He was here so long before we came. He will, or he did in Yorba Linda when I was a girl, race a buggy or even an automobile. Here he has decided that neither Spry nor I can provide him with such sport. He ignores us.

The cottonwood trees around my parking place are protected by heavy meshed screen supported by iron bands. I could not imagine why.

"Beavers," said Lily.

"Beavers!"

A beaver in the desert seemed as strange to me as a camel in the Everglades. I thought beavers were denizens of northern forest lands.

"All a beaver needs to be happy is water and trees. He's got both here."

I've never heard a beaver since I've been here, let alone seen one. Or if I heard one, I didn't recognize the sound he made. Does a beaver bark, grunt, hiss, chatter?

There is a bird I never see whose song is simply, "Tweek, tweek." Nothing more, though *he* does not seem to tire of it.

I have heard the wild burros, at last, and they sound like any burro, mule, hinny, jackass. Their sound is a domestic sound—not strange to anyone who has been around barnyards, but so harsh and rasping you want to reach for a throat lozenge.

.   .   .

Night before last I heard for the second time in twenty years a sound dearer to me than bird song, dearer than the sound any wild animal, bird, or beast can make: the cry of the coyote. I first heard it earlier this fall as we were moving east from Oregon to Idaho. We had stopped for the night at Cougar Camp, in the Ocho National Forest, some miles beyond Prinville. The only other camper there was a man in his sleeping bag, with his dog on the ground beside him chained to the car. The sound of a small stream reached us in the trailer. Above the pine trees Christmas-card stars were shining. Supper was over, and Max and I were listening to the stream, looking at the stars, and thinking about a game of Russian bank when we heard it, Max first.

"Listen," he said.

I did. The hair stood up on the back of my neck the way Housman said his whiskers did when he heard a line of true poetry.

"Coyotes!"

I slid the window open so fast and hard I took off the top half of a knuckle. In my excitement I didn't notice it until later.

"Coyotes!"

I had never expected to hear that sound again. I heard it often in Yorba Linda in the days when coyotes chased Old Silver back to the house. They could have pounced on him and eaten him at once if they had had any meanness in them, or if they had been hungry. But coyotes had full stomachs in those days of plentiful ground squirrels and jack rabbits, and Old Silver was not game to them, but fun-and-games. They laughed in their beards as they barked him out of their hills and homeward.

The last time (I thought) and the best time I ever heard coyotes was in 1950 when I was sleeping on the roof of my sister's adobe house, in the middle of a desert date ranch. I awakened one morning to grayness, but in the east the sky was beginning to brighten. I awakened to three sounds and one scent; and I don't ever expect to hear, see, and smell a combination like that again, or any other combination to equal it.

Near at hand in the garden (date groves are "gardens"), Juan, the Mexican worker, was cutting wood for his breakfast fire. His wife, inside the house, already had the stove going, and the air was filled with the raw, wild sweetness of mingled mesquite and greasewood smoke.

Juan, as he chopped, sang—one of those sweet, keening Mexican songs, or so they sound to us.

Then, suddenly, above the singing and chopping came a sound that mingled with the smell of the wood smoke: the sound of first one, then of several, coyotes singing in the sand hills south of the house. Were they answering Juan? Indians—and many Mexicans are at least part Indian—have great respect for the coyote. He is their little brother, but a little brother with miraculous powers. He brought fire to the Indians. He made the Indian tribes. He has visited the land of the dead. He changed the course of the Columbia River. Were the coyotes answering the song they heard and that they understood? The wood chopper never paused in his work or his singing. The answering cry of the coyotes was not a novelty to him. I wanted to rush down the ladder from the rooftop and ask him what song he was singing and if the coyotes often cried while he sang.

But I was sleepy and lazy, and my bed was warm. Presently the wood chopper went inside. The coyotes became silent. Nothing was left of that morning's beauty but the lingering smell of smoke and the growing light, to which I closed my eyes.

The coyote who sang from the rimrocks above Cougar Park was strong-voiced and alone. He called again and again, but there was no answer. He was the first coyote I had heard since that morning on the rooftop at Carmen's twenty years ago. Carmen is now dead. Coyotes are disappearing. I cried with the joy of hearing him, of hearing a sound I thought I would never hear again in this world. It was as if a past time had returned.

Next morning the man in the sleeping bag crawled out, gave his socks a good shaking, pulled on his boots, unchained his dog, and was off.

We traveled down out of the Ocho Mountains into sagebrush country, and into the land of the great rimrocks. On a barbed-wire fence a newly killed coyote was stretched, not yet swollen or bloated. Was he my last night's singer? If I had been alone I would have stopped the car, knelt in front of him, and said, "Forgive me, little brother."

The coyotes of night before last's concert here at the trailer were not sorrowful but playful, as the coyotes were who chased Old Silver home. It is difficult to judge the number of coyotes singing. Their voices echo through the canyons; they change pitch; they yodel. But this, if not a pack, was certainly the song of three or four. They would cut loose with their before-the-world-was-born cries; then they would be silent, while every dog on the Arizona side of the river barked its head off in furious, angry, domestic warning: "Stay away from our side of the river."

After the dogs had had their short, sharp say, the coyotes, with taunting good humor, would reply, "Back-yard brothers, we answer you from the hills and canyons you have lost."

Frank Dobie, whose *Voice of the Coyote* is the best book on coyotes I know, drew in my copy the Privia symbol for a coyote track. Then he added the most flattering words I have ever had written in a book given to me by its author: "Coming to know you has been as good as a coyote concert." To men who string coyotes on barbed-wire fences, that may seem a pretty backhanded compliment. But Frank Dobie was not a man for backhanded compliments. He was forthright. He could kick like a mule or kiss like a lover. I say this intuitively, having known neither from him.

I watched the river last night until the stars were out and

the river doubled them. Thoreau said, "I think it is important to have water, because it multiplies the heavens." Talk like that would make a dam builder snort. Thoreau never saw a desert or a desert river (or a dam builder). I wish he had. He sometimes feared that the sight of real grandeur would rob him of the grandeur he saw in grass and toads. Because I love deserts, not ponds, I sometimes feel like a woman rejected when Thoreau gets to harping on that little pond of his. "Man," I would like to say to him, "don't knock the desert till you've tried it."

Lily says that it is the river, not the desert, that holds her. It's the combination that holds me and fascinates me. The desert is a skeleton, and the river is the living heart that beats inside the dry cage. How can such a thing be? It's a part of the mystery of the desert.

"One would think that, by a very natural impulse, the dwellers upon the headwaters of the Mississippi and Amazon would follow in the trail of their waters to see the end of the matter." Thoreau—who else?—said this.

The truth is, I think very few people have had a "natural impulse . . . [to] follow in the trail of [rivers] . . . to see the end of the matter." Nothing would surprise me more than to see a procession of persons who live at the headwaters of the Colorado pacing down its banks in order to discover the "restless reservoir" where it deposits its waters. A far more natural impulse, it seems to me, would be to go upstream, in order to discover the beginning of the matter.

Son, on whose hands time hangs heavy, I think, has done a number of minor repair jobs on the trailer. The refrigerator no longer freezes the lettuce; the butane no longer escapes from the holding tanks; the pilot light on the stove burns.

The impression I had when I first saw Son—"What a beautiful, pitiful face"—is fading. I don't know about the beauty now. The yellow dye job on his long hair has gone, and his general look is of an aging Viking who has lost his ship. About the pity I don't know, either.

I have had a lifelong altercation with almost everyone I know about my use of the word "pity." I seem to be the only person in the world who doesn't mind being pitied. If you love me, pity me. The human state is pitiable: born to die, capable of so much, accomplishing so little; killing instead of creating, destroying instead of building, hating instead of loving. Pitiful, pitiful. I have even made a "Pity Anthology," a little book when it began, a big book now.

Two additions to my Pity Anthology came from books I recently finished reading. Catherine Drinker Bowen says that Bacon describes a man as "of middle stature and age, comely of person and had an aspect as if he pitied man." This phrase, says Bowen, "is wholly Baconian" and was "fashioned upon Sir Francis' ideal of what a gentleman should be. 'An aspect as if he pitied men.' " I pity men. I don't know whether or not I have that aspect.

The other quotation, from Belloc, whom I first read forty years ago, I came upon yesterday: "It is our duty to pity all men."

William Blake told a girl at a party, a girl he had just met, that he had recently been jilted and that he was suffering. She said, "I pity you from my heart." "Do you pity me?" asked Blake. "Yes, I do, most sincerely." "Then I love you for that," said Blake, and soon Blake married the girl who pitied him.

If I told Son that I pitied him, I don't know what his response would be. Certainly he wouldn't love me for it. He would more likely have thought, with Beerbohm, that "pity is a little sister to contempt."

I know nothing about Son, except what his face tells me, and what I observe of his life and his living quarters: living in the lean-to tacked onto his mother's one-room shack, without a job, not driving, walking, swimming, fishing, boating, reading. His mother sweeps up the leaves that blow in around and under his bed. It seems to me a pitiful life.

I said to him one afternoon as I passed the McCurdy place on the way to my canyon, "I wish I had a book on cactus. I feel tongue-tied not knowing the names of the varieties I see."

"Shit," said Son. "A cactus is a cactus."

# XIV

———◆———

After thirty years of scorn for houses on wheels and pity for my poor parents who were not content with what was to be seen in Orange County, California, Max and I had simultaneously, a year ago, a sudden conviction that we perhaps did not know what we were talking about. Why not rent a travel trailer for two weeks? Anybody can stand anything for two weeks, anything at least as discardable as a travel trailer. At the end of two weeks, having experienced what years of observing had not taught us, we turned in the rented trailer, bought our own—the Walden on Wheels in which I am now living—and began the journey that has paused here on the Colorado.

Husbands and wives learn to ignore each other when traveling together. They must to retain their sanity. They must die to each other to make a future resurrection possible. This is especially true for couples faced with the necessity of sitting side by side for ten or twelve hours in the front seat of an automobile.

Some states permit passengers to ride in the trailer. There one can read, lie down, take a nap, even take a shower—live, in fact, like a robber baron in his private car. There is no sense in the law that forbids this, with the pretense that the passenger's safety is what the law has in mind. If the law cared about passenger safety, motorcycles would be taken off the highways completely. The young men dead in motorcycle accidents must be ten thousand times greater than that of middle-aged ladies dozing in trailers. Death by, in, or even near a trailer is infinitesimal as compared with the deaths of cyclists, Easy Riders or no. I feel like an incensed pot user decrying the illegality of pot while alcoholics legally drink themselves to death. Who is responsible for such laws? Not the motoring public; not the trailer-using public. I could, as Lily did, buy a motorcycle and legally kill myself and half a dozen others—if I managed to get into the right lane for the job—within the hour. But doze on my own bed, endangering no one, while Max drives at a comfortable fifty miles an hour? If I do that, I'm a lawbreaker and can be sent to jail, whether for felony or misdemeanor I'm not sure. The fine for this kind of dangerous action is, in California, $500. California, where every kind of activity is countenanced and even encouraged, is thus oversolicitous of its trailer travelers. I am inclined to have a large sign painted—TRAVELER SLEEPING—and to hang it in the back window of our trailer and await the action of the highway patrol. Would they haul me off in a paddy wagon as a highway menace? Would they save me for my own sake from the danger I court, while water skiers risk (and lose) life and limb on the fake lakes and the liquid highways? I have $500 earmarked for such an emergency if they do.

For reasons other than legal I ride most of the day when we travel in the front seat with Max. During the day not much will have been said by either of us, so the occasional person with whom we talk when we pull up in the evening brings us some of the same pleasure a wayfarer brought to the cabin in the clearing.

We started our trip to Brownsville by a circuitous route that led us through Oregon. Oregon is, in some places, like a cemetery. The big stumps of the slaughtered trees stand up like headstones. In this land of water there are signs directing you to the "ocean beaches," a seeming pleonasm to a Californian who thinks, Where else is there water *and* beaches? Oregon is the land of the big decaying barns, barns no longer needed now that the stock is gone. When the last one falls, a great sigh will sweep across the state. In Oregon the churches, with all the Oregon wood available for building, have gone crazy: "That," we were told of one extraordinary spire, "is known as Mr. Nasmith's Erection." Mr. Nasmith was the architect.

"Pure raw honey" is advertised. The old red barns and the forest ghosts are now next door to retirement homes. An old man in the yard rides his wheel chair like the buck rake of his earlier years. There is a "Midget's Motel." What in the world can this mean? A movie marquee advertises, "Naked and Els." Even more mysterious.

In my youth I thought Oregon a second-rate state, inhabited by people who had given up before they reached California. I thought this, I believe, because local students who could not meet the entrance requirements of the University of California could get into the University of Oregon; and because Oregon teachers came down to California in the summertime to study in the California colleges and so earn California teachers' credentials. Teachers in California were paid more than Oregon teachers. I had never in my youth seen Oregon. Seeing it, I no longer judge it by college entrance requirements or teachers' salaries. I judge it by what I see, and what I see is awesome, though I say this after discarding what most travelers consider Oregon's glory: her great river, her enormous forests, and the rainfall that makes both possible. When we emerge from the forests, I write in my notebook, "Escaped." A man in a forest is a bug in the grass.

We moved out of the forests of Oregon into the high desert country, or at least the high and dry country. The land I love. The wheat country, the cattle country. The tawny, the golden, the brown country. Purple-blue cloud shadows move over the tawny hills. Marble clouds. Nine inches of rain a year at

Mitchell: about right. If you want to go through Mitchell, you take the "business loop." Not the busiest business loop in the world. We enter the land of the rimrocks, savage and strange; rimrocks edged like a Sioux war bonnet. There are no more dead animals on the road. No more buzzards on the fence posts.

October first, and into the sage country, at 4,000 feet. Gold-daisy floor in the valley below, lavender sage. Neat as an in-grain carpet. Rimrocks above like ramparts, like stone barri-cades of a vanished race; rimrocks covered with lichens. Ten thousand shades of russet, coral, sulphur, green.

In a Safeway in Burns all clerks are wearing the uniform of the New York Mets. I ask about it. "It's wonderful P.R. We've as good as got the long green in our hands when we humanize ourselves this way."

I spend a long time trying to find a bottle of wine I think drinkable. I find one for $2.25. The checker whistles at the price. "You must be hard up for a drink."

I never saw so many Old West magazines in my life as in this store.

"Who reads them?"

"The men," says the clerk. "They won't read anything else."

An elderly lady in the Safeway gets her third volume of a set called *Books of Knowledge*. These books come, I think, with purchases of merchandise.

"Oh," she says, "how I've looked forward to this."

I try to find a bottle of ink. "We don't carry it."

"How do people write?"

"They use ballpoints nowadays, honey. Three years ago a lady asked for ink, but that was the last request I've heard of."

Mountain pyramids show up everywhere on the horizon. One camel would convince me we were in Egypt.

Wagon Tire. Poverty Basin.

An enormous black ridge, battleship-massive, crested with rimrock, rising like the backbone of a monster above the grass plains. Had I been an Indian seeking explanations, this might have been one: "We are insects living on the hide of a dead monster."

Can you hear the wind in the grass? Yes, you can. In knee-high, old-gold grass, the wind passes through with a dull roar.

There is a store on the valley floor beneath the Abert Rim, the highest fault scarp in the United States, 2,500 feet high. That elongated shape, a crested snake, is more frightening than if it were perpendicular. It looks as if it could move if it took a mind to, and no move it made would be nice.

I say to the storekeeper, "You were not born in the West."

"No, in Boston."

"Why did you come here?"

"I saw it." He motions to the Rim.

"During the war?"

"Yes."

He sells groceries and gas and collects Indian artifacts. He has more cases of arrowheads than of cheese and hamburger. "I find them wherever I kick up the earth." People find what they want. I am lucky in secondhand book stores. "Desire," said A. E., "is hidden identity." Our own comes to us. "Some of those," said the storekeeper, his Boston accent still strong under the Abert Rim, "are ten thousand years old." Beautiful and lethal, chipped out by hand, of various colors and shapes. Some have done their job, penetrated flesh, opened arteries, embedded themselves, and learned to live a hidden and peripatetic life inside an elk. In 10,000 years, all we have learned, it seems, is to kill more efficiently. Will our weapons be collected one day like arrowheads? Napalm guns and antipersonnel shells? Not beautiful, but a curiosity of cruelty, like the Iron Maiden?

Outside the store two or three tumbleweeds run a ghost race. Two are held up by a picnic table; the smaller is able to hurdle it. It is tumbleweed weather. The wind is from the north, and the tumbleweeds are heading south for the winter.

A store's sign: AUTO PARTS AND SADDLERY. When will that store owner add LANDING STRIP to his sign?

Travel by auto is frustrating: able to see but not to experience. That is why it is emotionally wearisome. The imagination no sooner enters a sight or an idea to explore it than the mind is wrenched away by new sights and ideas. The Indians living under the rimrocks? The hands that chiseled the arrows? The expectations of those who planted the line of poplars leading to the house once white, now weather-beaten and windowless? Who was the first to arrive? The last to leave? How many coffins, with a bow of black on the front door? How many births, and the doctor's buggy standing in the rain? The mind bleeds. Put a blindfold on me and do not take it off until we have stopped passing through, have stopped, and can once more live as well as see.

What is living? It is, at the very least, experiencing with more than the eyes; it is being more than a moving eyeball. The rest of the body, ignored, aches. Let me feel the roughness of earth under my feet. Smell—a bay tree, smoke, cattle, water. Mama said, "I don't remember all I've seen, but I'll banter you I can put a name to everything I've ever smelled." She was a connoisseur of smells. She would rather have a bottle of perfume than a sack of gold.

I always want us to stop early so that there will be time to walk about; time to give the senses, entombed all day in a metal capsule, a chance to come to life; time to give the overworked eye a chance to take it easy; nothing going by at fifty-five miles per hour that it need note.

We drive at four o'clock through a gate we must open and close, because this is an Oregon cattle ranch. We can stop here because Max has had some correspondence with the resident manager about the ranch, which is for sale. Cows fascinate him, as gambling or women do other men. He would rather have a herd than a harem. The first picture he ever drew was of a cow. Thoreau died saying, "Indians and moose." Max will die saying, "Ranch and cow." He owns some cows now. Some land in Idaho. He wants to own more of both. I cannot look at a cow, at a bull calf soon to be a steer, with the same joyous openness Max can. I feel like the wolf disguised as Little Red Ridinghood's grandmother. "Why are your teeth so large, Grandmother?" the yearling asks. "The better to eat you with, my dear." Only, cattle are more innocent than Red Ridinghood. They don't notice my teeth; but my mouth, as I watch mother and child or calves frisking, feels full of big teeth.

When we stop for the night, we open the door of our little cabin and are at home. We walk about. The kettle is put on. The ranch manager comes to speak to Max. As they talk, I walk up and down the banks of a live and speaking stream; boulders large enough to insure some bass notes; speed great enough to keep the conversation going.

A man joins me. I respected him from the minute I laid eyes on him. He looked as if his grandfather on his mother's side had been St. Nick. On his father's side, Old Nick. He was large, white-haired, and grizzled, a man ordinarily clean-shaven, but who was waiting for Sunday to shave again. His build, his white hair, his amiable countenance, were St. Nick. The Old Nick looked out of his eyes, hard-blue, glinting.

"My name's Casey Brown," he said.

For a minute I thought he didn't know his own name. Before I could say, "You mean Casey Jones," he said, "I'm a horsebreaker, not an engineer."

He was sizing me up, too. "That your husband?"

Max is two years older than I but looks ten years younger. Once a man looking at a house we had to rent said, "Your son had to leave. He said you'd give me the key." Casey, a man used to fractious horses, showed the same care with women.

"He is." I answered Casey's question.

"Tell him eighty-five thousand is the *asking* price. The place ain't worth more than seventy at the most. It's been overgrazed. There's winters when you have to bring in a lot of hay."

"I don't think we'll do more now than look around. Do you live here?"

"I've lived here since 1917."

"Do you work for the manager?"

"I rent grazing land from him. I'm a horsebreaker."

"What's a horsebreaker do?"

"Breaks horses. Buys 'em young or untrained, breaks them, trains them, sells them. It's all I've ever done. I did it for the ranch when the owner was here and he had more land. It's my business now. The only one I got. I'm seventy-five years old. I'm too old for the business, but I ain't afeared of them. I make a profit. I live with the manager and his wife. Or at least eat with them. She's a nice woman. If you buy the place, I go with it."

"I wouldn't want it without you."

"I'm breaking a good little mare right now. She'd be just right for somebody not eager for a lot of cavorting."

"You've got my number. Who lives in the other house?" I pointed to a brown weathered house, as large as the white house we had passed on the way to our parking place beside the stream; better situated, really. The white house was out in the open, nearer the public road. The brown house was set in the curve of the stream, with a black butte behind it to protect it from the winds.

"Nobody," Casey said. "It's abandoned."

"It looks in pretty good shape."

"It is. It was when they moved out."

"Why did they move? I like the old house better than the new. Did the wife want something nearer the road? More up to date?"

"No, that was the least of her worries. She was satisfied where she was. It was her husband wanted to give her something grander. He had the money to do it. He was making it hand over fist in them days. Cattle was worth their weight in gold."

"Didn't she tell him she was satisfied where she was?"

"I wouldn't be surprised she did. But he thought a big new house might hold her attention. Might turn her mind toward him."

"Where was it turning?"

"Toward another man. Worthless fellow, as it turned out, as anybody could've told her. A drifter. A horsebreaker like myself. After you break a horse, you've finished with it. That horse don't hold no interest for you any more. Well, she ran away with the horsebreaker; he broke her, and then he was done with her. She came back here to live. I think I didn't mention she had children. She came back here to live and her husband let her, but she didn't live here as his wife. She lived at the white house, and he fixed up a room down at the old place."

"That's a sad story," I said.

"I ain't got anywheres near the really bad part yet," he said.

"What's the bad part?"

"It's pretty damn bad. Couldn't be worse."

"Tell me," I said. "When stories get bad they get real."

"There was an outbreak of foot-and-mouth disease around 1930, and the herd here was infected. They came out to tell Walt they'd all have to be destroyed. Well, Walt's home had been destroyed when his wife ran off, and his cows was about all he could claim he had left. So he got himself his shotgun and said, 'I'll shoot the first man who destroys an animal of mine.' And he stood up there about halfway between the two houses, with his gun leveled at the county men who were out to do their job.

"Clara, his wife, seen what he had in his hands, and she felt more than half responsible for the frame of mind he was in. She run out of the house and tried to rassle the gun away from him. He had it loaded and cocked, of course, and in the scuffle he shot her dead. When he seen what he had done, he turned

128

the gun on himself. Then the county men killed the herd, and that was the end of the old WC ranch. The kids left for California, though they still own it, and nobody but me and the managers have ever lived here since."

"Did you see all this killing?"

"No. I was away then, down in California myself. But shortly after, I came back and went on with the only work I ever knowed. And I've been here ever since. As I said, I go with the ranch."

Next morning while Max rode around the place with the manager, I went over to the old brown house.

It was large, gabled, had clapboards stained brown. A good deal of household equipment had been left in the house when Clara moved out. A wood stove in the kitchen of a kind I had used myself. Warming oven above. Water-heating tank on one side. Some dishes in the cupboard. A blue-and-white-veined enamel saucepan on the floor. A 1937 calendar was still on the wall. The walls had been plastered, and pieces of plastering had fallen here and there. A stand table and tufted sofa that the mice had been at were still in the sitting room. A bed with a fancy sleigh headboard stood in a bedroom.

It looked as if Walt had said to Clara, "Leave it all behind. Forget it. We're starting anew."

So they walked out into a new house with new furniture. But the horsebreaker they couldn't leave behind, so Clara threw away the old husband, too, and went with the horsebreaker.

There was one room in the house, a bedroom, that was still in use—maybe the room the husband had occupied when Clara came home. The bed had sheets on it. There was a pair of boots on the floor. On the bureau with other knickknacks was the picture of a woman in a sea-shell frame, round-faced, with a wavy pompadour and a net guimpe with stays in the high-necked collar. Clara, I thought. Put there by Walt and left there when Casey—I supposed it was Casey—moved in.

We stayed at the ranch two days. While Max hitched up the

trailer for leaving, I walked around the old faded brown house again: colorless, grim, lowering—and beautiful: lapped by the ceaseless sound of the river; a year-round spring behind it; the butte curving around it like a stone hand. In the kitchen, the "safe." My grandmother had one in Indiana, the doors of tin punctured in elaborate patterns for the circulation of air. In that room the last supper was eaten; the corn-meal mush that had been supper's dish was put into the safe to cool for slicing and frying for breakfast.

Did Clara think she could change her life by changing houses? Was Walt fool enough to believe she could? After he shot himself, Walt had enough breath left to say to the Department of Health men, "Kill the cows now. It doesn't matter."

Casey came down to see us off. "I was a prospector before I was a horsebreaker. There's gold back up there in them buttes. But I'm not the man to find it. I'll stick to the horses. I'm too old for the work, but I ain't afeared of them."

I was tormented because I couldn't find a name for the look in his eyes. He stood watching us as we drove out and didn't turn away until we latched the gate behind us.

Max said, "Maybe we'll be opening and shutting that gate a good many times in the future."

I said, "Don't bank on it." There was too much sorrow there.

# XV

———◆◆———

I awakened doleful this morning, sorrowful, abandoned, bereft. Then I remembered the dream I had awakened from and could say, "It was just a dream." I don't know whether it was "just" a dream or not. This is what I dreamed. I was standing outside the trailer facing the river and waiting for the sun to set the river on fire, as it does each evening. As I stood there a boat, somewhat on the order of the Mississippi river boats we see in movies, came into sight. There was music, singing, dancing, eating, drinking. The boat had wrapped about its prow a big banner saying, BROWNSVILLE OR BUST. It came near enough to the bank on which I stood so that I could see the faces of the passengers. Max was among them, glass in hand, talking vivaciously. He faced my way. If I could see and recognize him amidst the crowd of passengers, he could surely see me standing alone on the river's bank. If he did so, he made no sign. Then someone, a man, touched his arm and pointed in my direction. Max stopped talking for a minute, gazed in my direction, then waved in the kindly way one waves to children beside the railroad track as the train sweeps by. He immediately resumed talking. I didn't wave back. He wouldn't have seen me, anyway.

I salved my hurt feelings by thinking, They'll never reach Brownsville by traveling down the Colorado. Brownsville is situated at the mouth of the Rio Grande. Then in my dream it came to me that I had completely forgotten my geography. I was not only unloved; I was ignorant. The Colorado, of course, emptied into the Rio Grande; and Max and that whole crowd of merrymakers would be swept effortlessly into Brownsville, while I, whose goal had also been Brownsville, would be here in my cabin on wheels, counting mud hens.

When I remembered the dream I felt better. Max was not actually going on to Brownsville without me. He was at home working, as I was here working. I attributed the dream to the writer's—the female writer's, anyway—constantly guilty conscience. "Writing," says Lawrence Clark Powell, "is a solitary occupation. Family, friends and society are the natural enemies of the writer. He must be alone, uninterrupted, and slightly savage if he is to sustain and complete an undertaking."

This is true enough. But at night in dreams the female conscience punishes the female writer for her savagery. "In your tub, your box, your trailer, you think you have escaped from all that threatens you. Have a good look now at *what* you have escaped. Love and merriment and Brownsville on the great tropical ocean gulf. Count the mud hens, sis. Note the leaves that drop. Listen to the coyotes. Try to figure out Lily and Son. Meanwhile, with singing and drinking, life and those you love are giving you the go-by."

I felt better after I was able to account for my feeling of sorrow and failure, but understanding the cause didn't immediately cure the pain.

Thoreau paid attention to his dreams. He recorded them in his journals. "I easily read the moral of my dreams. Yesterday I was influenced with the rottenness of human relations. . . . In the night I dreamed of delving amid the graves of the dead, and soiled my fingers with their rank mould."

I would like to know the degree to which our dreams color our days. I have heard people say that they never dream. Such people seem as strange to me as those who say they have never had a headache. What are heads and nights for? To ache and to dream. I sometimes do not have a headache, but I think I never sleep without dreaming. I go to sleep dreaming. I wake up dreaming.

Here in the cabin I have not known that knot of sorrow and despair that sometimes fills my throat in the early morning. "What do I have to be sad about?" I would ask myself. Is this the blues Mama sometimes spoke of? No reply. "The rottenness of human relations" had not occupied my mind the day before. Since the feeling was a physical one to which I gave the name "sorrow," I began to wonder whether or not sorrow might be the symptom of physical distress; not the other way around, as I pictured it. Finally, remembering dreams I had on awakening (which I don't very often do), I wondered if the morning dejection might be the result of the night before's dream.

The dreams I can remember are those I have had over and over again. Some still persist. Most I have outgrown. One that is still with me is the dream of what may be called Public Failure, though sometimes the title should be Private Disorder. That dream began, or at least I associate its beginning, with piano-box days when I was failing as a piano player. It is easy to be glib about that failure now, but at the age of ten I was truly humiliated by my inability to play "Marching Through Georgia" fast! A friend my own age consoled me. Her name was Bernadine Heilman, and like so many of Yorba Linda's residents, young and old, she died of tuberculosis: Richard Nixon's older brother, Harold; my mother's only brother, Walter Milhous; John Buckmaster; Nettie Mozier; Robert Shaw. Oh, among the beautiful hills we went around with burning cheeks and hacking coughs.

Bernadine told me not to worry about being unable to play for Mrs. Leaman. She said that I had only to believe that doing so was a matter of life and death and I would be able to walk out onto the concert stage and play Beethoven's "Moonlight Sonata" flawlessly before an audience of thousands. Was there any real need, she asked me, to play "Marching Through Georgia" fast? The world would not topple, I had to admit, if I did not. Bernadine persuaded me to stop worrying about "Marching Through Georgia" and to remember her formula. "If it's a life-and-death matter, you can do it." She, poor exponent of will, was probably whistling to keep her own courage up. She was soon dead; in her own life-and-death struggle she lost.

She convinced me, however; and from that time to this I am constantly in my dreams being put to the test, and failing. I am in a play. I neither know my lines nor the story of the play in which I'm appearing. For hours it seems I struggle to make up lines that will fit the unknown play in which I have a part.

Equally sharp and bitter but shorter are my failure as opera star and public speaker. The audience is waiting for my speech. I am at the lectern, but I have no speech. Even shorter is my agony as opera star. I have no voice. Why can't I dream that, using Bernadine's formula, I succeed? Or why can't I stop trying?

In any case, and even if the dream is not remembered, I don't think that after a night of such dreaming one could awaken merry.

Two other dreams, dreamed over and over again when I was young, one pleasant, the other unpleasant, I no longer dream at all.

The pleasant dream was occasioned by World War I. In this dream I parachuted (from where or what I do not know) to a detachment of our beleaguered troops, bringing them a message that would enable them to escape their besiegers. This, or something like it, I suppose, is a frequent dream of adolescents in wartime. "Alone and unaided I saved our brave men." I was, however, a kind of Mata Hari parachuter. I parachuted naked. The reasons for my being unclothed I never knew or questioned. Nor did our brave men. Naked as a jay bird, I floated down to them, and I must say I never enjoyed a dream more. I felt, insofar as I can remember, like a dove from heaven, plucked but comely, Eve before the fall; and with the knowledge that I was bringing a message of life. All eyes were upon me—that, of course, was part of the pleasure—and everyone's thought was, What a brave girl to have embarked upon so dangerous a mission without a stitch of clothes to her name!

The minute I hit ground the dream dissolved. And it ceased altogether after World War I had been won and my services were no longer needed. War gives many people an opportunity to perform acts that they enjoy, and that peace does not justify.

The second dream was one of terror. I didn't, when I dreamed it, associate it with what I now think was its source. When I was nine or ten, I heard a roomful of men housebound one winter afternoon by rain say that sooner or later a tidal wave would engulf Southern California. It was bound to happen, they said, because the oil that held up the crust of the southern part of the state was steadily being pumped out. Soon, with nothing below to support it, Los Angeles and Orange County would drop into the abyss where once the oil had been. Then, over the engulfed counties (and cities and people, even over *Yorba Linda*), the great tidal wave would sweep.

I believed them. It seemed the likeliest thing in the world to me. I had seen it happen with pies. Spoon out the filling of a pie and the upper crust falls in.

For ten years I dreamed of that tidal wave; or perhaps "dream" is not the right word. For ten years any sound—Pacific Electric car, heavy wind, door banging—that awakened me after I had gone to sleep was interpreted as, "The tidal wave has come." I suppose I did have a dream that lasted for a second or two. But the dream and the leap from my bed to peer out of my south-and-westward-looking window to check the progress of that wall of water must have been about simultaneous. No daytime sound ever made me think, Tidal wave. No nighttime experience of false alarm ever cured me from believing that any unexpected heavy sound was the long-expected wave.

I never went to bed without reviewing in my mind the location of every floatable object on the place: tubs, wash boilers, wash bench, ironing board, Papa's house props. I was no Noah. I never told anyone of my tidal-wave fears. I had no plans to save anyone but myself. I don't know why this dream disappeared. When I had a class in geology? When I went to Northern California, which is confident that it will escape the catastrophes Southern California invites? I don't know. But that dream of fear and heart thump is gone.

On October 26, 1851, Thoreau wrote in his journal, "I awoke this morning to infinite regret. In my dream I had been riding, but the horses bit each other and occasioned endless trouble and anxiety. . . ."

The biting horses were only the beginning of Thoreau's bad dream. No sooner was he rid of the horses than he was in a boat "learning to sail on the sea, and I raised my sail before my anchor, which I dragged far into the sea."

He saw the buttons "which had come off the coats of drowned men." He saw his dog, "when I knew not I had one—standing in the sea up to his chin, to warm his legs. . . ."

Out of his boat, he found himself walking in a meadow, listening to Bronson quoting "grand and pleasing couplets"; better than biting horses, but perhaps not much.

I have often wished it were possible to have a complete record of every dream we dream: every act, every word, every feeling. How would this dream record compare with the waking record? Would there be a visible relationship between what a man does in his dreams and what he does in what we call his life? Would we be amazed at the disparity? Does one compensate for the other? Amazed at the duplication?

Thoreau inclined to the belief that his dreams were occasioned by the day's happenings. I am interested in the effect dreams may have upon our lives. I do not care much about what my living does to my dreams, but I would like to know how my dreaming shapes (if it does) my life.

.   .   .

When we came here in January, the cottonwoods along the river had not yet shed their last leaves. Those that remained seemed intent on making up for the absence of their fallen brothers. They were pure gold, and they danced when the smallest breeze struck them. There was so much activity you failed to notice how few the dancers were. They behaved like a handful of survivors in a besieged fort, doomed and knowing it, but still trying to fool the enemy with the rapidity of their gunfire.

In spite of everything the fort fell; the last gold leaf went seaward with the Colorado. Now the trees are in bud, or perhaps in bloom. It is difficult to tell which, gazing up at them against the dazzle of sun and sky. In bloom I think, since this morning, when I awakened, I thought I heard bees swarming. There were bees all right, but harvesting, not swarming. Each cottonwood tree was a carillon, a tower of sound. Desert bees make honey with fierce intensity; the desert blooms only momentarily, and bees have to make honey while the blossoms are there. I never heard such an uproar. A million bees must equal the sound of a jet. This was no Tennysonian murmur from immemorial elms. This was the roar, every seat filled and engines laboring, of a 747 entangled in a blossoming cottonwood.

A wind came up in the night, and I was glad that the trailer did not catch its force broadside. If it had, I think I would have—remembering Papa's example—hunted planks to prop it up. I'd like to see Brownsville, but this is not the cabin, with wheels, not sails, I want to be in as I pursue Max down the river.

This morning I saw that the metal awning that protects the window at the front end, the dining-room end, of the trailer, and one that is closed when we travel, had been wrenched loose at one corner. The pilot light of the heating system (a propane furnace) had also blown out. There was no heat in the cabin. No one here on the edge of the desert will freeze without heat, but it is chilly, morning and evening. I can re-light the pilot light, but my experience has been with wood and electricity. The one time I worked on a pilot light in a gas oven I had my eyebrows blown off. So I postponed the furnace, preferring to be a little cool, but with eyebrows.

Toward afternoon the wind let up and I drove into Mesquite for supplies. There was still enough wind for me to feel the buffeting when I passed a draw through which the wind could sweep. When I got home about five, I saw that the Mc-Curdys, who had been away in Scottsdale, where Lily was having a showing of her pictures, were back.

While they were gone, a boy from across the river took care of their animals. The feeding has been unceremonious: food into one pan for the dog—bang; food into two pans—wham —for the cats; water bowls filled, and the boy was off on his motor bike to the bridge downriver. No arabesques of cats leaping to their assigned boxes; no hymn singing following the communion with Kal Kan and Kitty Krunch.

Son, as I drove past their place, was singing "Sweeter as the Years Go By," while the animals finished their meal. I waved to him as I passed. I don't much enjoy seeing those animals mince away at their food as they have been taught to do. A dog wants to gulp; a cat's tongue is not a slow organ. But if they want to eat, the McCurdy animals have all been taught to Fletcherize. And they all want to eat.

The hymn singing, I suppose, is what makes me think that Son may be an ex-preacher. It and his lack of a job, for preachers without pulpits have no profession to fall back on. Perhaps I have read too many Graham Greene novels, seen too many Burton movies. Son looks a little like Burton, as a matter of fact. Perhaps my casting him in my mind as a fallen priest is perfectly natural. I am but casting an imaginary movie based on a Greene script.

I had put everything away and was ready to take my evening

seat for the mud-hen sunset ballet when I saw Son coming up the path toward the trailer. I was sorry to see him. I am as bound to my routine as one of his trained animals. I was ashamed to say, "Will you wait, please, until I watch the mud hens roll up the sunset?" What kind of nut would Son think *I* was? The result of this kind of reluctance and the shame for it ("People . . . need people," the song says, and aren't you people?) is often an exaggerated heartiness: "Come in, come in," the reluctant call out, as if you were the one person they had been yearning for, and your presence will be their day's crown and flower.

"Come in, come in"—I answered Son's knock—"welcome home."

"I see we missed the big blow," he said.

"How did you know?"

"Sand all over our place. Your shutter was loose."

I noticed for the first time that it had been fixed. "You fixed it?"

"Who else? Five minutes' work. I didn't think you could do it."

"I wouldn't even have tried."

"The next time a blow starts, lower the shutter at once and fasten it down."

"It started in the night."

"Well, you can get up in the night, can't you? There's nothing to be afraid of around here."

"Well, there is one thing," I said. "The furnace pilot light went out, and I'm afraid to light it."

Son had the pilot light going in two minutes, eyebrows intact.

"There's nothing to it," he told me.

"For you." The chilly air was already feeling more comfortable.

"You certainly light my fire," I told him.

Son laughed and laughed. He sat down on one of the divans.

His unmarked ruddy face—no bitterness about the mouth, no furrows on the forehead—crinkled with pleasure.

"You ass-hole, you," he said.

I was too astonished to speak, but my astonishment must have showed.

"*I am* an ass-hole," Son explained, as if this would reassure me. "Everyone's an ass-hole. We're all a bunch of ass-holes together."

Was this Son's way of saying that the human condition is pitiable? Since I didn't ask or say anything else, and the shift had been made without comment, Son continued in what I discovered was his second language.

Son is bilingual. He must have learned the language I had heard him use up to this time as a child. Lily is a religious, Bible-reading teetotaler. Son had obviously not learned obscenity at her knee. But he was far more fluent with four-letter words than I had ever heard him with five or seven. The minute he began to speak what sounded like his native tongue, he *could* speak. His life story could be told only, it seemed, in that language.

I know a man, a writer, who says he has three languages: decent, indecent, and literary. He learned indecent language as a boy in Utah; he picked up decent language at Berkeley (the free-speech movement would have been lost on him); and, as a writer, his sentences are more than decent: they are literary. I doubt Son has a third language. If he does, it cannot surprise me as much as his second has. The chief surprise was not that Son used these words but that I understood them so perfectly. I had read them all, of course. As far as I was concerned, Son's second language *was* literary, but I had never heard it spoken before. I can still read Latin after a fashion, but I have never heard Latin spoken as the speaker's native tongue. If a man appeared before me speaking Latin, *that* in itself would amaze me. If I understood him perfectly, the surprise, though great, would perhaps be less. I had only read the words of men who spoke as Son did.

There was nothing personal about Son's language. That was the pity of it. Language should be personal: words particular to me that seem appropriate for you. At some time they had, I suppose, been personal for Son. "Ass-hole," when first used, had meant an opening for offal, and he had used the two words with full knowledge of the fact. A woman he called an old cunt was reduced to another opening, and the first time he had used that epithet, an indignity had been intentionally done to a woman. Now Son's indecent language was impersonal.

I understood his words all right; what I didn't understand was why I wasn't outraged. I wasn't outraged for the same reason that I wouldn't be outraged if a lunatic threw kisses to me. He wouldn't be throwing them to *me;* he would simply be expressing himself in a way that had become routine and was meaningless.

I was brought up in a generation, a locale, and a class that used language—nice language, genteel language—as one of the chief signposts to designate who they were. I never heard any "bad" words in my youth.

Nancy Mitford wrote an article on U and non-U—upper class and nonupper class—as these terms apply to the English vocabulary. Certain distinctions of more or less the same kind prevailed in Southern Indiana. We never learned a kind of false diction, which, Miss Mitford says, is the sign of the lower classes trying to appear linguistically elegant. A napkin was never a serviette; false teeth were never dentures; when we misunderstood, we didn't say, "Pardon?" There were certain words, however, that nice people never said, and one did show one's upbringing and "class" by his language. These words had to do, for the most part, with bodily functions. Ain'ts and hain'ts flourished in our neighborhood; these were certainly non-U. They were not the mark of a dirty mind but of a lack of education. Linguistically, Southern Indiana had broadened when I was a child and since my mother was a girl. *She* had been sent to her room for not skipping, as she read aloud to her parents, the words "bucking bronco." I don't know what Grandpa and Grandma thought a bronco was, but a "buck" was a male animal; and a male animal meant sex; and a well-brought-up girl found ways of side-stepping words that suggested that unmentionable fact.

There were words, when I was a girl, that I occasionally heard which were never used in our family and which I knew were not nice because we didn't use them. We had bottoms, but not butts or asses. We had stomachs, but not bellies. We had bowels, but not guts. We did not piss, we peed, when young. Later we went to the "outhouse" and still later to the "bathroom." We certainly did not shit. In avoiding that word in our family, Mama used for us children a term that ruined an otherwise unobjectionable word. We did not, as children, have BMs or "do number two" or defecate. We were told to "grunt," and I shuddered through the primary grades with a series of stories of grunting pigs. What words our parents used for sexual intercourse we did not know, because we didn't know that such an activity existed. Whatever that word was, I am sure it wasn't Son's.

Recently in a magazine rack I saw a magazine with a fine color reproduction of a picture of Thoreau on its back and a quotation from him under his picture. I knew that the interest in Thoreau is great nowadays, but I didn't know that there was now enough interest to support a monthly magazine. The quotation was, "I lose my respect for the man who can make the mystery of sex the subject of a coarse jest, yet when you speak earnestly and seriously on the subject is silent." I took the magazine to the check-out stand. Practically anything Thoreau says interests me, and I was ready to converse with him "earnestly and seriously" on the subject of sex. No coarse jests would be attempted.

When I got to the stand, the checker flipped the magazine over. What I was buying was a magazine called *Sexual Behavior,* and the subjects considered that month were: "Drinking and Sex"; "Are American Men Afraid of Women?";

"Clothing and Sexuality"; "Homosexuality in the Movies." Thoreau was simply the shill. I should have known that in any popularity contest with sex Thoreau would be the loser, though on all of the above subjects he has had pertinent things to say; on some of them, however, he was probably unconscious of having done so.

The Quakers of backwoods Indiana were not prepared to speak "earnestly and seriously" of the mysteries of sex. Unjesting *and* silent was their attitude toward the subject. This was Victorianism. It was also part of the faith of those people. The body was the Lord's holy temple. And while a cunt and a cock were part of the holy temple, one did not for a minute consider them the entire edifice.

Leslie Fiedler says that he has taught his children that the only "dirty words" are those that belittle people: kike, nigger, Polack, and the like. "Nigger" and "kike," while possibly intended by their users as demeaning, whittling down the individual as they do, cannot subtract from those so designated the enormous realms of history and accomplishment that is theirs and of which the hearer is aware. The woman called an old cunt is reduced to a function, and a secondary one at that. I'd rather be a nigger or a kike than a cunt, though the last word is now socially more acceptable than the first two.

So for various reasons we talked "nice" back on the Muscatatuck in the early part of the century. All of the reasons for so doing weren't holy. A nice-talking child no doubt felt superior to one who talked of his butt and his belly, who puked instead of vomited, and possibly who even et instead of ate. Today there has been a counterrevolution. Puke and shit and fuck are chic. The Anglo-Saxons have, for the time being at least, conquered the Normans. Honest island plainness has supplanted the Latinate multisyllabled sexiness of the invading Normans. The English lost the battle of Hastings in 1066, but now, almost 1,000 years later, they appear, if you read the new novels, to have won the war.

I do not know how Son picked up his second language; for

he, I am sure, as much as I—perhaps even more than I, for Lily appears to be verbally more conventional than my mother—spoke the language of Victoria when he was young. He is not influenced by, and probably has never heard of, radical chic. Yet he has made that turnabout in language that is impossible for me, and that, in a way, makes his language more literary than mine.

Perhaps if I had been a man and in the army, as Son has been, a change in my language would have been automatic. I have some word envy of those men novelists who command this second language.

Jean Genêt says (he is speaking of homosexual society in which all the members are male, but only some are called men), "Slang was for men. [Genêt uses "slang" as Mama used "dirty."] Like the language among the Caribees it became a secondary sexual attribute. It was like the colored plumage of male birds, like the multi-colored silk garments which are pre-rogatives of the warriors of the tribe. It was a crest and spurs. Everybody understood it, but the only ones who could speak it were the men."

I was like that listening to Son. I understood his language, though I couldn't speak it.

The upbringing of girls of my generation, wrong in a good many ways, was also wrong in that it taught us to believe that dirty words were purely a masculine prerogative, a man's "crest and spurs." Believing this, a filthy mouth seemed to us, as to Genêt, "a secondary sexual attribute," on a par with big biceps and a hairy chest. Thus taught, I looked forward to hearing some strong language from Max when we married: a damn or hell or two. I never imagined anything worse. Max's language, since Max was a Quaker from a college town, was, at the very least, as nice as mine. So I tried a damn or two myself. Max's reactions were those reported by Genêt when Mimosa (male but not man) stepped out of character: "One day at one of our bars when Mimosa ventured the following words in the course

144

of a sentence, 'his screwing stories,' the men frowned. Someone said with a threat in his voice, 'Broad acting tough.' "

Neither Max nor I knew the word "broad" then, but "acting tough" was familiar and summed up the situation accurately. We both knew that I was "acting," and that toughness, if there was to be any in the family, should be displayed by Max, not me. "Broad acting tough." That is still the opinion when a woman writes wearing the "crest and spurs."

Son was never profane, never blasphemous. He belittled woman, reduced her to a single act and a single organ, but neither God's name nor His Son's did he ever take in vain. What he had learned in Sunday school stuck with him: "Thou shalt not take the name of the Lord thy God in vain." Okay. He didn't. In Sunday school there had been no other prohibitions about vocabulary. Somewhere, somehow, Son had acquired his second language. He used it—it seemed to me, no judge— with a considerable flair and rhythm. The trouble was, I listened to him the way I used to read Pater and Firbank: too aware of style and vocabulary to pay much attention to content.

Did he ever preach? I don't know. He both married for the first time and entered the army at seventeen. The generalizing nature of his vocabulary made it impossible for me to retain any clear picture of the women he talked about. Organs, except to a clinician, are so similar.

At six Lily whoo-whooed to let Son know that supper was ready. I thanked him for what he had done and told him that I had found what he had to say interesting. I didn't mention the fact that I had found his manner of telling astounding, or that I was equally astounded not to find it revolting. I had been taught to believe that I should have been revolted. As it was, what I had heard might as well have been told in Esperanto.

"I haven't come to the bad part yet," Son said, like Casey before him.

I didn't know what resources of vocabulary he would be able to dredge up for "the bad part"; but the simplicity of the statement let me, for the minute, forget the language and see the man.

"Come over sometime and tell me the bad part," I said. "I'll give you a drink."

Day before yesterday I decided to go home. *Walden* ends, "Perhaps it seemed to me that I had several more lives to live, and could not spare any more time for that one." I thought about the lives I was missing here and drove to the airport to charter a plane to take me and dog to Las Vegas. At Las Vegas I could make connections with a San Francisco-bound plane. At San Francisco Max would meet me, and two hours later I would be home. I was packed and ready to leave in the morning, but when I drove to the airport to check the weather— for in these small chartered planes one flies with the weather— I was told that there would be no flying to Vegas for a couple of days. There was wind, rain, and snow out Vegas way. I could, as Max had done, fly the next day or the next to Phoenix; take a plane from there to Los Angeles; and from Los Angeles, where planes, grounded by nothing but fog, fly every hour on the hour to San Francisco, make the forty-five-minute flight north.

The indecisive are always open to signs. They solicit portents; seek guidelines in the sky; open Bibles to find prophetic verses. They even (I did once) walk down a row of books in a library, with eyes closed, and point to a title that will provide guidance. Eyes closed, I touched a book and found, when I opened my eyes, that I had chosen the perfect text for the indecisive: Frank Stockton's *Lady, or the Tiger*. That portent stunned me, so that I sat down at a library table to read the ending again. Which *did* the hero choose? Stockton never says. By the time I had finished reading, *my* decision had been made by the book that refused to reveal *its* decision. The hour for the meeting had passed.

I decided to go the way the wind blew. I had been thinking for years of being alone in a lonely place. Surely I was up to three months. I didn't book another flight. "I'll stop by again when the weather is better," I said to the airport manager.

# XVI

———◆———

Last night, not sleeping, I had two thoughts; the second, in a way, casting doubt on the first. My first thought took the form of a question: are all of my moments of ecstasy based upon what is visual? Could those moments—I don't know how to name them—of utter delight, illumination, transportation, stillness, come without sight? Sight, it seemed to me, was always their cause. The order, the quiet, the peace of the tank house in St. Helena; the living room here: candles lighted, a vigil light big as a star burning; dusk coming down. Alone on a river in a unknown country; new grass, fine as baby hair, growing between rocks in the wash; the sun going down, burnishing a cove like a transparent shell. Moments of seeing— every one of them.

The first of these moments I remember (there must have been many such moments earlier) came in the house on the hill in Yorba Linda. It was winter, a dark day, cold and raw, rain threatening but not yet falling. Mama was in the hospital with appendicitis. Papa had been in Los Angeles all day on Water Company business. Carmen was staying with a relative. Myron and I came home from school, I expecting a cold, untidy house—which I would clean and warm before Papa came home. We found the house already clean, already warm. Walter Cope, an old bachelor who kept house in a tent nearby, had been over, swept, dusted, mopped, started a fire in the base-burner. A man who can keep house in a tent can keep house anywhere. He had put everything away—a job almost beyond Mama (who did not live in her eyes). When we arrived, he left (he was too careful to leave an untended fire burning), and I was alone with the feeling I have never been able to name. The rag carpet on the dining-room floor was striped with bars of jeweled light. The ingrain carpet on the living-room floor was a stained-glass window, soft with firelight shining down onto it. Everything was right, and nothing need ever change. I was the room's center, and its color and orderliness and warmth filled me. My fingertips pulsed with the rise and fall of the flames. My cheekbones were softened by what I saw. I went back in time. I was boneless, filled with life, but with my life yet to be lived.

Into this order and warmth came Papa, home from the hurly-burly of Los Angeles, with food for our supper so that I didn't have to cook, and with gifts for Mama, whom he would visit after supper. The food was a man's idea of what would be good for supper: pickled pigs' feet nestling in mounds of delicatessen sauerkraut, like pigs in clover. Myron and I had never tasted such food; we didn't know it existed. It was the perfect food for that evening: gnawing around a pig's toes! Who could have expected fun or flavor in that? They were some special brand of pigs' feet. I've never found their like since. It will take another raw December day, with the house unexpectedly warmed and cleaned by another old tent-keeping bachelor, to provide it.

The books Papa brought home were novels he thought would entertain a woman still weak from an operation. They were secondhand and cost twenty-nine cents each. I don't know about Mama, but they entertained me. One was *The One Woman*, by the author of *The Clansman*. In this Papa had written, "For Grace: The One Woman in My Life." The other was *Castle Craneycrow*, by the author of *Graustark*. Papa had to work harder on an inscription for this, but he made it: "For Grace, who makes our home a castle."

Last night the thought that had never come to me before

was: do these moments of bliss come to me as the result of what I see? Or when the feeling comes, are the things I see transformed?

There are only two times I can remember when it seems to me that the feeling might have transformed what I saw.

One spring morning when I was somewhere between thirteen and fifteen, I walked home from where I had spent the night with a friend. The walk was, perhaps, three miles long, and I started early, not later than seven. I didn't follow a road but went through groves of half-grown orange trees and across uncleared ground where cactus and sagebrush still grew. It was at the height of the spring blooming, and on the uncleared hillsides and in the arroyos and around the ragged edges of the fields there was a wildfire rage of flowers. Yellow violets, though not the most showy, were my favorites. Mustard was perhaps the showiest simply because of its height, but it couldn't compete in color with lupine or California poppies or Indian paintbrush. There were stands of brodiaea, which we called teakettle stems, and carpets of inch-high baby blue-eyes, which I tried to avoid trampling as much because of their name as because of their fragility. I walked fast, because I did not much like "staying overnight," and because there was always lots of Saturday work to be done at home.

On Reservoir Hill, my walk was almost over. I had climbed the gradual slope from my friend's house, which was near the Santa Ana, and could now see, a quarter of a mile away, my own home. What remained of my journey was short and downhill all the way; so, the long haul over, I had earned the right to pause and catch my breath.

Then it happened. Then, I think, what I felt transfigured what I saw. Not the other way around. I had been walking, aware that it was a fine spring morning and that flowers were blooming, but my mind had been on the he-saids and she-saids of the night before's party. There on that hilltop a feeling burst my body apart, and its fragments became one with yellow violets and Indian paintbrushes.

Mama had a round paperweight that she had won as a girl in an elocution contest. It was a heavy glass ball filled with fluted columns of gold and rose, fountains of glass that sprayed stars of blue; and in the center of all this tangle of glory and glassy fireworks was a single little flower, a periwinkle, but white, not blue. I was not this flower, but what I felt *was:* my feeling made me the world's flowering center. I turned around and around. There was smoke from the home chimney; and in the same way as I was opened to the spring world, the chimney smoke opened the house to me so there was added to the world I could see an invisible world. The walls of the house became transparent: Papa in the kitchen making baking-powder biscuits and singing, "Oh, that will be glory for me."

What I felt was beyond crying or laughing or rejoicing. It was almost beyond feeling. It was very near to being. After a while whatever it was faded, and I walked, slowly now, on toward home. I have never before spoken to a soul of that hill or of what I felt there. But I will remember it as long as I remember anything.

The second time when what I felt transformed what I saw, I was also out of doors and climbing a hill. I was homeward-bound from the newly opened Yorba Linda Library with an armload of books. This was an autumn night, after nine o'clock, for I had stayed until the library closed. A clear night, with a blaze of stars in the sky. I was not thinking of them, but of my great haul of books stacked from the crook of my arm to my chin, which I had clamped down on top of the stack to hold the books steady. I was climbing the dirt road of a hill when suddenly the feeling I had had on Reservoir Hill came to me, and I said out loud, "You are M. J. West." This is how I thought of myself in those days, for my name is Mary Jessamyn, and I was in love with what was spare and cut to the bone. It was as if I had told myself a great piece of news. When I said those words, *then* I noticed the heavy clotting of the Milky Way, and the brow of the hill a dark curve against the starlit sky. *M. J. West noticed them.* Who had been noticing them before, because I hadn't lived starless until the age of thirteen or fourteen, I don't know; but on that night I knew who was doing the seeing: M. J. West.

I can never, as some women can, sign myself to anything that is part of myself, otherwise. Legally, socially, conventionally, locally, I am Mrs. H. M. McPherson. But the truth of the matter is that I am M. J. West; and I was told so and accepted the fact long ago.

M.  J.  WEST

*Writing my name I raise an edifice*
*Whose size and shape appear to me*
*As homelike as the hexagon the bee*
*Builds for his own and honey's use.*

*Wasp nest or palace is a home*
*If you're a wasp or king. The mole*
*Is happy in his little hole*
*And I within my written name.*

I no sooner jot down an insight of my own—one that shakes me with its truth and newness—than I discover that it has been expressed by dozens of writers before me, and felt but unrecorded by how many millions of others who think without pen in hand!

The note I made in my journal two nights ago was this: one frequently acts because two persons apparently are involved: a twin who, however much the other suffers, is determined to know the nature and effect of a particular act. So the actor, the one who suffers, undertakes the repellent, the nasty, the distasteful, with eyes wide open. He knows the character of the action and his feeling about it, but he cannot resist the compulsion from the other, the observer who drives him on.

At times the action appears to proceed from some appetite for irony; from some predilection for the unlikely, the wry, the twisted; from a need to create an opportunity for the observer to say to the self who acts: "You who so loathe this sort of thing are now in it up to your neck." And then the two of them, actor and observer, marvel together at the irony that has joined aversion and commitment.

No sooner had I written that than I encountered two similar statements. First, in McLean's *Life of Hazlitt*. There Hazlitt is quoted as observing (his subject is the attraction of persons for each other) "how far the greater portion are joined together not infrequently by the very fear of the event, by repugnance, and a sort of fated fascination."

". . . by repugnance, and a sort of fated fascination." Yes, that is what I had in mind.

Next, in Thoreau: "I . . . am sensible of a certain doubleness by which I can stand as remote from myself as from another. However intense my experience, I am conscious of the presence and criticism of a part of me, which, as it were is not me, but spectator, sharing my experience, but taking note of it; and that is no more I than it is you. . . . This doubleness may easily make us poor neighbors and friends sometimes."

To say nothing of poor lovers, which Thoreau no doubt realized.

There are few human beings, I should think, who have not felt this doubleness: the self that acts; the self that watches. Fewer perhaps will have experienced Hazlitt's (and my) propulsion by the observer toward the repugnant, or the strange, bitter amusement and irony upon which the observer feeds.

Why does this doubleness "easily make us poor neighbors and friends"? And impossible lovers? And untrusted politicians? (Tricky Dicks without a trick up our sleeves, simply because on the lens of the TV camera the shadow of our other self, the omnipresent observer, is visible; and surely one who is double is capable of double-dealing?) Poor neighbors, poor friends, impossible lovers, mistrusted politicians, because the other is present in all situations. No one cares to play second fiddle to a voyeur, to an observer for whom the whole drama of heart's blood spilt, passion spent, affection bestowed, was "a work of the imagination only."

For one who is double, another is not necessary. The friend, the lover, does not relish this. Even the constituent is inclined to teach the politician a lesson of his need of another by withholding his vote. Thoreau was double; he even refers to himself as *hermaphroditic*.

### TWO-SEEING EYE

*Two-seeing eye*
*See one, see one.*
*Not black and white,*
*Not moon and sun.*

*See day or night.*
*See like or loath:*
*Two-seeing eye*
*That stares at both.*

*Two-seeing eye*
*Your double sight*
*Bids me to go*
*Forbids my flight.*

*Bids me to love*
*And shows the flaw;*
*Evokes the purr,*
*Reveals the claw.*

*I am a ghost*
*Homeless, adrift*
*Seeking the dark*
*From light to sift.*

*Two-seeing eye*
*See one, see one.*
*In doubleness*
*Your will is done.*

*Until I'm lost*
*Mired deep in night*
*Blinded by my*
*Two-seeing sight.*

I who live alone by this ancient, once destructive, now dammed and impotent river am never truly alone, because of this doubleness. Solitude may be what I seek, but the other, the observer, will never permit it.

There is, says Harrison Sage, author of *The Quest for Solitude,* a way by which the true lover of solitude can be recognized. Is he alone because he is running away from something? Or is he alone because he is running after something? A man on the lam, though often alone, may not be a true lover of solitude. But the true lover of solitude may also be running away from something—something that will never permit him to experience what he has known only when alone.

One of the curiosities of history was the banding together of groups of men whose goal was the solitary life. Societies were formed, the purpose of which was separation from society. It is as curious as fighting for peace or waging a war to end all wars. Peace is achieved by not fighting. Wars not waged end wars. Solitude is the result of being alone. "Brothers, I love solitude. Let us band together for that purpose." As contradictory as, loving peace, to join the army.

Colette understood very early, if we can trust her memory—and we can—that love is the enemy of solitude. She speaks of "the jealous and anxious passion I had for solitude. O solitude of my young days! You were my refuge, my panacea, the citadel of my youthful pride. With what might and main did I cling to you—and how afraid I was even then of losing you! I trembled at the mere thought of the more ruthless and less rare ecstasy of love! At the thought of losing you I felt already demeaned. And yet . . . who can resist the pull of love? To become only a woman—how paltry! Yet I hastened eagerly toward that common goal!

"Did I hesitate a minute, one solitary minute, standing between your beloved specter, O solitude, and the menacing apparition of love? Perhaps. I don't know, it is still too close to me."

I had not, among other of her possessions, Colette's logic. I did not see that love and solitude are opponents. I hastened as eagerly as she toward the common goal, without in the least understanding, as she did, that though solitude could, love could not, live in a tub, a box, or a trailer; not without ousting solitude first, anyway.

# XVII

The last overnight trip I took with my parents started in July, when I was still seventeen, and ended in October, when I was eighteen. I was three weeks late for the beginning of my second year in college—which daunted my parents not at all. If college wasn't teaching me how to cope with college, what was it teaching me?

I had avoided many of their innumerable camping trips. There can never be another decade like that between 1910 and 1920 for young people (I am thinking of my father and mother now, not of myself) who wanted to travel, and who had an undreamed-of machine with which they could cover the ground at twenty-five to thirty-five miles an hour! They had in addition an unknown countryside to explore: a countryside almost empty of people, but containing towering mountains, vast deserts, extinct—it was hoped—volcanoes, geysers that for fifty cents could be turned on and off for the astonishment of tourists. There were exotic fruits and flowers, never dreamed of by poor benighted Hoosiers living in and off their back-East apple orchards and corn patches. If these were the cats of Zanzibar, they were another breed of cat, and everyone was too busy looking to count.

So they packed and they went! Again and again and again!

Some of these trips I was able to avoid. I missed Yosemite. I was too young to join the Women's Land Army, but old enough at fifteen to go with a group of high-school girls to cut peaches in a cannery at Van Nuys. The Italian women working in the cannery celebrated Allied advances on the Italian front by pounding on their dishpans with their knives—an earsplitting rat-a-tat-tat of victory. I, like Hemingway, was with the Italians at the time of the fighting on that peninsula.

My father and mother came out of their way to Van Nuys to try to persuade me to go with them. But I had a room to myself in the home of a widow who, also helping the war effort, gave it to me free. And I was rolling in money. We were paid by the box, and I was a fast peach pitter. I felt graveside sorrowful to see Papa and Mama leave without me. I had one fact to sustain me, a fact that had prevented them from giving me outright orders to abandon peach pitting: I was part of the fight to make the world safe for democracy. They could not accept the responsibility of losing that fight because a daughter of theirs was missing from the peach-pitting front. My post was not important, true. But because of a nail improperly placed, the horse had lost his shoe and stumbled; the messenger who was to have carried the news that would have turned the tide of battle lay unconscious by the roadside. So for the lack of a nail the battle was lost. For the lack of a pitter, was democracy to be endangered? They couldn't risk that. And I, in addition to my real concern for democracy, had my darling little room at the widow's to keep me steadfast in my patriotism.

The room had casement windows, dimity curtains, a window seat, and shelves of Zane Grey, Stewart Edward White, and Ernest Thompson Seton, the library of the widow's late husband. I was halfway through *The Riders of the Purple Sage* when asked to abandon peach pitting for Yosemite.

I had visions of Vernal Falls and El Capitan (Mama played this Sousa march on the piano) and Half Dome, and memories, too, of campfire hours, with Mama's fried camp biscuits and "Tenting on the Old Campground" on the French harp to follow. But they could not prevail against Zane Grey, democracy, and a room of my own. I bade my family a tearful farewell: a young soldier doing his duty, but who would have been heartbroken if duty had commanded him to leave his book-lined room.

Off in a tent, the other members of the junior land army, all nine of them, were living in community hilarity. I felt sorry for them. They felt sorry for me. They sang—I could hear them: "Pack Up Your Troubles in Your Old Kit Bag" and "There's a Long, Long Trail A-winding"—then went to the movies. I read *The Riders of the Purple Sage* and watched the cooling night air lift the white dimity curtains.

There are many beautiful movements in the world: a wave cresting; a pacer responding to the call of "Rack on"; a buzzard riding the air currents. But there are two available to any dweller in the West—perhaps I should say the Old West—that cannot be bettered: curtains lifting in the cooling air off the ocean after a sultry day; and outside the window a stand of volunteer oats, now green, now silver, as the ocean wind bends and releases them. I had the proper curtains at the widow's. Here on the Colorado I have the volunteer oats. Do I hypnotize myself watching such movements? Do hours pass without my knowing it?

I escaped another trip, this one to Yellowstone Park, for reasons advanced as Christian rather than patriotic. The real reason was that I did not want another trip: four of us crowded into the back seat, and Carmen snuggled up spoon-fashion against me at night in a camp bed built for one and one-half. I went to Asilomar, which was then owned by the YWCA, to work as their "pantry girl." The pantry girl sliced bread, made pats of butter, and took care of leftovers. I was so good at this part of my job that though I arrived at Asilomar a 120-pound pantry girl, I left there a 145-pound pantry girl, unrecognized by my parents when I arrived at Union Station in Los Angeles.

Into Asilomar for conferences, for rest, for reports to be made to the various organizations that supported their work came

159

YWCA secretaries from all over the world: from India, from China, from South America. Some were neat, trim, handsome young women, who spoke foreign languages, carried Bibles, and wore suits, which had been tailored for them in Hong Kong or London, as they went about the world on the King's business. They impressed me mightily.

I had never thought of being a YWCA secretary. But I had thought that in case marriage failed me, I might go to China as a missionary; a rather special kind of missionary to women. Some women of China, I knew, had their feet bound. I believed that after their feet were unbound, they would need to be taught to move about, to develop muscles never used. I, who was All Southern California Girl Basketball guard, would go to China and there teach basketball to the women of China. This, as I saw it, would be fine for all concerned. I was saddened by my supposition (correct) that my basketball days would end with my school days. In China on such a mission I would be able to continue playing basketball, the girls whose feet had been bound would have their muscles strengthened, and all would be done to advance the Kingdom of God. Who was to finance this basketball missionary tour, I do not know. Basketball players are millionaires today. Fifty years ago there was little money available, even to players expertly dribbling and energetically catching rebounds for the glory of God. Nevertheless, this plan of mine for good works (and fun) in far places made me feel at one with the homecoming secretaries.

The homecoming secretaries had individual rooms. The "stuck-ups," as the girl workers were called, slept in a long screened porch, bed next to bed like soldiers in a barracks. The secretaries' rooms were never all filled at once, and I soon took over one near my end of the barracks; not for sleeping purposes —I saw that this could cause endless trouble with bed linens or with unexpected secretaries arriving from Tibet in the middle of the night. I slept in my assigned cot beside a girl from Pomona who came in from dates breathing hard and saying,

"Oh, I am all Al's and Al is all mine." But for all purposes other than sleeping, I used a secretary's room.

I was only once disturbed. I was seated on the bed, books around me, when Mrs. Leonard, the Asilomar housekeeper, came into the room.

"What are you doing here?" she asked.

There didn't seem to be much purpose in dissembling.

"I am here to read," I replied.

"So I see," said she, and without another word she left. Since she hadn't said, "Don't let this happen again," or, "These rooms are for the secretaries," I continued for the two months I was at Asilomar to have as my private study a secretary's room. I came to need it. I spent all I earned, except for one Japanese tea set with handleless cups, on books.

I had never before been where there were books for sale. At Asilomar there was a book store. It was irresistible. I needed someone to come to the book shop singing, "Sister, dear Sister, come home with me now." I was drunk with the tipple of buying and reading. I don't remember what the available choices were. A good many religious books, I suppose. Daniel Polling and Rufus Jones and Bruce Barton. I bought nothing, however, but poetry, the poetry of women. I don't know whether the YWCA, as a kind of forerunner of Women's Lib, stocked women writers more heavily than men, or whether my own tastes ran that way. I still have the books I bought that summer: those by Sara Teasdale, Angela Morgan, Lizzette Woodsworth Reese (Mencken thought highly of her), Adelaide Craspey. No Millay. Did the YWCA consider her too erotic for pantry girls and secretaries?

I bought anthologies of poetry: *The Little Book of American Poetry; The Little Book of Modern American Poetry*. If I want to know what a pantry girl thought about love, I have only to look at the poems and lines checked thus: ∨. Never underlined. I think underlining detestable. I do not want to be hit in the eye when I reread a book by what hit me in the eye years ago. I want to be a new reader. I bought E. V. Lucas's *The Open Road* and *By the Campfire,* because I can read almost anything in prose or verse so long as the subject is nature.

Almost all travel is lost on teen-agers. They are all Byrons for whom scenery is only a background for their own emotions. Since (to judge by myself at that age) they are all either in love or hoping to conduct or display themselves so that someone will fall in love with them, they can more comfortably do this suffering and acting in front of hometown scenery, thus sparing expense to parents and wear and tear on the nerves of all less young than themselves.

It is difficult to understand the generosity of parents. I have never been a parent, but faced with a rebellious fourteen-year-old clamoring to pit peaches or be a pantry girl or visit Grandpa, *anything* rather than take a trip with me in my already overloaded car, I would, I think, say, "Stay home, miss, and good riddance." But Papa and Mama could never say that. They could not look on greatness with pleasure unless they shared their pleasure with their children. Every good thing in their lives they wanted us to have a part of.

The young do not discover the world. They discover themselves, and travel only interrupts their trips to the interior. Dr. Livingston didn't mind being *greeted* by Stanley, but if Stanley had insisted that he interrupt his trip to the interior, he would have had another reception. Parents don't understand this. They unselfishly insist that children abandon *their* trips to join adult junkets.

My parents' junkets occasionally revealed to me wonders greater than those the most energetic teen-age Columbus could discover inside himself. But I missed many. I traded natural wonders for the four walls of a widow's spare room and the excitement of commandeering the knotty-pine bedrooms of globe-trotting YWCA secretaries. I listened to "The Preacher and the Bear" in Grandpa's parlor when I could have been hearing the wind in the pines of the Sierras.

I escaped more trips than I took, but I did not escape all. I was unable to avoid going with my family on the trip to see the sequoias. Grandpa was remarried, the war was won, and there was no real opening for me in China. There was no reason to criticize *that* auto trip, because it was fast. We crept up the narrow dirt road, with its hairpin curves that led along the sides of the mountains of the Sierras. Mama sounded the Klaxon constantly. She had no faith in Papa's sense of danger. He was an easygoing West, with the addition of an Indian's stoicism. He did not anticipate danger. She did. She played the Klaxon as she did the Kurtzmann, *con spirito,* as we mounted.

The sequoias, as soon as we caught sight of them, silenced the Klaxon. Even its echo was forgotten. Those great trees absorbed all echoes past and present. They said, "Be still." We breathed quietly, spoke in whispers, walked carefully on the spongy carpet of needles out of which they grew. We touched the great shaggy boles of the trees. They did not seem to be trees; true, they were called trees, but they were unlike any other trees we had ever seen. They were, of course, not people or animals; but like the rimrocks of Oregon, they were perhaps spirits who had assumed tree shape and decided to rest for a while, unmoving. They had been here, we knew, for hundreds upon hundreds of years. When Christ was born. When Shakespeare wrote. When the glaciers retreated. Speak. Tell us about it. From far above us, from their skyscraper tops, came a murmur we could not understand. We were cricket people at their feet. We could not interpret their sky-high language. But we listened, silent.

If I had not been pushed into that Klaxon-equipped car and told that I *must* go, I would have missed those trees.

I would have missed also, except that I was given no choice, my first boat trip. Even on that occasion, the first time I was ever water-borne, what I remember is not the Golden Gate, then unbridged, or the bay itself or the white city on the hills above the bay, but my own emotions. I remember what I felt as we crossed by ferry from San Francisco to Sausalito. I do not remember what we crossed. I got out of the car and stood on the wind-blown prow of the ship: a Viking sighting Vinland, a Columbus with the gray Azores behind, Captain Cook heading for unknown natives and death.

I heard and saw the first writer of my life on one of these camping trips I didn't want to take. We were camped someplace between Carmel and Pacific Grove. Papa, as he always did if one was available, bought a paper in Monterey, as we passed through. In it I read that an author was to speak that night in Pacific Grove. Not only had I never seen a living author, but I had also never seen anyone who *had* seen a living author. Pacific Grove was only two miles from where we were camped. The speech was to be given in a church.

Papa and Mama didn't think much of my traipsing off at night, but since the speech was to be made in a church, they said that I could go if I would take Rusty with me. Rusty, at six, didn't think much of tramping off anywhere to hear an author. I bribed him with promises of ice cream afterward, and we set off in good time to see the speaker arrive. This was my *first* writer, and I intended to see her as well as hear her. Few handsomer women can ever have picked up a pen. She had dark hair, pink cheeks, and a smiling, rosy mouth. She wore, that summer evening, a lacy-looking dress with red roses tucked into its ribbon belt. If this is the way a writer looks, I thought, her words will be honey and gold. I had read enough to know that looks were nothing most lady writers were noted for. Even Elizabeth Barrett, who undoubtedly looked beautiful to Robert Browning, resembled her spaniel, Flush, to me.

I expected a writer to speak about writing. Writing was what I was interested in and what I had tramped two miles to hear about. Then the beautiful Kathleen Norris, for she it was, announced the subject on which she would speak: "The Necessity for the Passage of Legislation Prohibiting the Manufacture and Sale of Spirituous Liquors in the State of California." And she did. She did. I could have cried. Rusty didn't care. He was asleep. This was for me the greatest transportation of coals to Newcastle ever attempted. I was as much a teetotaler as Kathleen Norris; and my parents were, if anything, more so.

On one of the Sunday-afternoon drives that were the custom of the country when cars were new and the countryside had not yet been ruined by them, I, inflamed by roadside signs and the heat of four in the back seat of a topless car, had said, "Papa, I wish I could have a bottle of root beer."

My father stopped the car immediately. This tells you how long ago this happened. No one can stop a car immediately in the state of California today without causing a twenty-car pile-up, numerous deaths, and a possible conflagration. But, as I say, this was a long time ago, and Papa stopped the car immediately. He did so in order to turn around and look me square in the eye. "Jessamyn," he said, "little did I think I'd ever have a daughter who would ask for a bottle of beer. And on Sunday afternoon, too."

Papa's feeling about beer was mine exactly. Whiskey was wicked; but beer was not only wicked, it was vulgar.

"Papa," I explained, "root beer has nothing to do with real beer. It is nothing but root juices."

"Why don't they call it root juice, then?" Papa asked.

I had no answer to that. But Papa had. "I'll tell you why," he said. "They want to lead the unwary step by step downward toward the real thing."

In the long run, of course, he was right. But it took a while. As a young woman in Paris in my mid-twenties, I had a room in the home of a female botanist, a woman with a degree from Oxford and decorations from the French government for her work in World War I. One day each week she took the train out of Paris into the countryside to botanize. She took me with her. Those were the days of twenty-five-mile walks. At noon we would stop to have lunch in a country inn. I was told that since the water in these inns was not safe, I should drink wine.

That was unthinkable, so I walked through France during the summer of 1928 washing down my omelettes and bread and cheese with an English soft drink called Lemon Squash. The waiters grinned; my landlady shrugged; and I, without the sense to know it, passed up a chance to drink the wines of France under the tutelage of a woman who knew those wines well.

I was a product of my upbringing, and I had been brought up by parents who had never known anyone in their backwoods life who drank for any other reason than to get drunk. And these persons wanted to get drunk so that the inhibitions that, when sober, prevented them from raping the hired girl in the hayloft or giving their contentious neighbor twenty whacks with an ax would be stilled. *That* was what one drank for; that was what drink led to: murder and rape. So I stayed away from it, as they did.

Until I was a graduate student at Berkeley, I had never *seen* anyone who was drunk. Then in San Francisco one night I saw a sailor progressing sideways down Market Street, his back against buildings for support and his feet feeling the way with less confidence than a tightrope walker over Niagara. I was awed, repelled, fascinated; I was disgusted with myself for wanting to look. What was I? An eighteenth-century barbarian gone to a madhouse to laugh at the antics of lunatics? But my head *would* turn in his direction. A man had done this to himself. He had swallowed something that made it impossible for him to control his body. Death itself, my grandmother dead in her casket, had not aroused in me so much feeling.

Later, at the end of my twenties, I was sent home from a sanatorium for tuberculars to die amidst my loved ones. My new doctor suggested that a bottle of beer a day might improve my appetite. Papa would not buy the beer without a prescription from the doctor. This was not necessary, but Papa would not have it thought that anyone was drinking beer in his house for pleasure. No one did. Warm beer on a stomach already queasy was no pleasure. It was immediately rejected.

As Papa had predicted, the unwary are led downward step by step toward the real thing. I was pretty wary, but by the time I was in my mid-teens I was drinking root beer. On one of those camping trips I had been unable to avoid, I decided to take the next step—to go beyond root beer; though not far.

We were headed for Mount Lassen and were camped for the night someplace beside a river. The valleys of central California are very hot in summer, and the river, while doing little to cool the air, made me think of a cool drink. Downstream about a mile, we had passed a general store plastered with signs for soft drinks. I decided, tremulous with daring, that I would walk back there and order ginger ale. Real drinkers, I knew, put liquor in ginger ale. No one I had ever heard of put *any-thing* into root beer. It was a child's drink. I was fifteen and beyond that sweet brown suds. Or I thought I was. The doubt made me tense. I changed my dress into something I thought worthy of a ginger-ale drinker. I put my fifteen cents into my pocket. Ginger ale was no five-cent drink for kids.

When I was ready to go, my father said, "Take your little brother with you."

Ordinarily I loved to take little brother with me. But this was to be what nowadays is called a rite of passage. I was moving from childhood to adulthood, or at least to maidenhood. I was celebrating the event with an adult drink. I intended to say, "Make mine ginger ale," in a cold, hard voice. This was not the place or the time for a little brother. Papa had never heard of the rite of passage; nor had I, for that matter. I knew only that this was an important and formal matter—and that I needed to be alone. I was not permitted to be alone.

When we reached the store, I said in my cold, hard voice, as planned, "A bottle of ginger ale."

"I want root beer!" Rusty wailed.

On any ordinary occasion I would have bought Rusty whatever he wanted: Nu-grape or Nesbitt's or Hires. But this was special. "I am buying ginger ale," I told him in my hard, cold voice.

I gave him half, of course, which may account for two facts: first, that Rusty got to the real thing earlier than his older sisters and brother; second, that the rite of passage, thus interrupted and flawed, may have delayed my own maturing.

Today young people take to the road while their parents stay more or less put. I was a hippie in reverse. I differed from my parents by refusing to take to the road. I stayed home and let them do the driving.

If I had it to do over again, would I still choose, as I did when young, the solitude of our empty house? Or the empty room in anyone's house, rather than go with my parents on all those camping trips? If I were the same girl, I suppose I would.

I have never understood those who share the sentiments of the man who wrote, "Make me a boy again just for tonight." Being boys, they would be as incapable the second time around as they were the first to understand the meaning and quality of what they possessed. So I never sing, "Make me a girl again just for tonight." I had that once. I did with it what I did, and without becoming another girl, I would do what I did before and remember it as I remember it now.

I have sometimes thought that I would like not to be young but to see myself, my parents, brothers, and sister when we were all young together. I have thought that I would; but given the chance, I'm not sure I would take it. The sight might drive me crazy with sorrow or self-pity. What would it be like to see that girl (knowing, as I would, how soon some of us would vanish from sight) choosing time after time to be with Mary J. Holmes's English Orphans or Tarzan or David Copperfield rather than with them? What if I saw myself bullying my little sister? Sowing the seeds that made her say before she died, "I have resented you all my life." What if I recognized the reason it was impossible for me to say even once in my life to my father, "Papa, I love you."

Perhaps if I could see but not hear a word, there would be no problem; see under the blue skies that have also vanished the young father and mother and their four children in the house on the brow of the hill, the house that swayed in the wind and had bagpipe music played through its unbattened walls when the Santa Ana was at its height.

Yes, I would take a chance on seeing, but not on hearing.

I might feel sorry for myself, for the rest of the life that remains to me, if I were to hear Mama say now, as I did then, "Myron is my favorite child"; say that, in answer to an aunt's question, in my hearing. I wasn't hurt by it then. Then, Mama's preferences were mine, except in such matters as housekeeping and trip taking. She had some kind of magic by which she had made me her partner, a junior mother. If she liked Myron best, that was no repudiation of me, but our joint choice among the children. Rusty was certainly cuter; Carmen prettier; but our favorite was Myron, for exactly what reason I was never sure. Being the favorite seemed to me a good position to be in: the favorite got the largest piece of pie; got a bicycle; got a job I had wrangled for myself as the janitor of the elementary school because it was more suitable for a boy to be a janitor. That job had suited *me* to a T. The pay was good; I swept in time to Sousa's marches played on the school Victrola; I read the crumpled-up notes the kids had written to each other and thrown in the wastepaper basket. I resigned nevertheless in favor of Myron, and without ill will.

Being the favorite, Myron tells me, is *not* a good position to be in. I (along with Mama) had chosen Myron as the favorite. He had had no voice in the matter. He did not choose to run and didn't run; standing still, he was elected. His sense of fairness (and what had happened didn't seem fair to him) was injured. His sense of his own worth was undermined. Was something wrong with him that all these concessions had to be made to him? Wasn't he able to fend for himself?

I inclined to this belief myself. We had to be especially good to Myron because he *was* so slow, so backward (this is Southern Indiana for shy), so quiet, so lacking in aggressiveness.

If I were to hear now Mama's answer to Aunt Rose's question, would I see the result in my own actions? Girls take care of boys, not vice versa. When a boy, my age and Myron's, was teaching Rusty (in Mama's language) "bad" words, I was sent out to give the boy his comeuppance, not Myron. I have often wondered what those words were. I got a bloody nose but no information out of that encounter. Perhaps in listening to Son's rich vocabulary I am giving Mama *her* comeuppance: "I don't have to protect Rusty from hearing dirty words any longer. I can listen to them myself."

If I were given the chance to see myself as a girl, I would not want to be able to hear *or* see what happened on the occasion when Mama read in one of my notebooks, "My mother is a slattern." I don't know where, at the age of ten or eleven, I had picked up that unchildlike word; perhaps in one of my English novels: the same one that had taught me to say, when asked to help pick green beans for supper, "Don't ask me to work in the fields."

Mama was heartbroken and angry because of what I had written. Papa had tears in his eyes. I know now what I didn't know then: Mama was an actress. Everything she put on was a costume. She handled clothes the way she handled words; she added to, twisted, reversed. She dressed for an occasion she had in her mind; she completed the costume she had caught a glance of in a mirror. Old sweater like a scarecrow? *Be* a scarecrow. Scrunched old hat like a man's? *Be* a man. Skirt caught up and petticoat showing like a scrub lady? *Be* a scrub lady; wave a frayed napkin fastidiously like a scrub lady, saying farewell to a departing friend. This was Carol Burnett arrived for the home screen fifty years too soon. This was hippieism without any Haight-Ashbury to stroll in. How could I be expected to see into the future?

I knew quite well that for an occasion Mama would be as well turned out as any woman in Yorba Linda. When ladies wore Cuban heels, her heels were Cuban. When they wore slit skirts, her skirt was slit, way up and with an accordion pleat of acid-green taffeta snaking out at every step, with a kind of warning hiss.

I had no understanding at twelve of any of this. I knew and still think Mama was untidy. But "slatternly" was a dirty word for her, and for a child to have used it about a play-acting mother making do for an audience with a dignified husband and four small children was cruel.

After the evening of reading that sentence, Mama never referred to it again. But she remembered it. I wrote a story in which I said that the neck of the mother's nightgown was dirty.

"Why did it have to be the *mother's* nightgown?" Mama asked in a sorrowful voice.

I don't know why. The nightgown with the grimy neck was not Mama's. Hers might be hanging from the chandelier or in the wood box or *on* at twelve noon, but it would be clean.

Children today bemoan their square parents. That's the accepted rule for parents. A high-spirited mother with a square child is a far worse case. I think I was not truly square; I simply longed for a square parent, which is not so much square as childish.

I had my own collection of oddities to which Mama, kinder than I, gave no generalized downgrading name. I do not even know how to characterize a girl with such preferences and practices.

I could not bear to drink out of a glass or a cup or indeed any kind of container. The feel of the rim of a container in my mouth was as unpleasant as the feel of a bit in the mouth of an unbroken horse. I drank from the flow of a faucet indoors or out.

I would not carry a pocketbook or a purse. That, I thought, was the mark of a stodgy, careful, middle-aged housewife. I carried what money I had in my shoe, and anything else loose in my arms. This necessarily resulted in a good deal of loss.

I would not use a washcloth. Why drag a rag across your

face? Soap the hands, get both hands full of water, and splash and snort.

I chinned myself whenever I passed a projection that made this possible. This was possible in every doorway in our home-made house.

I wanted to eat beans at least once a day. I had read that Indians had more endurance than any other race as the result of their bean eating. I wanted to be able to endure.

I wanted all windows left uncurtained at night as a sign that we had nothing to hide.

I scorned all those who carried handkerchiefs, because I scorned runny noses. Men with bandannas were all right. Bandannas were for sweat, and sweat was admirable. Snot (a forbidden word) was not.

I wanted no ant, fly, spider, bee, flea, or mosquito killed. I wanted them shooed or herded to safer places. So long as an animal was quiet, it had nothing to fear from me. If it got noisy (blowfly, mosquito), I might kill it.

I wanted all sickness ignored. Go on as if it didn't exist. No handkerchiefs, no sanitary-belt harness (walk the right way, and it wouldn't be needed), no concern about whether the cat had eaten from a dish or the drumstick had fallen on the ground. Take a chance.

I wanted to stand and sing the verse of a hymn before every meal.

I wanted to read the last two-thirds of yesterday's book and the first third of tomorrow's book every night before I went to bed. That way, no matter what happened in life, there was always something to look forward to in fiction.

I wanted to copy into a notebook every verse, line, paragraph, that struck me as beautiful.

I wanted to live underground.

I wanted to be a lady pugilist and to fight, masked, against men. I wanted to win.

If given three wishes, I wanted (1) everyone to be a healthy

Christian; (2) all wars to cease (I wasn't quite sure that healthy Christians could bring this off without some magic); and (3) for me, after the other wishes had been granted, to be as wise as I was beautiful, and both beyond human recollection.

Who did this girl think she was? William S. Hart? The Girl of the Golden West? What was her sex? She obviously didn't know. She knew she wanted a square mother. It was lucky for her she didn't have one.

# XVIII

———◆◆———

Max, in a letter yesterday, said, "Perhaps we made a mistake in not going to Brownsville. Sandstorms on the Colorado and rainstorms in Napa. The pump house is afloat and the bridge underwater. You like wind better than rain, so you won't be sorry you're there instead of here. I should be finished with the Oakland job in two or three weeks and we can head toward Brownsville again. What do you think?"

I don't know what to think. Oh, to be in Brownsville now that April's here? I don't know one thing about Brownsville, except its location on the map and the newspaper accounts of its temperature: in the low 80s, right through the year. I see it on a blue gulf, with palm trees creaking in the off-sea breeze.

I'm not sure whether my desire to stay put is a hatred of travel or a case of always, or at least usually, falling in love with the spot I'm in. What can I find at the mouth of the Rio Grande that the banks of the Colorado do not offer? The wind of the last three days has blown itself out. The river was as blue this morning as if it had not absorbed those tons of sand. At noon the sky clouded over, and the river turned milky. Water does what the wind says; it looks the way the sun wants it to.

Last night for the first time in my life I saw Orion setting. It splashed down in the bend of the river. At home we have no horizon. We're on a knoll, surrounded by hills, with oaks and madroñas and black acacias for a rooftree! If I want to see what's happening on the horizon (and I often do), I have to get into a car or onto a horse and ride out to some cleared spot. I do this if I want to see the new moon. I am superstitious about this. I have come to feel myself a midwife to new moons. If I'm not where I can see that ghostly curved wisp in the western sky, I fear for the twenty-eight days ahead. I've not done my part in the month's send-off. So I see the new moon often. But Orion's setting is not at an hour when I want to ride out in search of a horizon. I felt like a shepherd last night, a Chaldean, someone tree-free.

Yesterday the beer-drinking Indians not only said, "Hello, Woolly," to Spry; they said, "Hello, Pima," to me. Is this respectful? I have already decided that I don't want "She was a pitiless woman" carved on my tombstone. Do I want "No one respected her" there? What is respect? How is it shown? How is it lost? Did I lose it by talking to the Indians? By marveling at Son's vocabulary instead of clapping my hands to my ears?

When I came home from town last night through folds of amethyst and coral and gold, I found Lily and Son up on the riverbank: Lily painting; Son on a stump, watching.

"Some fool will pay five hundred dollars for that," Son said, pointing to his mother's fire-opal canvas.

It was the moment of the glory's fading.

"Sing, Son," said Lily. "It will help me to catch it."

Son began to sing "Day Is Dying in the West." Son, no Caruso, or even a Johnny Cash, knows the words and the tune and has a strong voice. He went on to "Now the Day Is Over" and "There Is Sunshine in My Soul Today."

"Help him," said Lily. "You know the words."

I knew every other word, at least, and I love to sing. I need a strong voice like Son's, sure of every word and as convinced of their truth as if he'd written them himself, as cover for my breathless voice and uncertainty about tunes and words. I hoped no boaters would pass us on the river. They might con-

175

clude that what they heard was some impromptu revival meeting and put ashore to be saved. I doubted that Son was up to the job of saving anyone. I knew I wasn't. Lily probably could, but it would be a pity to interrupt her painting. We went from one song to another. Pretty soon, I thought, we'll be talking in tongues. Son, when he shifted from high to low in his vocabulary, was already very near the borderline of something far beyond the dictionaries.

We were singing "Throw Out the Life Line" when Lily put down her brush. Since we were merely background music, violins throbbing while the artist emoted, we stopped singing.

"Oh, don't stop," Lily pleaded. "Don't stop. You sound so sweet. Just like the old camp-meeting days in Iowa."

That's exactly what I feared: Son the traveling evangelist, and I the village choir member.

"I'm too out of wind to sing any more."

Lily doesn't want to make a nuisance of herself, and she'll keep Son from doing so if she can.

"Come, Son. I've got a pot roast in the Dutch oven, and Jessie, I'm sure, has work of her own to do."

"Pima" downtown and "Jessie" here. Lily is the only person in the world who calls me Jessie.

Jesse was Mama's father's name. Mama's mother insisted that I be called "Mary Jessie." Mama accepted the Mary, but fought against what she considered the dullness of Jessie, and finally compromised with the considerably fancied-up version of "Jessamyn." Jessamyn was her own concoction, and she made me promise never to let anyone call me Jessie. And until Lily, no one has. Lily hadn't asked when I first arrived, and I had expected to see her so little that *what* she called me hadn't seemed to matter.

The McCurdys went home, and I went back to the car to gather up my groceries and to rescue poor old Woolly, left alone in the car and forgotten during the hymn singing. That's the way it goes: "Praise God from whom all blessings flow," while the poor dog sweats it out alone in the airless car.

176

The clouds, which had turned the river milky at noon, piled up in back of the mountains while I was putting away the groceries. I went outside to have a look at what was going on. Rain was falling forty miles away on the peaks of the Panta-mints. I could see the elderberry-colored rain scarves curved inward by the wind off the sea. But what was most remarkable was the scent of the rain-soaked mountain flowers flowing down the slopes with the runoff from the storm above. Once before in Nevada, on the dry eastern side of the Sierras, I had experi-enced this same mysterious flow of piercing sweetness. It was then, as now, a flash flood of fragrance. I could account for it, but this didn't prevent me from marveling. I was engulfed by a sweetness whose source was invisible and miles distant.

I stayed outside until it was dark. I inhaled so much perfume I thought that I would surely exhale fragrance for a day or two.

It was time for lights when I went in, closing the door on the sweetness.

I feel most alone in an empty house. A house was made for people, and their absence makes the rooms more empty than any forest can ever be. Or even any desert. In a way you can never be alone outside. Outside is too populated. (Is the moon "outside"?) Inside, emptied of its inhabitants, is a shell whose original tenant has passed away. Completely. You are alone and an intruder in a house not your own, and this doubles the aloneness. Perhaps burglars are solitaries, and theft is only a sideline with them. The real high comes not from the money or the tape recorders, but from being alone where they ought not to be.

Here in the trailer I am the snail in its own snail shell. It shuts me in; it shuts others out. It is truly exclusive. The mud hens have long since rolled up the day sheen. Son and I hymned the sun to rest. I light the vigil lights, and the bliss that must never be sought and can never be depended upon fills the room. A silence louder than sound throbs in my ears. The flame's waver envelops both rooms in a watery come-and-go. My veins respond. We sit down, Woolly and Spry and Pima and Jessie and I, and watch. As we watch, colors grow brighter, forms more distinct. Meanwhile and contradictorily all blend, blur, and become one.

# *XIX*

———◆———

I was seventeen when I took my last camping trip with Papa and Mama. At the time, I didn't know that it would be the last.

*There is a line of Verlaine I shall not recall again,*
*There is a nearby street forbidden to my step,*
*There is a mirror that has seen me for the last time,*
*There is a door I have shut until the end of the world. . . .*

So writes Jorge Luis Borges in "Limits."

The door I shut until the end of the world on July 1, 1920, was the door of an auto loaded for one more camping trip with my family. I never opened that door again. And much as I wanted to be alone and not to travel, this was a camping trip I couldn't resist. We were heading back East. We were Indiana-bound. We were going back to see the Old Country: the land where it snowed, where the pawpaws and service-berries grew, where spring beauties and Johnny-jump-ups blossomed; where they said "redd up" for clean the house, and "clever" for hospitable, and "meechin" for humble; where men were called "pretty," and streams "branches" or "runs"; where dreaming was "mooning." Back there people "perished" to death, and you did a job "slap-dab," and the weather always "faired off" before morning. Oh, yes, back there they said some people were always thirsting for water from other folks' wells; and I was one of them. I was one of them. I thirsted for a drink of branch water or from that living spring behind Great-Grandpa's house, the spring that never went dry, the spring that had the sweetest, coldest water in all Jennings County. I would see the house where I was born; see the house where Papa and Mama courted; see where Grandma raised her guinea hens and Grandpa his oxheart cherries. This was the land I had imagined and dreamed about. This was the land Mama's words had created. And such lands, built of words, you build yourself into with your own heart and gristle. You calk up the chinks between words with parts of yourself as you never do the land you actually live on. The back forty of the ranch you live on has none of you in it (unless you're a farmer and have plowed and sweated there). God made that loam without any help from your imagination.

So I looked forward to this camping trip and the Indiana I had mooned about. I never saw it on that trip. Or I saw only those parts of it vivid enough or sharp enough to break through a mooning even stronger, a mooning over love; for I was engaged and in love. Indiana, through Mama's decade of talk, was a territory already half-known to me. Love was territory incognito. No one, except the romantic novelists I had read—Elinor Glynn and Zane Grey and poetesses like Sara and Edna—had said a word to me about love, and their words were misleading. Ernest Thompson Seton, in *The Life of a Grizzly*, had actually been more to the point, but I hadn't the sense when I read it to realize this.

We crossed the Colorado south of where I now live. I didn't give it a glance. The Petrified Forest had rainbow-colored hunks of ex-trees, heavy as lead and free for the taking. I couldn't be bothered to touch them, motivated not by ecology but by love centered elsewhere. The high desert country of juniper and piñon was all cloudland to me. At Wagon Mound a flash flood roared by, with a miner's shack riding its crest. It could've been the Ark for all I cared. Even the banks of the Wabash, long-imagined, were nothing when we reached them compared with the remembered pressure of Max's two arms.

Our first date had been half-blind. He had seen me, but I hadn't seen him. We went to a football game. In the back seat of the car coming home he gave me a tremendous hug, just as the car went over a jarring bump.

"I saw that coming," he said. I had never imagined such a combination of appropriate action and quick-witted justification.

Max, like me, had helped save the world for democracy. He had worked as a combination ranch hand and cowboy on a ranch in Inyo County. This was before Los Angeles had stolen (the Inyo County word) Inyo County's water. He was back there again for the summer that I was seventeen, his heart lost, as it still is, on cattle. Since I wouldn't be seeing him anyway, Indiana seemed as good a substitute as any if I had to play second fiddle to cows.

We certainly had the car to make the trip in. Papa had two cars that summer. He had traded one-half the oil rights on a second ranch he then owned in Yorba Linda to a Kansan for $5,000 and a Franklin auto. The Kansan never got any oil, but then, Papa didn't get a very good Franklin, either.

The second car, acquired I know not how, perhaps bought new, was a beauty, destined to convince relatives in Indiana that local boy had made good, and farmers en route that people in California had really struck it rich. It was a Paige, "The Most Beautiful Car in America," its makers advertised; and I really think it may have been.

I remember for beauty only two cars besides the Paige. Both, as it happens, were yellow: they were my grandfather's Hupmobile and my own first car, a yellow Dodge convertible, with red-leather upholstery. The first time I made a tour of the town, top down, a man from a rocker on his front porch yelled, "You're going to have to charge more than five dollars now!" I drove home very slowly, wondering if a yellow convertible *was* too gaudy a turnout for a middle-aged Quaker writer.

The Paige was apple-green, with a deeper green-leather upholstery. It had something I have seen on no other car and don't know very well how to describe. Sedans were still in the future, but this was a kind of semisedan. In front there were glass wind wings to deflect the wind from those in the front seat. Between the front seat and the back was a plate of glass, and to this there was also attached wind wings. Behind this bulwark of glass, we sat on our seats of green leather, cozy and stared at. It was, Myron tells me, an "assembled car using a Gold Seal Continental Motor." What this means I don't know. I do remember that the wheels with which the Paige came equipped had wire spokes. They looked very racy to me. Racy they may have been; practical they were not. The wire spokes were constantly breaking. So Papa, before we left on our journey, had them replaced by wheels with wooden spokes.

The car was a big one, but how it expanded to carry the cargo it had to hold is still a mystery. I know where the bedding went: the seats were taken out, and we rode on the bedding, pillows and all. Where did the beds themselves go? There were three of those metal contraptions, each of which folded into three sections and were cranked taut at bedtime. Where were they placed? On the seats under the bedding?

The cooking equipment was carried in what was called the grub box. This was attached to the running board of one side of the car. In this was stored dishes, pans, cooking supplies, a grate for cooking, a two-burner Coleman stove, and a collapsible oven. Someplace there was a dishpan, because I took baths in it. There were suitcases full of clothes, for Mama had no idea of returning to the land of her birth unfashionably attired, with a bunch of ragamuffins at her Cuban heels. I had a hat that needed a covered wagon for transportation. How and where all this was carried, I don't know.

The cooked food with which we started was enough to daunt a less calm man than Papa. I can understand almost everything (that I can remember) about my youth except my passion for cooking. Boiling, parboiling, soaking overnight, shredding, mincing, blanching, steaming! These may be suitable occupations for the aged, whose other appetites have faded and whose muscular tone inclines them to work that can be carried on while sitting on a stool. But what was a nice girl like myself doing cracking walnuts and pitting cherries? If I had a seventeen-year-old who wanted to mount a stool and whip eggs until they peaked, I'd take her to an analyst. There are better things to do at seventeen. There are better things to do at any time of life, as a matter of fact.

Why is it that we consider it sane for a young female to make a Lady Baltimore cake? To make scrapple? This requires first boiling pork neck bones, next making a corn-meal mush with the neck-bone broth, and stirring into this mush the pork flesh, which has been shredded, and such salt, pepper, and sage as taste demands; then finally, after allowing an overnight hardening of this conglomerate, slicing it and frying the slices in hot oil. I thought this sane when young, before it had come to me that I was mortal and my days were numbered. When this *did* come to me, rather late in life, I ruled out scrapple.

A young woman can spend her time this way and be applauded. If one of my brothers had set about making his own razors or boiling up soft soap in the back yard for his lathering or burying potatoes and turnips in the ground to preserve them through the winter, he would have been thought mad. A young woman doing something comparable on a stove is thought sweet.

I outgrew my cooking madness late. I remember this period of my life with the same wonder I would experience should I read that for several years Norman Mailer wanted to be a certified public accountant. My conclusion is that there was, unduly prolonged in me, a period analogous with that which makes little boys want for a few years to play at being cowboys or cavemen. This imitation primitivism, however, is not encouraged among them as is cooking among girls.

Unaccountable as it now seems, when I was seventeen I

wanted to cook; and a camping trip was the perfect excuse for a culinary orgy. We never ate at restaurants when traveling, never bought sandwiches, hamburgers, soft drinks, slurpees. In the first place they were expensive; in the second, with cooks like Mama, Papa, and myself along, why buy food less good than we could produce?

Before we left home, Mama and I cooked the food we wouldn't have time or equipment for on the road. Mama did bake peach cobblers in the collapsible Coleman oven when we went through peach country; Dutch apple pies when the crop was apples; but there wasn't time or equipment for producing jelly rolls, marble cupcakes, rocks, travelers' pies, rice puddings, and tamale pies.

When I think of the time and care it takes to make a jelly roll, and of how little you've got when you've made it—nothing any better, actually, than a slice of good buttered bread with jelly on it—I wonder that a girl who would spend hours mixing, baking, and rolling this thing could grow into normal womanhood. Perhaps she didn't. I wonder who invented the jelly roll? Some male who hated women? Who laughed up his sleeve when the damned cake broke in half in mid-roll and the unhappy housewife had to cut it in squares, then cover the squares with boiled custard and pretend that cottage pudding was what she had had in mind all along?

The problem of storage en route for this precooked food was not of long duration. We were all hearty eaters. It disappeared soon. When it was gone, we drove across the land buying whatever was ripe and for sale. It had to be for sale. No foraging, not even for a worm-eaten windfall. We lived high on the hog crossing America: eating roasting ears, green beans, succotash, fresh strawberries, blackcap raspberries, pies dripping with pink juice of pieplant (now called rhubarb), catfish, baked carp, fried chicken, and cottontails. The meals figured out at twenty-five cents a head a day. One-fifty a day for food for a family of six. When traveling, we didn't stop for lunch. At noon we ate crackers and cheese or bologna and bread handed over the glass divider by Mama in careful proportions to prevent fighting among the diners in the back seat. Carmen always saved hers until the rest of us had gobbled ours. This was maddening, but not, we had to admit, unfair.

The big meal took place at night when travel for the day was over. Before it was dark, we stopped in some quiet spot off the road: schoolyard or churchyard or graveyard. Or riverbank. Or woods-lot clearing. Or abandoned barn. We had no tents. While the men cranked up the beds and made them, Mama and I cooked. We ate on tombstones or stumps or the steps of schoolhouses. Or on a rock down by the edge of a stream whose tune we learned but whose name we never knew.

The Paige's exhaust pipe contributed its share to what there was as yet no name for: pollution; but we crossed America without littering. We were not affluent. We had nothing to throw away. Our plates were pie tins, and no one wanted to part with his. The only tin cans we carried were those containing Carnation milk, Van Camp's beans, Libby's salmon, and Hills Brothers coffee. Papa dug holes for these. Toilet paper was still a Sears Roebuck catalogue, and we were as careful as cats in leaving no trace. There may have been a few cinders, some coffee grounds not yet blown away when we left camp, to tell where a family had spent the night. We followed the old Santa Fe Trail. We did not even leave bones, as many of the first travelers on that route had done, to show the way we had come.

After supper the children—and I, too, if the dishes had been washed—played duck-on-rock or hide-and-go-seek or follow-the-leader; or simply wandered up to the top of a rise to see the sun setting, someplace out west, nearer home; or perhaps to get a glimpse of a coyote starting out on his evening hunt for his supper; or to imagine that a shadow was a mountain lion, considering *us* as a possible meal.

After supper I took a bath. This was the part of the day

when being in love made me disregard the rest of the family. Being in love prevented me from truly seeing anything or participating in anything. This was no one's loss but my own. The abstraction of my being in love was, for the others, a means of keeping me quiet, unargumentative, and biddable. Until it came to the after-dinner bath in the dishpan, my family had never had a better traveling companion than I was, when in love.

After having experienced "being in love" a few score times, one would think it would be a state easy to describe. It isn't. If one could describe it and analyze it, one wouldn't, I suppose, experience it so often. It would then be like a virus cold. One could recognize the symptoms, load up on vitamin C or Contac, and avoid the disease; or, if not avoid, at least recognize it as a disease.

I don't know that "being in love" has anything to do with love, though there may be cases—happy ones, I should think—where the two coincide: loving and being in love.

I first fell violently in love at the age of nine. The boy was five years older than I, and the president of the Christian Endeavor. He went on to become a Quaker minister. I had a tendency to fall in love with scamps or saints, Joaquin Muriettas or Junipero Serras. I, who am temperate myself, was drawn to those who practice excesses. I still admire those who say (like Mama), "How can I tell what is enough until I know what is too much?" Amos was pious. He was good, clean, soft-spoken. When Harold, the boy who later taught Rusty dirty words, gave one of my long braids a scalp-jarring jerk, Amos gave Harold a good talking-to. He said, "Do unto others as you would be done by," and Harold said, "If I ever have long braids, I hope somebody jerks them."

The year before he came to Yorba Linda, Amos had almost died of typhoid fever. I would look at him sitting with the eighth-graders—a real Galahad, with his pink cheeks and honey-colored hair—and think how death had almost claimed him. Then I would put my arms on my desk and my head in my arms and sob, sob because I had not been there to nurse him. This daydream of nursing him to health was typical of my daydreams of being in love: intricate, detailed, involving me in all kinds of effort and sacrifice and insight, and not at all erotic. My nursing would finally bring back the glow of health to Amos's dwindling cheeks, and hair to his balding head (hair that he had lost when his fever went to 106.5 degrees). Then Amos, fever abated, hair regrowing, would take my hand in his own poor, wasted hand and say, like Lincoln of his mother, "Dear girl, I owe it all to you." I wanted no other reward.

One of the great differences (falling in love aside) between young people and older ones is that the young do their thinking —if it can be called that—in scenes of action, while older people think in words. It is the difference between being in a movie in which you play a leading part and writing a book in which you may also play a part. It is the difference between talking and acting. Older people do not truly day "dream." A dream is not talk, not soliloquy, not dialogue. It is action. With age the time comes when situations are thought about, not participated in. This makes the mind a linguistic millrace. It leads to insomnia. I have, in an effort to sleep, often forbidden my mind to use a single word. I have determinedly, calling nothing by name, walked through a house known and lived in long ago. I see cupboards, rocking chairs, windows, the flicker-shadow of a pepper tree's moving, minnow-shaped leaves, the fading light, the velvety mold on a jar of marmalade, never letting my mind name one of these things. I see, smell, touch. I glide through the room speechless as a snake; when words are lost I find sleep.

Amos's father was a carpenter. One day, walking into town from the ranch in an outfit that I thought was not worthy of the love I felt for Amos, I saw him on a rooftop with his father, helping with the shingling. In this still, treeless land every moving object, unless it kept to the canyons and arroyos, could be seen for miles around. I kept to the canyons and arroyos. I crept into town by a six-mile, cactus-strewn detour so that Amos would not see me at less than my best. My feet bled for Amos. He had, I was thankful, climbed down from the roof and gone home by the time I reached town.

I was constantly in love. To a psychologist the clue to my state might have been apparent. It was never noted by parents, teachers, or school friends. The clue was that I never looked at, spoke to, or touched the one I was in love with. I got near him. I wanted to be in his orbit. I suffered when near him. My heart pounded, my lips trembled, my eyelids fluttered. Since I truly suffered, why did I seek suffering? I do not know. There would be no recompense for the suffering: no talk, no touch, no companionship. Male and female, created He them, and I seemed to have been put on earth to suffer the consequences.

By a process unclear to me then and now, I would gradually fall out of love with one boy and into love with another. Suddenly, characteristics in someone thereto unnoticed would strike me with overpowering charm. Amos would wane and Wendell wax.

The most painful of all of my fallings in love were with teachers. This began after I had graduated, at the age of twelve, from the eighth grade. Up to that time, the only man teacher I had ever known was the grammar-school principal. He had a mobile upper plate. Because of this, I regarded him rather as a mechanical wonder than as a human being. I had been in love with half a dozen boys besides Amos, none of whom had ever known of my feeling. I was in love for a time with a young man in his twenties who was preparing to be a Quaker minister. At this time a splinter group called Pentecostal had control of the Quaker Bible College at Huntington Park. This college was located in a small town in the dairy country east of Los Angeles. These people at Huntington Park (and elsewhere in Southern California) believed in what was called the second birth. I was never, and am not now, very clear about this. One could be saved; this I had myself experienced. If saved more than once, one experienced a second birth. This was a religious experience that made it impossible for the twice-saved ever again to sin. The Quakers in charge of the Huntington Park Training School believed that a man proposing to be a Quaker minister should have experienced the second birth and have passed beyond the possibility of sin. Lee Vernon, the young man I revered, never believed himself incapable of sin. For this reason he did not receive the approval of those in charge of the selection of Quaker ministers. He became, instead, a Presbyterian minister, a body that has never lost its belief in the possibility of sin for clergy and laity alike.

The teachers I fell in love with were always English teachers. Surely there must have been a comely geometry teacher, a swashbuckling teacher of civics? Were all the teachers of Latin and chemistry and world history crumby, shaggy, dusty little men? And were all the English teachers great, yellow-haired Vikings? Or splendid Heathcliffs with black curls and smoky eyes? Were all the English teachers men who had personally known Charles Nordhoff and James N. Hall, the co-authors of *Mutiny on the Bounty,* or who had portrayed Hamlet for three seasons with the Ben Greet players? Why were *they* the ones who repeated with throbbing voices, "I must down to the seas again, to the lonely sea and the sky"? Why were they the ones who read to us from the sonnet series written in celebration of their own honeymoon trip in a buckboard through Yosemite Valley? Did chemistry teachers never have honeymoons? Or the librarian? If so, they kept quiet about it in class.
My eyes suffered most in my years of undeclared passion for my English teachers. It was difficult for me to take my eyes off a male English teacher once I entered his class. It was a tropism. My eyes followed him as Blake's sunflower followed the sun. In order to prevent this, which embarrassed me and no

doubt made the teacher uncomfortable, too, I chose, the minute I entered class, some object to look at: a doorknob; the map rack, which hung on the wall; a tree outside an opened window. And I *looked* at it—while I recited, while others recited, while teacher lectured. Doorknobs and map racks were easier on the eyes than Vikings and Heathcliffs. One's glance bounced off instead of sinking in. Nevertheless, at the end of fifty-five minutes of staring, my neck would be stiff and my eyes glazed. I was eager for the release of hygiene or algebra class, where the teacher could be looked at and my eyes take a rest from glory, passion, and doorknobs.

Emotionally things were calmer at Whittier College, as they should have been at a school founded by Quakers and named for their bachelor bard. I went there for all the wrong reasons. I wanted a doctorate in English. Whittier didn't give one, and even its A.B. was not then recognized by the Association of American Universities.

Each year Whittier College celebrated May Day with the election of a May Queen and the winding of a Maypole. One of my reasons for going to Whittier was to be its May Queen. The sister of the Quaker who turned Presbyterian because he felt he could still sin had been May Queen. I thought he might take some notice of the girl who had followed in his sister's footsteps. I would never have been elected May Queen at Whittier College (but at sixteen we are all Mittys, and nothing is impossible). So it was just as well that the year before I enrolled at Whittier someone took a long look at these Quaker maidens bounding around a garlanded Maypole and said (I suppose), "This may be friendly, but is it Quakerly?" In any case, May Queens and Maypoles had been done away with by the time I reached Whittier, and I was spared the disappointment of non-election.

Though there was no doctorate in English at Whittier, there were some English classes and one male English teacher. I naturally fell in love with him. Herbert Harris was as lovable as any of the other English teachers with whom I had been infatuated, but since he was the only teacher and choice was thus limited, the emotion I felt for him had some of the calmness and even monotony of marriage. I could bear to look at him.

Except for English teachers, I found teachers as a whole resistible. I don't understand students today who complain simultaneously of the stupidity of their elders and of the lack of opportunity afforded them by the multiuniversity to get to know their professors better. As an undergraduate, I agreed with today's young: the middle-aged have lost something. But unlike them, I had no desire to probe this loss further by getting to know my professors outside class. I saw enough of them in class.

When I went to Berkeley as a graduate student in English, I left behind me the gentle monogamy of Whittier's one-man English department. At Berkeley there were more teachers in the English department than there were on Whittier's entire faculty. There were great men at Berkeley—scholars, writers, lecturers; men who wore the scarlet robes of the ancient English universities; men who had taught men of renown. J. S. P. Tatlock (called Jesus St. Paul by his students), the great Chaucer scholar, was there, still carrying his books in his green baize Harvard bag. Benjamin Lehman, who was married to Judith Anderson, the famous actress. Kurtz, of Gayley and Kurtz, who together had published more textbooks than any one of us had read. Bertrand Bronson, who played a lute and sang madrigals. Arthur Brodeur, another Chaucerian; if he had been the Round Table's Arthur, Guinevere would never have fallen. Tall, lanky T. K. Whipple, the youngest full professor in the university.

These men knew and were excited by the writers who were just making names for themselves in the twenties, writers of whom I had never heard at Whittier: Joyce, Eliot, Lawrence, Mansfield, Woolf, Hemingway, I. A. Richards. There is some special magic for the young in being able to watch and celebrate the emergence of new writers, to recognize new ideas and new ways of expressing them. It is a pity to have been young and book-loving and to have missed this.

The study of English literature began at Whittier with Shakespeare and ended with Browning and Tennyson. There were no classes in American literature. Harris admired the stories of O. Henry and read them aloud to us. The tenacity of my obsession for English teachers can be judged by the fact that my love for Harris survived this severe test.

Perhaps it was my conviction that in our 200 years of writing, America must have produced something better than O. Henry that caused me to elect to work in the American Studies division of the department of English at Berkeley. I did so without knowing that T. K. Whipple headed this division. I immediately fell in love with him, and might have done so even if he hadn't been an English professor.

Edmund Wilson, who was a freshman at Princeton when T. K. Whipple was a senior there, writes of him in a preface to Whipple's *Study Out the Land:* "He was a long-legged loose-jointed fellow with pale blond hair and a Missouri drawl, whose expression, with its wide grin, was at once sad and droll . . . his devotion to literature was never dilettante-ish, as it is likely to be with undergraduates, nor did it ever become a matter of routine as it is likely to do with professors: it was something fundamental to his life. He presented an unusual combination of Princetonian and Middle Western—of pleasantry, casualness and elegance with homeliness, simplicity and directness . . . he had something that is very rare and a little hard to define. He diffused a quiet kind of light that accompanied him like a nimbus."

When I was his student, the pale, blond hair had darkened to pewter, but otherwise Wilson's description holds. I saw the Princetonian elegance rather than the Middle Western homeliness and simplicity. (We are quicker to recognize what we do not possess rather than what we possess.) But his expression—

"sad and droll"—and his nimbus of light I saw and responded to, though I could not have described them as accurately as Wilson.

When I entered T. K. Whipple's graduate seminar in American literature, I did not know that he had already published *Spokesmen,* which Wilson calls the first criticism to "study the new novelists and dramatists and poets at the same time appreciatively and calmly." I did not know that he had been a Marine during the First World War, or that he had at that time had his first bout with the cancer that was to cause his death twenty years later. I did not know that he had declared himself a socialist.

I thought of myself as a socialist then, too. I had been converted at the age of fifteen, sitting on the sands of Newport Beach, reading John Spargo's *History of Socialism* and a life of the Belgian socialist Jean Jaurès. I still have the notebooks that I filled that summer with what seemed to me the self-evident truths of socialism. Mama, who knew without being told that I was not, as was the rest of the family, a true-blue Republican, asked me, when Al Smith was running for President, if it would not be possible to keep the fact that I would vote for him from my grandfather. Al Smith bore for Republican Quakers a double stigma: he was not only a Democrat, but a Democrat who was for liquor. This was too much. I told Mama that she could tell Grandpa that I would not vote for Al Smith. I did not tell her that I intended to vote for Norman Thomas.

So I entered Whipple's class without knowing anything about him, except that he was the man who was head of the American Studies department and hence the man under whom I should study. I did recognize in Whipple the quality that Wilson calls "a stoicism, a kind of resignation." I then considered myself a stoic as well as a socialist. Now that I know more about both, I admire myself as young socialist more than I do as young stoic. The young stoic is often a cop-out. His "I can endure anything" is often only another way of saying, "I will risk nothing."

Wilson remembers Whipple as a young man quoting from *Rasselas* "seriously and not merely for the phrase *the characterization of human life as a state* [I may not have it quite right], where much is to be suffered and little known."

In his essay "Aucassin in the Sierras," which is in the book *Study Out the Land*, Whipple quotes from *Rasselas* again and does so presumably correctly: "Human life is everywhere a condition in which there is much to be endured and little to be enjoyed."

In the same essay Whipple says, "I have never been able to share the common antipathy to hermits." I didn't know that there was such an antipathy; but if there is one, I am glad Whipple didn't share it and would not condemn me, hermit-like, alone in my cabin on the bank of a deep, slow-moving river. On the subject of hermits he goes on to say that he is not talking of misanthropes or "nature lovers like Thoreau, who spend more time listening to bullfrogs and woodpeckers than listening to the still small voice . . . I believe that a sprinkling of hermits might be highly beneficial to the United States. Out of our few hundred million we could afford to spare a few hundreds who would make us ask ourselves questions and say to us: the things you care for are valueless; your world is not only contemptible, but a positive nuisance; you know nothing of real happiness, and you are not on the way to learning anything about it."

This is downright astonishing in Whipple. He was the man who introduced me to Thoreau (you don't count "The Battle of the Ants" in a high-school textbook a real introduction). I cannot believe my eyes, reading his characterization of Thoreau as a bullfrog and woodpecker listener rather than as one who preached, "The things you care for are valueless . . . you know nothing of real happiness." There are some bullfrogs and woodpeckers in Thoreau, to be sure. But you can scarcely hear them for the thunder of his denunciation of a money-changers' world, which is "not only contemptible, but a positive nuisance." This is one of Whipple's earliest essays. I can believe only that as he read and taught Thoreau, he got to know him better.

Academically, I had no business in Whipple's seminar. My training in Whittier's limited English department was superficial. I had never had access to a good library. I entered my first library at the age of twelve, and it consisted of a collection of donated books on the shelves of a reconditioned janitor's closet in the Yorba Linda grammar school.

As it was, I got into the class by the skin of my teeth. If you were not a graduate of the University of California, it was necessary, before you could become an official candidate for an advanced degree in English, to pass an examination called the comprehensive. This consisted of three hours given to answering questions on the history of English literature, with an additional three hours of writing an essay on an assigned subject. The comprehensive had to be passed with a grade of $B$. I don't remember which part of the comprehensive came first; whichever it was, I received a $B$, which was automatically lowered to a $C$ because of poor spelling. This meant that on the second part of the examination I *had* to make an $A$, and make it using words I could spell. This severely limited my vocabulary; but by using "jump, Jane, jump" words, I got my $A$, became a Ph.D. candidate, and had my application to Whipple's class accepted.

In 1942, thirty years after he had first known Whipple at Princeton, Wilson still remembered that young man of 1912 vividly: bearing elegant, expression sad and droll, a socialist, a stoic, literature fundamental to his life.

In 1929 I found myself sitting across a seminar table from this man. I immediately fell in love with him, and as a result, I never really knew him. The romantic greensickness of being in love blinds, tongue-ties, prevents any kind of human communication except touch—which was not only out of the question, but would have been a very partial way of communicating with a man like Whipple.

The combination of the subject Whipple taught and his regard for it, added to the man he was, encapsulated me as firmly as a child in a womb. I was alive, my heart was throbbing, but I could not kick out of the tough, restricting entanglement of lovesickness, though Whipple gave me the opportunity to do so.

I had not been in his seminar for many weeks when Whipple asked me if I would like to be a reader for his undergraduate class in American literature, a mob 500 or 600 strong. I was too ignorant to understand the functions of a reader. Professors at Whittier did their own reading. Whipple explained to me that a reader attends the professor's course, takes charge of the class at examination time, reads, corrects, and grades the examination bluebooks, stays after class, becomes in fact that person to whom modern students so greatly object: the buffer who separates them from the professor they feel they have a right to know.

Whipple's invitation made me feel a little like Cinderella being asked by Prince Charming if she would mind trying on the glass slipper for size. Not only did this job offer me a chance to see T. K. Whipple more often, but it also released me from a job for which I was not suited. Max and I were both at that time playground directors. I could play games. My idea of teaching children was to go out and play the game harder and faster than they could. This kept me lame and them uninstructed. To top it all, I could earn more money being Whipple's reader than I could being a playground director—and earning money was the point of our playground directing.

I said yes immediately.

I was immediately in trouble. Whipple wasn't teaching O. Henry. Or even Bret Harte. He was teaching Nathaniel Hawthorne and Herman Melville and Mark Twain and the James brothers. I had never read a word of Melville, so I had at once to plunge into the depths of *Moby-Dick,* attend the undergraduate classes, and, as a result of the night before's feverish reading, be able to shed a little light for a student on the process of blubber processing aboard a whaler.

The seminar was something else entirely: twelve of us around a table, all writing papers on Early American writers: Emerson, Hawthorne, Thoreau, Whitman. I wrote for reasons forgotten on Hawthorne. Whipple read my paper, the result of a semester's work, aloud to the class. When he finished, he said in his deep-chested, resonant voice, "I don't know whether you realize how wonderful this is or not."

My paralysis in Whipple's presence was now complete. I was afraid that he would be filled with embarrassment because of his outburst about my paper. He wasn't. It was evidently not an outburst but his measured judgment. Later he said to me, the first and only person ever to do so, "You ought to write, you know."

It was in Whipple's class that I first really read Thoreau. At that time, Whipple did not emphasize the Thoreau who listened to bullfrogs and woodpeckers. I learned of the Thoreau who was, above and beyond everything else, a writer. His greatest passion was for words. Thoreau wanted to spend at least four hours a day out of doors. That left him twelve hours for the pen. What his consciousness recorded in Concord weighed heavy as an overdue child on Henry Thoreau until he shaped it forth in words. Henry could have survived without the woods and the woodpeckers, but without his pen he would have been a man mortally maimed. Housebound during the days of his last illness, he wrote about the house tabby and her kittens. He was born with the necessity of saying to others how it had been with him. His world was not Proust's, but like Proust, he gave us his remembrance of things past.

I have always wished that the paper I wrote for T. K. Whipple had been on Thoreau, not on Hawthorne. A paper on

Hawthorne was a literary exercise for me. A paper on Thoreau would have been heart's blood, which was what I wanted to give Whipple.

Whipple died young, as dying goes these days, in 1939. His wife, when I was his student in 1929, was ill with tuberculosis. Two years later, when the date was set for my doctor's orals, I had a lung hemorrhage. The doctors told me I had far-advanced tuberculosis. Three days later I was in a sanatorium.

Thoreau, when his brother died of lockjaw, developed all the symptoms of lockjaw and lay for days duplicating the agony of his brother's dying without himself ever having lockjaw. In my first days in the sanatorium I sometimes thought that, separated from the university and my degree, I was still trying to stay near Whipple by developing his wife's disease. I know now that one woman with tuberculosis is more tuberculosis than any man would choose to have in his life. Nevertheless it was a link, though tenuous (and becoming more so as I became more ill), with the past.

I never saw Whipple again. I bought in a secondhand book store in Berkeley a few years ago a New Testament, inscribed, in the hand I had often seen on bluebooks—a hand as tall, elegant, and upright as its owner—with the name "T. K. Whipple."

So, a New Testament, a love of Thoreau, the disease of a wife, the injunction "Write": a pitiful inheritance when, if something in my nature or nurture had been different, I might have known this man who could have spoken to me on many subjects of which I was ignorant. Being in love prevented that. Being in love was a constant, radiant euphoria. It was as much an enchantment as that I experienced alone in a room with twilight and firelight mingling. It had nothing to do with love, and it prevented loving, lovingness, even loving kindness. Even kindness. Kindness would have made it possible for me to talk to this man.

Whipple gave me every chance to know him. He gave me *A*s, made me his reader, trudged up the steps to Max's and my

198

studio apartment on La Vareda to bring me bluebooks about which there were any questions, told me to write. But when the shoptalk was over, I was speechless. Whipple the real man, the man who had come from Kansas City to Princeton, who had been a Marine, who had cancer, whose wife was ill with tuberculosis, for whom literature was life—this man was a stranger to me. In the end Whipple must have thought me dotty, a competent student, but not a fully developed human being, which was the truth.

There is one other aspect of my two-year fantasy that interests me now. Hidden knowledge is power. The murderer's "high," which Capote talks about in *Cold Blood,* lasts only so long as the murderer knows something no one else knows: "Back there in that house lie bodies dead and bleeding." The crushes, the "beings in love," that girls chatter about are superficial. They are leakages. The organs most involved are irritated speech centers. These do not generate power. The high comes from the hidden. So I, looking at Whipple (I had at least, since my high-school days, learned to use my eyes without pain), felt power. I knew something he didn't know, that no one knew, could guess, or would ever know.

The power generated by secret knowledge need not be a knowledge of love unrevealed; it can be a knowledge of hate, of scorn, of disgust. Hitler, before his final solution was revealed, no doubt felt it for Jews with whom he talked. "If only you knew what I have in store for you," he said with his eyes, while the high of hidden knowledge mounting from his chest to his throat almost choked him.

Only one person has ever spoken to me about being in love. She is one of the persons I meet here—usually at the mailbox. Here, where I am not known, where I am a transient, a riverside squatter, people speak to me more openly than they do at home. I don't know their names; they don't know mine. We are as anonymous and free as the wild burros.

The mailbox is on the main highway, a quarter of a mile

from the trailer. Usually I walk there to pick up the mail or post my letters. When I drive into town for supplies, I stop there on the way home. While going into town last week, I passed two young men—bearded, long-haired, wearing sandals and tunics. One was pulling by means of a rope harness an eight- or ten-foot wooden cross, which was mounted on a wheel. The second young man, with what appeared to be a leather-thonged whip, occasionally lashed the man who pulled the cross across the shoulders and back.

When I reached the mailbox last week, they were not far from me. I waited until they arrived. I stood outside the car with my mail in my hand, uncertain as to whether I should speak to them, and uncertain as to what I would say if I did. "Hot day, isn't it?" seemed, under the circumstances, inadequate. If they didn't pause, perhaps I would say nothing.

When they were even with me, they stopped, and the young man in the harness took it off his shoulders. There were a few rusty stains on his tunic. That whipping wasn't play-acting. I don't care for beards because they hide so much of the face. Between hair and beards two eyes and a nose was all I could see of the actors in this roadside Passion play. Both young men were blue-eyed, with dusty brown hair.

They said, "It's a hot day, isn't it?"

I said, "You hurt my conscience. I feel that I should help pull for a while."

"Good," said the burly one who had been doing the pulling. "That's what we want you to feel."

"Feel but not help?"

"No. You can't pull. That's our job. You can walk along and use the whip for a while if you want to. That's what most people are doing today!"

"I don't think I could do that."

"Why not? It's what you do every day, isn't it?"

I knew what he meant, but I waited for him to say it.

"What are you doing about the war?"

"Voting for the right people. I hope."

"That's all?"

"Money for those who oppose it."

"Money." There was so much saliva in the word the young man spoke that it didn't completely clear his beard.

"How would my whipping help?"

"Show people that somebody besides us knows right from wrong."

"Come on," said the young man with the whip, handing it toward me. "I'm next. Lay it on."

"I couldn't do that."

"Afraid to make a show of yourself?"

"I expect so. Partly, anyway. But I'd rather be whipped than whip, I think."

"That wouldn't make sense to anybody."

They were from Los Angeles and were planning to walk up through Las Vegas and the Owens Valley and Reno, then cross over one of the passes into California and head home down the Sacramento Valley.

I didn't want any more saliva directed more or less in my direction, but I asked the question anyway. "How are you fixed for funds?"

"Not too good," the burly one said.

I gave them ten dollars. Not enough, but it would buy them a meal or two.

"You really think you'd rather be whipped?"

"I think so."

"Turn around."

I did so. I had expected a light slash, the kind of symbolic blow a man receives when he is knighted. The blow was not symbolic—a stinging clout that made me hold onto the car. When I turned around, there was no apology in their eyes. The burly one, now using the whip, gave the new cross bearer a slash that brought an immediate stain through his shirt.

"You're one of us now," said the man with the whip.

I wasn't sure with whom I was one. Madmen, charlatans, saints. There wasn't any blood on my blouse, but the welts were finger-thick.

One day I picked up a young couple thumbing a ride just outside town. They were both University of California graduate students taking a year off to "experience freedom." Progress by ride thumbing isn't my idea of freedom. Your freedom is subject to anybody's whim. The girl left her shoes in the car, and I lost some of my freedom following the couple, after I got home, to return the shoes. They were sitting by the roadside, "thinking what to do."

I picked up a Mexican boy heading for Nogales and home. He couldn't speak a word of English, nor I more than a word or two of Spanish, but we were able to understand each other pretty well. He was nineteen, a big fellow, with a broad face and an agreeable smile.

A Mexican shop owner and I had talked of the difference between Spaniards and Mexicans. His father, who had been born in Andorra, had come to Mexico and married a Mexican. "It's our Indian blood," he said, "that makes us Mexicans sweeter than the Spanish." Since I have Indian blood, too, I was glad to believe this. The Indian blood of the boy I picked up was plain to be seen, both in the width of his face and in his courtesy.

He looked at my bag of groceries. *"Pan?"* he asked.

*Pan* is bread. I picked the loaf out of the bag and handed it to him. By rubbing his hand on his stomach and holding up three fingers he told me that he had had nothing to eat for three days. He drank that loaf of bread. It went down like water. He did not seem to chew it. The loaf was half gone before I could get the carton of milk out of the grocery bag. He seemed undecided as to whether he should slow down the eating with drinking.

I asked him if he would take a bus to Nogales. "Bus" he understood, as I understood *pan*. "No, no. Mucho leggo," he said. "Mucho leggo" is good Esperanto anywhere. I bought him another loaf of bread, a pound of bologna, and a half-dozen candy bars before I let him out. I gave him a dollar bill. He shook my hand. Mexicans are great handshakers. He said that he had no mama and no papa, but that I had been mama and papa to him. I told him that he was a *bueno muchacho* and bade him go with God. He was an admirable offspring. We waved each other out of sight.

The lady, the only person who has ever talked to me of multiple fallings in love, was a roadside mailbox encounter. The mailbox is placed in a little swag in the road so that the mail carrier will not be endangered by passing cars. In this little lay-by a car was parked when I went for the mail one late afternoon. She was out of the car, watching three children playing on the bank, which sheered off abruptly from the road toward the river. They were under ten years of age, and that romping around above forty feet of water kept my heart in my mouth.

"Don't worry," the young woman said. "Swimming is my life."

This meant something more than "I can swim well" or "I am the US backstroke champion." But what, I didn't know.

I wanted to ask, "How do you mean, your life?" but didn't. Instead I said, "Are you having car trouble?" This wasn't an orthodox place to stop, or to let children play.

"There's nothing wrong with the car. We ran out of gas. My husband has gone for some."

"I have a car nearby. Should I go pick him up?"

"The service station will bring him back."

At first glance I had thought the young woman plain. She was taffy-colored, skin and hair. Her face was angular, her bosom not noticeable, her mouth thin-lipped. At second glance

I still thought her plain, but with eyes as remarkable as hers, plainness didn't matter. Eyes like those, set in a skull, would be compelling. It is possible to talk with many persons for hours without once having been admitted past the frontal bony structure into the life behind the eyes. These eyes were moss agates, with flecks of gold, and they were as open as uncovered wells. If swimming wasn't *your* life, you shouldn't have gone near them.

"Why do men resist putting gas in their cars until the last minute?" I asked.

"There's not much left in life for men to gamble about. They can gamble about the gas."

"It can be irritating," I said.

"It does not irritate me. I have a fine husband."

"It irritates me."

"The fine wife perhaps has the right."

"I'm not a fine wife."

"I'm not talking about being perfect. I'm talking about me. I fall in love all the time. Passionately in love."

"What do you do about that?"

"Do? I do nothing. I cry in the night."

"Does your husband know?"

"Certainly not."

"Why does he think you cry?"

"Gallstones."

"Do the men know?"

"My God, no. I don't want pity."

"Don't any of them fall in love with you?"

"They wouldn't dare. I'm a good wife. The mother of three children. I don't want them to."

"If one did, and proposed, would you marry him?"

"No. I don't expect to find a better husband than Leland. What would be the point? Another husband wouldn't stop my falling in love."

"Don't you ever talk to these men?"

"Some. Some are men I see only once or twice."

"What do you talk about?"

"The weather."

"Don't you suffer?"

"I told you I cried in the night."

"In the daytime?"

"I'm happy. I told you, swimming is my life."

There was a car coming up the road. "Is that your husband?"

"I expect so."

I didn't want to see him. I thought he might read my face. I didn't want the mystery solved, if he was the solution.

"I have stuff on the stove." It was the truth. She didn't bother to say good-bye.

Usually I'm impatient about mail. I never get over expecting some extraordinary communication inside an ordinary envelope. But I didn't open any of my mail—occupied, as I was, thinking of the passionate swimmer. Robert Louis Stevenson said, "Marriage is a sort of friendship recognized by the police —if they only married when they fell in love, most people would die unwed." On the other hand, it seems to me, if everyone married when he fell in love, polygamy would have to be recognized by the police.

There is a great difference between loving and being in love. I should not have said that when I took that last camping trip with my family I was in love with Max. I wasn't. He had seen me before I saw him; he had hugged me and said, "I saw that coming," before I knew I wanted to be hugged. I never had a chance, fortunately, to "fall in love" with him before I began to love him.

One of the differences between loving and being in love with is that when one is in love, one's daydreams are all of the loved one. Storm Jameson, in *Journey from the North*, says of a Texan with whom she was in love, "I thought about the Texan the whole time whatever I was doing. When I sat down to write

I was forced to drop my pen and give myself up to thinking about him, re-living endlessly tiny details, a tone of voice, a phrase. Now that I am incapable of behaving so fatuously I regret the loss of a sensual trick so little harmful to anyone except myself, and so absurd and pleasant."

Jameson continues with the speculation that dying begins "not when our body fails, but much earlier in the moment when we can no longer run the risk of a total folly. . . . A part of me was gross, violent, sentimental, wanting change and excitement more than it wanted things in the end infinitely more important to me."

Storm Jameson, in love, thought continuously of the Texan. In true loving, oddly enough, the direction of the thinking is reversed. You think about yourself: Am I worthy? In the poetry anthologies I bought at Asilomar and in which the faint checkmarks are still to be seen, I chose those lines that spoke of the woman's dedication to the man she loves and of her determination to present him not only with her devotion, but with perfection. "I love my life, but not too well/To give it to thee like a flower." So sang Harriet Monroe, when not busy editing *Poetry*.

It was this determination to give my life in flowerlike condition to Max that made me so obnoxious on the trip to Indiana in 1920. It was very difficult on dirt roads, in an open car and in midsummer, to stay flowerlike—which meant, to me at seventeen, being at the very least fresh and clean.

My costume alone made floweriness difficult. With the exception of Papa and Rusty, who wore civilian clothes suitable to the season and their ages, the rest of us—Mama and I, Myron and Carmen—wore World War I army-surplus uniforms—or at least the surplus pants. The doughboys were able to wear those pants and help win a war. But Carmen, Mama, and I were not able to get to Indiana in them without making changes. The bottoms of the pants legs laced up so that they were close-fitting about the calf and ankle. Then from ankle to just below the knee, two- or three-inch strips of pants material were wrapped in an ascending spiral to form a kind of puttee. Carmen could manage that spiral, but Mama was too impatient and I was too clumsy to achieve an overlap neat enough and taut enough not to require constant rewrapping. We were not far along the Santa Fe Trail before the female part of our expeditionary force discarded puttees. Myron, as proof that it takes a man to make a soldier, wore his well wound the entire trip, there and home again. Mama and Carmen just laced up their pants and let it go at that. I, convinced that some kind of unfaithfulness was involved if I, who had been flowerlike in Max's presence, was slovenly elsewhere, wore golf stockings where the puttees should have been. If not exactly flowerlike, they were at least tidy.

Loving and being loved is more demanding than being in love. You can be in love with someone who knows nothing of your feeling and endlessly permit yourself "the sensual trick" of which Storm Jameson writes; never worrying whether or not your costume is worthy of the one of whom you daydream. If you are loved, have been told so, and have replied, "Me, too," responsibilities have been incurred. I wore golf socks with my surplus pants for Max's sake. Max would, I believed, want me to be garbed like a tidy traveler.

The pants situation, Max excluded, became more complex as we traveled east. In the West no one cared how we were clothed from the waist down. The fact that women were as bifurcated, if not a little more so, than men had long ago been accepted. Pantaloons of any kind were acceptable. East of the Mississippi, this was not true.

In a country store in Kentucky a grocer refused to sell Mama a loaf of bread because she wore pants. It was his moral duty, he explained to her, not to accept her as a customer. He was foregoing the profit he would make on the bread in order to combat the growing deterioration in the moral tone of America as evidenced by women in pants. Mama was abashed, not only for herself but for this narrowness on the part of a resident of her own cherished "back East."

"Everyone," she explained, "wears pants in California."

"You're from California?"

Mama said yes. Back East was the Old Country, and she would always be loyal to it; but after eleven years in California, she was a Westerner.

"So you're from California," the grocer exclaimed. "That explains a lot. Quite a few things, from the reports we get, go on out there that we wouldn't put up with for a minute back here."

Mama, as she left the store without bread for our bologna, heard the storekeeper say to a cracker-barrel crony, "What did she expect? Dressed so's we could see her clear up to her fork."

It was possible to see that she *had* a fork, I suppose; but all was well covered, first by cotton drawers—split to be sure, but amply designed and with edges overlapping—and, on top of these, heavy-duty, army-issue pants. That grocer was really fork-minded.

Pants troubled Kentucky and Southern Indiana, but it was my determination to be dainty that caused trouble in the family. Daintiness requires, first of all, cleanliness; and cleanliness requires water; and water in a dry camp was hard to come by. We had two canteens: one a desert canvas bag, which was hung over the radiator cap; the other, a five-gallon rounded metal can covered with Roman-striped flannel, was kept inside the car. Canteens, children, and radiator were filled wherever there was a supply of good water.

We crossed the Mojave Desert at night. The Paige's needs, when it came to water, were always considered first. Without it, we could get nowhere. After it was taken care of, cooking and dishwashing were next in order. Face and body washing were not considered absolutely necessary, and, necessary or not, were not possible in a dry camp.

Mama didn't care about washing. She was making the entire trip well lubricated with Ingram's Milkweed Cream. She also wore a big hat and veil to protect the already protected surfaces. It was impossible to understand how in that getup the grocer had been able to get his eyes below her neck. Hoosiers believed that the California sun turned a woman's skin to leather, made her look like a field hand. A California cousin had returned to Indiana for a visit, and the report had come back to California that to Hoosiers she had looked "much broken." Mama did not intend to look like a field hand, or to be considered "broken." She was a sight on the road; but in Jennings County she would wash, powder with Java Rice Powder, take off her surplus pants, and in a flowery dress and white gloves show the Hoosiers how real Californians looked.

This was fine for Mama. The Hoosiers we would see were pinned down along the Muscatatuck. Mama had no conviction that they were omniscient. I, however, was a different case. I felt required to live as if Max could see me at all times. I was like a Christian newly converted, determined not to be a Sunday Christian only. I had been courted and proposed to in the guise of a clean, fresh, sweet-smelling girl. If a very small wash-pan of water for me meant that there was no water for the breakfast coffee or for cleaning the skillet, surely I had made the only possible choice. What was coffee or a clean skillet compared with being true to my true love? The journey progressed along the lines of a Western scenario depicting the encounters of embattled ranchers fighting over water rights. It never occurred to me that an omniscient Max might think there was more virtue in family harmony than in cleanliness at such a price.

Love (or my idea of it), not cleanliness, was the cause of the strife. As children we had been permitted to do pretty much as we liked in the matter of keeping the dirt down. I have no ingrained habits of cleanliness to this day. I like the feel of water (though swimming is not my life), and I have some regard for the sensibilities of others. But I don't keep clean as a matter of habit. The routine was never established. "Brush your teeth." "Wash your hands." "File your nails." "Shampoo your hair." "Take a bath." Were such words ever spoken to us? I cannot remember them.

I went to school once, in the seventh or eighth grade, with my dress on inside out without noticing the reversal until the teacher called my attention to it. I was in college before I learned that people brushed their teeth after each meal.

Apart from what I may or may not have learned at home, I had a distaste for all that was finicky in the way of cleanliness. Washing fruit, for instance; spreading paper towels on toilet seats; refusing to drink from fountains where the jet didn't completely clear the fountain. I thought life would punish those who refused to take any chances with it, who tried to protect themselves too carefully from it. Careful men were downright revolting. The first time I saw a man put on a pair of galoshes, he might as well have been putting on a corset. I did not know anyone who owned an umbrella or a raincoat. To delay a journey because of rain was old-maidish. The first Christmas present I received from Max was a big handsome wool stole, picked out, I am sure, by his mother. I never wore it once. What did he think I was? He might as well have given me an ear trumpet.

Being loved and in turn loving had, however, convinced me that cleanliness was nice, if not necessary. I still did not think that the sky would fall or that I would break out with impetigo if I missed a daily tub. Cleanliness was part of being physically appealing. This made sense to me. So the journey progressed amidst these heated feuds over water rights. *I* was a complete Westerner. Who owned the water? The one who got there first, and I was a quick one at the canteens. What could my poor parents do? Seventeen is too old, or at least too big, for whipping. They couldn't abandon me beside a cactus clump on the Santa Fe Trail. They could appeal to my sense of honor. And did. What they could not seem to understand was that on my side I had love; and that for love a few sacrifices—like coffee, clean skillets, and even honor—might have to be made. By everyone.

# XX

———◆———

Who of the family was totally present on that back-trailing trip? Perhaps no one is ever *totally* present at any time. Mama lived less in deserts and mesas and pueblos than in the vision of herself appearing lily-white and "unbroken" before her relatives and former neighbors. I lived in a constant parade of my daintiness before Max. Papa, with an eye for a panorama, as the old Hoosiers called it, had to pay more attention to the Paige than to the scenery: the leaf of a spring broke in Colorado; the wonder being, considering the load we were carrying, that it had held up that long. A blacksmith repaired it.

In Kansas there had been unseasonable rains, and at those places where the road became bog, farmers with a couple of mules waited to pull travelers out of the mud. Their price was one dollar if hired to hitch onto the car before the crossing was attempted; five dollars if hired after the car mired. Papa, though no gambler, bet on the most beautiful car in America and always won. He had, of course, his children as a work crew —shoes off, surplus pants rolled up—paving the way for him with bushes and branches across the quagmires. We did so well that travelers tried to hire us instead of the farmers with their mules. Myron and I were tempted, but Papa didn't have time for roadside enterprises. I hoped that Max would understand that rules for daintiness didn't hold in disaster areas.

My feeling is that none of us truly noticed the land through which we passed until we reached New Mexico. Deserts, mountains, lakes—we had seen them all in California. We had not seen a petrified forest before, however. There we stopped and marveled. We walked through a rainbow-colored wreckage of stone that had once been a forest. We stroked stone, shut our eyes, and tried to imagine the thrum of sap through those bones before they had hardened and the sough of wind through the leaves that would have canopied us 2,000 years ago. It was a graveyard of trees. The great ribbed torsos lay stretched like warriors at rest, emblazoned with the colors of the standards they had carried when they fell. The dry wind whispered around what it had once moved. Sand drifted where once moss and lichens had grown. Papa didn't have film to waste; on the whole trip he took not more than a dozen pictures. The Petrified Forest was one of the dozen.

The stone of the Petrified Forest was public property. Anyone could pick up a chunk of hardened rainbow and walk off with it. Everyone did so. Our chunk would have been larger except for the Paige's flattening springs. I have the stone now. I do not think of it as tree any more, but as part of the desert and of the Indians who made their home there. If you can hear the sea in a shell, in this wood-turned-stone you can hear the desert wind, the spitter of dry sand, the cry of Apaches.

We noticed something new in the land, even before we left the West. World War I was now a year and a half past. Already the war memorials honoring the heroic dead were going up in the little Southwestern towns. Most of them were ugly; all pitiful. When the war was in progress, I had, in the beginning, felt it my duty to read the names of all fallen Californians, printed in the Los Angeles *Times,* to say each name slowly to myself, then repeat, sternly and passionately after every name, somthing like this: "It should never have happened. I will never forget you. God rest you and keep you."

As the lists of the dead became longer, I had to content myself with simply reading the list, not pronouncing each individual name; and finally only reading and saying for all the fallen together, "God rest you and keep you." Now in little towns, on plaques affixed to red-brick monuments and to concrete drinking fountains, the lists of names were smaller. I went back to my earlier practice of saying each name under my breath. I felt that by doing so I gave the fallen soldier an instant of the life of which he had been robbed. I gave him my breath.

At the age of ninety my father, speaking of the Vietnam war, said, "In a way no war since the First World War has seemed real to me."

It was the same with me, though I was twelve and he thirty-five when that war "broke out."

"Why?" I asked.

"I haven't recovered from *that* shock yet."

A first war is like a first falling in love. Nothing resembling it has been imagined possible. First love with anyone at all arouses emotions that are memorable; if the loved one is vivid and daring, all that follow may seem pallid. The First World War came when America's last great war was fifty years past. We had believed that there would perhaps never be another war. Then the First World War happened. *It* was a war, we believed, to end all wars. We were not then cynical about the efficacy of wars. The Civil War had preserved the Union, hadn't it? The Revolution had given us independence, hadn't it? We didn't then ask ourselves whether or not independence and union might not have been won by less bloody means.

The First World War was the last in which the individual was visible; the last in which emotions were felt that could be sung about: "There's a Long, Long Trail A-winding." "We Won't Be Back Till It's Over, Over There." "Roses Are Blooming in Picardy." Poems we would remember came out of World War I. "If I should die think only this of me." "All the hills and vales along/Earth is bursting into song." "Nor need he any hearse to bear him hence,/Who goes to join the men of Agincourt."

We had read:

*There is no fitter end than this*
*No need is now to yearn or sigh*
*We know the glory that is his,*
*A glory that is his,*
*A glory that can never die.*

This was our first war, dashing as a first lover. We had not yet been betrayed; not yet discovered that the world isn't made safe for democracy by killing men; that the last thing to prevent a future war is a present war. So I cried at the war memorials, where men were remembered with so much less grandeur than dead trees; and my family, who grudged me water for love, didn't grudge me the time for tears for the dead. They remembered the dead themselves. They, too, mourned.

Fifty years and three wars later, Papa could say, like a widower of many marriages, that the first was the only one that counted.

We always camped before night fell, on a level spot, near water if possible, and outside towns. One night we stopped where a week later the county fair would be held—a fine camping spot: water in faucets (no fight at the water hole that night); grass mowed; even privies.

This was a gathering place for crowds, and even though we didn't promise the townspeople anything the equal of a Ferris wheel or a string of trained ponies, we were outlandish enough to attract a crowd. The car alone, with all of its unusual glass and California license plate, insured that. How long had we been on the road? Where were we heading? Didn't all that glass rattle around a lot? In case of collision wouldn't it be dangerous? How was crossing the deserts? Had the car boiled a lot climbing the Rockies?

The onlookers stayed while the tarp, which was spread on the ground under the beds, was laid; while the canvas, which was attached to the top of the car, then stretched to two supporting poles, was put in place. They stayed, more and more of them, until Mama was ready to start supper. Then she marched out and faced her audience. She was a self-conscious woman on premeditated occasions. If she had been told that morning, "At six tonight you will have to address a group of fifty people," she would have been in bed with a headache and a mustard plaster. But that unexpected, peering crowd got her Irish up, and she focused their attention by banging on the skillet, in which she was about to fry camp biscuits, with her mixing spoon.

"Folks," she said, "you'll be glad to know that the big show doesn't start until eight o'clock tonight. That will give you and us time to cook and eat supper. Then you can all come back and watch us get ready for bed. There won't be any lights, but the moon will be up for a while, and maybe you can figure out who's wearing what and sleeping where."

They got the point. We were people like themselves; we didn't relish having an audience watch us get supper and eat it any more than they would. They drifted away, trying to give themselves and us the impression that they had paused only in passing by.

I hadn't felt like a carnival freak until Mama made her speech. She was a barker in reverse. She said, "Go away, folks," instead of "Come in, folks." She spoiled my appetite. Since there was all kinds of water, I retired to a privy with a bucketful and had a long bath. It was a warm, bright privy, gilded by the westering light, already cleaned up for the fair to come. There was lots of time. The papery cells of a wasp's nest hung in one corner; pictures of flowers cut from seed catalogues were pasted on the walls. I never had a bath in a nicer place. I had come in mad and humiliated, but the splash of water, the suds of a bar of Fairy Soap, the little prairie wind that whistled through the privy cracks, made me stop hating Mama and start wondering about my love of privacy—which was inconsistent.

Carmen and I on one side, Mama on the other, had a difference of opinion about privacy. Mama wanted the blinds pulled at night. Carmen and I wanted them left up. We ranked people by whether or not they hid themselves after dark. When we passed houses with the blinds pulled, we thought, There are people whose lives don't bear inspection. We wanted everything open, lamp-lit, and the residents arranged in harmonious tableaux. I don't know what hunger this satisfied in us, whether it was a substitute for the theater or whether these lamp-lit pictures of the life of our neighbors reassured adolescents who knew that soon they, too, would be stepping into just such rooms, living out their own domestic pictures for passers-by.

I repaid those who staged living-room dramas for me by doing as I would be done by. I do not suppose that any passer-by ever saw in me or what I did the drama I imagined I mimed for his seeing. If I sat at a table, writing, I wrote for the eye of the passer-by—one who would think, She writes to her soldier boy, far, far away. If I crossed the room with a glass of water, I did so with delicate, hurried steps so that the passer-by would think, She cares for her mother, who lies feverish in her bed.

The self-consciousness and exhibitionism of adolescence has lessened, but not completely disappeared. When Spry and I walk, we walk with a zest we know is visible. Perhaps that is one of the reasons solitude is so appealing. I am no longer an actor. I am the eye that sees instead of the person observed.

"The consciousness of security kills life," someone—not Thoreau this time—has said. The consciousness of security against intrusion doesn't kill life—for me. It intensifies it. These two small, spare rooms: what is the opposite of claustrophobia? What is the word for delight in the small? Tonight there is a strong wind out of the northeast rocking the trailer. The last of the cottonwood bloom has spattered down on the roof. I see many small things usually missed in the daytime. I have lit my two little kerosene lamps, both to enjoy their smell and for the softness of their light. Max is afraid to have me use them. He thinks I'll burn the place up. But our mothers, grandmothers, and great-grandmothers used them without mishap. I consider myself, in the care of lamps at least, their equal.

Lamp light is not absolutely steady, so the highlights reflected in the brown earthenware pitcher waver like water. I see the angle with which the end pages of a book meet the side pages. The little wooden woman and the carved wooden cat are reflected in the Formica of the table top. The canvas contour chair, which I brought inside because the wind was blowing it about, has curves my wrist and hand want to imitate.

There was no hint of this wind when I went walking at four. There seems to be a contradiction between wanting a landscape as big and open as this country provides and a room so small. I exult in this landscape. I love light, variations in light. I love distance, immensity, tranquillity, contrast of mountain and plain, desert and water. I love a dry land and water in a dry land.

Lily was coming home in her Scout from a painting jaunt as Spry and I crossed the road, and I was able to open the gate for her. She will live to be a hundred and ten. Why do painters and composers live for so long? Because they are joined in love with their subject matter—as writers often are not?

Son helped her with her gear, then came down to show me that gas was again escaping from one of the trailer's butane tanks. He did so by putting a little soapy water over one of the connections. The connection immediately began to blow soap bubbles.

"Haven't you smelled it?" he asked.

I hadn't.

"The next time you go to town, have the fellow who brought these out come out again and fit them on properly."

Son says a number of things, even when he uses dictionary English, I don't thoroughly understand. His mother has been having a girl pose for her, and I said, "She's very pretty."

Son answered, "I don't know that I could agree to that.

Sometimes she looks kind of like a nature lover to me." What does that mean?

"She was a child of circumstances," he said; of his first wife, I think. "I was just an idol to her."

This was the first of the telescoped Washington and Lincoln holidays. I don't know whether the Colorado can take care of so many eager to honor these two men. One thing I have learned this weekend: half of the world lives and drives in vans. Campers, I knew. Trailers, I knew. Motor homes. But the van, I still thought, was a vehicle properly used to deliver bread and pick up laundry. Now I wonder if there is anyone in the state of California between the ages of sixteen and twenty-five without one. The vans congregate at the river's edge like turtles at mating time. The occupants sleep with the van's back doors open and with their heads in the opening. In the morning, with four or five asleep on the floor, the van's cargo appears to be mostly hair. Down it hangs. The boys have had the permanents. Theirs are the corkscrews and curly locks. The girls' hair hangs lank and long. I was born into the wrong hair age, the age that still had to "do up" its hair. This is no longer necessary; you just have it and toss it about a bit. A wig shop could lay in a good supply of raw material by sending an operator out at dawn with a pair of shears to one of these encampments of vans.

Until I saw these vans, I hadn't realized that thirty-five years ago Papa and Mama were hippie forerunners: too restless to stay home and report proudly, "We are much traveled in Yorba Linda."

No, not they. They bought, thirty-five years before its time, a green hippie van. They put a mattress on the floor for their bed. They bought a folding table, two folding chairs, and a Coleman stove. With these they had an outdoor dining room-sitting room. Thus equipped, they set out to be well traveled in the United States of America. And were. They saw the great houses in which the famous had lived, and the small houses in which they had been born. They saw all the natural wonders: geysers and falls; the bridges made by erosion; Indian mounds and Indian petroglyphs. They set foot in stands of virgin timber. They camped in the Badlands and the Great Smokies; on Kentucky's dark and bloody ground. They stood where Pickett charged and Custer fell. They didn't miss much.

Their thick letters came back fragrant with a dried red clover, a buckwheat blossom, a Cherokee rose. "Write us next," they said, "c/o General Delivery at Deming, New Mexico; San Antonio, Texas; Sioux City, Iowa; Wilmington, Ohio; Ashville, North Carolina."

If our letters didn't get there, they wrote, "Waited a day at Wheeling, hoping for word from some of you, and were well repaid. Letters from all, and we were able to continue on our way with our minds at rest. We hope to be in Tampa on the tenth."

Not yet Jesus Freaks, still they went to church on Sunday. They attended whatever church was at hand, whatever denomination, whatever color. Quakerism in California was not very quiet, and they were not offended by a pulpit-thumping preacher or an amening audience. They listened attentively to the sermons they heard. They had a duty to find some word amongst those spoken that would speak to their condition, help them lead better lives.

Well, they had the blood of Quakers in their veins, which *is* hippie, with these exceptions: first, that everyone in the seventeenth century, Quaker and non-Quaker alike, had the name of God on their mouths; second, that no one, young or old, then doubted that the example set by Jesus Christ should be the measuring rod for their lives. There were these differences between seventeenth-century Quakers and hippies, but the emotions aroused in others by the two were much the same. Quakerism in its beginning was, like hippieism, a youth movement. George Fox was nineteen when he left home "at the

219

command of God," to search for "a way." At twenty-four he heard a voice say, "There is one, even Christ Jesus, who can speak to thy condition." At that moment Quakerism had its beginnings. The parents of England were dismayed by their offspring who became his followers; the jails of England were filled with Fox's converts.

Samuel Pepys, hearing that the son of his navy colleague Admiral Penn had become a Quaker, sent the Admiral a letter of condolence, saying that he was sorry to hear that William had become a Friend, or "had fallen into some such melancholy state." There probably never was a generation gap as wide as that between the early Quakers and their parents.

They began, these young people, by rejecting the authority of the Church of England and by refusing to pay the state-levied taxes for its support. For this they were thrown into jail. They held meetings of their own; for the most part silent, but in which anyone—men and women—*could* speak. Pastors were not "ordained," but merely "recognized." Quakers traveled to their own meetings on Sundays, and such Sunday travel was forbidden. For this they went to jail.

They refused to bear arms. They believed that "Thou shalt not kill" was a command that was not negated by murdering thousands and calling it war, instead of killing one and calling it murder. For this they went to jail.

Their marriages were not recognized by church or state. No man "married" a Quaker couple. The couple, before witnesses and in the sight of God, affirmed their intention to live together. Such "marriages" were not recognized by state or church; children born of such unions were bastards. Quakers could not be buried in hallowed ground.

They had hair trouble then, too. It was the age of the wig, and Quakers insisted on wearing their own hair, shoulder-length and unpowdered.

They had hat trouble. It was customary to doff one's hat to one's betters. Quakers believed that all men were brothers.

They believed that God judged men by what they had in their hearts, not by what they had on their heads. They kept their hats on even in church.

God might so judge, but Thomas Elwood's father judged his son's respect for *him* by the position of his son's hat. When Thomas came into his father's presence, hat on, his father beat him, and the beating was stopped only when Thomas's sister threw open the window and threatened to scream "Murder." Thomas's father finally solved the hat problem permanently by burning all of his son's hats.

Quaker language was not only peculiar; it was downright revolutionary. It was customary to use one form of address for commoners, another for the gentry. By using "thee" and "thy" to all, Quakers refused to recognize class differences.

Quaker garb was outlandish. It was the age of the male peacock, the female lyrebird. Quakers believed that there were better ways of spending money and more appropriate ways of showing where the heart lay. They put on plain clothes, usually of drab colors, though George Fox bought for his wife a bolt of crimson-colored cloth for a cloak. Fox never got Christ and color mixed up.

The seventeenth-century Quakers had many hippie characteristics. They were never, however, militant. They believed that those who take the sword shall perish by the sword. They would not attempt to better the world or others or themselves by force. No trashing, no arson, no bombing. They believed, with William Penn, "A good end cannot sanctify evil means. Force can subdue but love gains, and he that forgives first wins the laurels."

Thoreau, who in so many ways was himself Quakerly, did not have much use for the plain folk. In his journal he wrote, "There is a Quaker meeting-house there [New Bedford]. Such an ugly shed, without a tree or a bush about it, which they call their meeting-house (without a steeple of course) is utterly repulsive to me, like a powder-house or grave. And even the quietness and perhaps unworldliness of an aged Quaker has something ghostly and saddening about it, as it were a mere preparation for the grave."

"A powder-house or grave . . ." In some ways it *was* a powder house. The Quakers blew asunder many a rigidly held religious and social concept. But it is strange to find that these people, who more than any other of Thoreau's time shared his views, elicited so little sympathy from him. He is now the hippies' culture hero, though God knows what Thoreau would think of the hippies. The artist, and particularly the artist who is a genius, doesn't need any synthetic vision producers in the form of drugs. This capability his genes have given him. What he needs is the discipline, the concentration, the technique, to body forth the vision he has in a form that can convey meaning to others. This discipline he cannot find by sniffing, ingesting, mainlining, or smoking.

Thoreau would not have touched the hippie commune with a ten-foot pole. The commune is an old American fad, which everyone who has his own work to do avoids. The Quakers, for all their success in united efforts of one kind and another, never tried to live together. They met in their "ugly sheds," practiced there a kind of group mysticism, then went to their own homes —somewhat more sizable but less ornate than mine—and there "centered down" to what appeared to them to be life's truths.

I am glad that Papa's and Mama's green hippie van came after my time of traveling with them. The touring car was bad enough; but we got outside of that, slept in our separate beds, bathed behind our separate bushes (or I did), and had some privacy.

The trip in the Paige was not hell on wheels, but it was, for the most part, wasted on me. I was jarred from my daydream of love only on occasions when something unusual or dangerous happened. The journey through the West was very much like a repetition of what we already knew: cactus and mountains and sagebrush and blue skies. When that flash flood at Wagon Mound went by, I saw *it*. Perhaps that is where I picked up my respect for flash floods. It could have demolished a car in a minute; a human being would have been pounded as flat as a flapjack. I watched and remembered.

Acts of God might have menaced us when traveling in the West, but the natives were friendly. When we reached the East (east of the Mississippi), human beings themselves were frightening. We crossed the Mississippi at St. Louis. On the eastern side, where land began but the bridge had not yet ended, I looked down into a face I have never forgotten. In the open door of an empty and littered shanty, a man sat on a box. The man was neither white nor black, but a combination of the two, which had produced a muddy yellow. I had never seen a face so desolate, so hopeless, so menacing. I had not known that flesh could be so shaped. I had often wondered what would happen to a human face if every thought and impulse of its owner from birth had been compassionate and loving. I saw two faces, belonging to an old farmer and his wife, in the county courthouse at Vernon, Indiana, once, that seemed to answer that question: beautiful, beautiful. As different from Main Street faces as apes from men. The face of the man in the shanty on the Mississippi has haunted me for a lifetime. I could pick it out of a line-up now. I think my feeling was less fear than wonder: "This can happen to a man." We were going very slowly, and he looked straight at me, feeling equal wonder, perhaps, at my round, freckled, and unmarked face.

In Illinois we stopped for the night at a country schoolhouse; no security guards in those days. We put up our beds on the schoolhouse porch and settled down once more to the luxury of running water and privies.

In the middle of the night we were aroused by a woman's screaming—the most terrifying sound I have ever heard. I did not know then and do not know now whether those screams were caused by pain, madness, or fear. The screams came from

223

a car that had been parked in the school yard after we had gone to bed on the school porch. Papa endured those sounds for a few minutes, then he shot the .22 he carried into the air. The car pulled out quickly. Papa was angry at himself afterward for doing that. "I wasn't much help to that woman," he said.

He reported the happening the next day to the police in the first town we passed through. The police were not interested. "The miners around here get drunk and yell," the officer said. "This wasn't a miner," Papa reminded him. "Miner's woman," the officer said. "They all get drunk and yell."

After the car left, those screams still echoed in my ears and along my nerve ends. I shook and couldn't stop shaking; and when I shook, the springs on which Carmen and I slept rattled. The rattling annoyed Carmen. "Mama," she called, "make Jessamyn stop shaking!" Mama didn't know how to do that. The best she could do was to tell Carmen to keep quiet and perhaps I would go to sleep. I couldn't go to sleep, and I couldn't stop shaking. After a while Carmen became accustomed to the clank of the hardware we were lying on and fell asleep.

Next morning I walked around and around the spot where the car with the screaming woman had parked. The ground was littered with amber-colored bone hairpins. I picked them up one by one until I had a handful. I thought, When that woman put these hairpins in her brown hair last night (she must have had a lot of hair, and she must have worn it in a Psyche knot or a French roll to take so many), little did she think that they would be picked up off the ground in a public school yard by a girl from California. I was struck by what had struck me before: the strange chanciness of life. The hairpin for a party becomes a school girl's souvenir. The mirror that reflects that smile will never see that smile again. The good-bye that is only for now turns out to be farewell forever.

What had been happening to that woman? Something she

didn't want to happen, surely. Something painful? Something a man was doing to her? I didn't know. Had it something to do with sex? I didn't even know the word; and either I was not curious enough to ask, or I had been taught not to ask questions about such things.

# XXI

———◆———

There are times, looking back on my youth, when I feel that I was distinctly retarded in my sexual development: comparable in that area to a child who doesn't talk until five or is still wetting the bed at ten. Why wasn't I more curious about the mechanism of sex? I heard a female child of four say the other day to another child, "I'll stick that up your poo-roo."

"What's a poo-roo?" I asked the mother.

"Vagina," said the mother.

"How does she know she has one?"

"Investigation. Didn't you investigate your body when you were a child?"

"I didn't. Not nostrils, ear holes, anus, mouth. And certainly not vagina, which I didn't know existed."

Training or retardation? A slow learner, a late bloomer? Perhaps some of each. The training was undoubtedly not only Victorian but the crude Victorianism of a backwoods border country, which in 1925 was just beginning to face up to Darwin's discoveries, which England had debated and suffered over seventy-five years earlier.

Why was the woman in the school yard screaming? I knew that there was a bad and humiliating thing for which men wanted women. Because of this, I must never accept a ride with a strange man. There *were* men who prowled about the countryside gathering up women and girls to ship to South America for this bad and humiliating purpose. Such women were called white slaves. The woman in the car could not be a white slave —as I had envisaged them.

These women, white slaves, were not ordinary workers: cooks, window washers, and the like. Such work was drudgery, but it was not "bad." A man could wash a window or cook a meal; these slaves were employed in some activity that only a woman could do. Now the only two things I knew about that a woman could do that a man couldn't was to have babies and to produce milk with which to feed a baby. No man, however depraved, I figured, would want a bunch of babies on his hands. One, from my experience with Rusty, was a full-time job. So the only use depraved men could find for women, insofar as I could make out, would be to milk them. This struck me as a witless occupation, but witlessness was possibly a prerequisite for depravity.

These depraved men collected herds of women, installed them in dairy barns, and there had them milked like Jerseys or Holsteins morning and evening. These men were known throughout their own countrysides as rakehells and high livers. No ordinary cow milk served at their tables! Nothing but woman-milk.

Sometimes these white-slave owners took their guests out to their barns. There, like eighteenth-century milords showing off their blooded horses, they displayed their herds of women-cows. The women, I thought, would not be naked. They were too valuable to risk losing with pneumonia or pleurisy. They wore over their backs a kind of horse blanket. Most of them no longer stood upright. Their breasts, from constant milking, were udderlike.

Usually a refined rakehell did not take his lady guests to his lady-cow barns, any more than he would take them to inspect his bulls. The ladies who were guests knew that something rather strange was going on out in those barns, something they would be just as happy not to know about. It was rather like the concentration camps of World War II: something quite unpleasant was rumored to be going on out there, something that was men's business. In the first place, it surely couldn't be true; in the second, if it was true, there was nothing a woman could do about it.

These women-cows, as I imagined them, never spoke. Chained, treated as animals—not ill-treated animals; well fed, though of course not on hay—without reading material, they had sunk into the torpor and humiliation of animals. Their eyes were big like a cow's, submissive, defeated. They were used. They submitted. It never crossed my mind that their owners ever thought of them as other than exotic dairy animals. It was like the corrals Myron and I had made for ladybugs, stinkbugs, potato bugs, grasshoppers, crickets: wrong, but amusing. The men, with their women-herds, were cruel and depraved, of course, as all slave keepers were. And I could easily understand why this was called the fate worse than death.

With such a fate possible, I only once accepted a ride with a strange man. Mama was in the hospital in Anaheim, three miles away from Fullerton, where I was a high-school student. I bought her, with my lunch money, a squat, flowered cream pitcher (I seemed to have been obsessed with milk products: my ideal Christmas present was a case of Carnation evaporated milk). I was hastening on foot to deliver the pitcher to her. A man, a strange man, offered me a ride. He didn't look like a white slaver, but when he took a short cut, unfamiliar to me, I told him, "Here is where I get out."

He made the mistake of trying to argue with me, of trying to convince me that this was indeed a short cut to the hospital. Exactly, I thought, the tactics of a white slaver. I was resolved to throw myself out of the car if he didn't stop. In doing so I would break the pitcher and quite possibly some bones. But far, far better a few broken bones than endless years yoked to one of those stanchions in the far-off Argentine.

The driver stopped the car, shaking his head in pity. He

had no designs on me of any kind, and I still had two miles, carrying my precious pitcher (I still have it), to walk.

At seventeen I no longer thought often of the white slaves in South America. But the vacuum the white slaves had filled was still empty.

The only sex education we had from Mama were a few prohibitions: don't talk about it; and, to the boys, I suppose, don't play with it. This was not uncharacteristic, I am sure, of many families of that time. What was probably less characteristic was my lack of curiosity. I couldn't very well talk about a subject of which I was completely ignorant. Why didn't I listen and learn? I didn't want to; partly because I thought I already knew all there was to know—God planted a seed, etc.—partly because I relished the idea of sex as mystery. No one, I think, considered me prissy. They may have thought me peculiar, and I may have been.

A few days before I was to be married, the mother of my best friend, evidently thinking that for my own sake I ought to know a fact or two, took me into her bedroom for a heart-to-heart talk. I refused to listen. I, on the eve of reading a book that, I had heard, was romantic and exciting, didn't want anyone telling me the plot before I had finished even the first paragraph. I had been in love for half my life; wasn't this all the preparation one needed for marriage? The answer is no.

In addition to the two prohibitions, "Don't talk about it" and "Don't play with it," there must have been one more positive command: "Keep it covered up."

In our first days in Yorba Linda, while Papa was still hauling all of our water in barrels from Anaheim Lake and storing it in the concrete weir box, which would later hold and distribute irrigation water, Myron and I, alone, on a hot day of dry Santa Ana winds, began to look more and more speculatively at that weir box. I was eight or nine; Myron, six or seven. The box had just been filled. There was a canvas stretched across it, held down by stones on each side, to protect the water from dust and leaves. But under the canvas was clear, cool water, which would reach about to our chins. It was our drinking water. But if no one knew? We had heard all of our lives that what we didn't know wouldn't hurt us. What bothered us was not hygiene but morals. We wouldn't harm the drinking water by swimming in it. Would harm come to us if we went swimming together in the weir box naked? We had no swimming suits, and underwear in the drinking water did seem unclean.

We solved the problem by making ourselves bathing suits from the sacks that had held rolled barley. All that is necessary to convert a barley sack into a bathing suit is to cut, in the bottom end, three holes: one large for the head, two smaller for the arms. The suits, so made, reached from shoulder to toe. Swimming in the six-by-eight-foot weir box, to say nothing of the sack-sized suits, was impossible. All we could do was jump up and down, which we did for about two hours. Then we clambered out and prepared to replace the canvas. When we did that, we saw floating on top of the water a film of lint from the barley bags.

For the next hour we skimmed lint from the weir box. The weir box was soon only half full of water, though the amount of lint seemed never to diminish. We were still skimming, still in our barley-sack suits, when Papa and Mama came home. No one had a word of praise for our modesty.

Papa, before he drained the weir box and set off with wagon and barrels for a new supply of water, said, "Next time you take it into your heads to swim in our drinking water, leave off the barley sacks."

Mama said, "Eldo!" But even she, after lint kept showing up in the drinking water for two or three weeks, was against swimming in barley sacks.

There were some pitiful gestures in the direction of sex education at college. The dean of women, whose husband, our Bible professor, was also a part-time chiropractor, asked me in to have a talk with her. What she had to say was this: "If you and Max continue to be together so much, the association will lead to marriage." This was exactly my plan, and I was happy to find that she thought it was succeeding. Marriage, however, was not what she was really talking about. When she went on to speak of the dangers of "queening," as necking was then called at Whittier, I knew that what she had in mind was something different from love, cherish, and obey. Different in what way she never said. So I was none the wiser for this little seminar on sex education.

At the end of each college year the engaged girls in the dormitory where I lived met in one of the rooms to hear a talk from the wife of the local Quaker minister. Since I was engaged at the end of my freshman year, I heard this talk over and over. It never improved. Nor did the ceremony. First, all the girls sat in a circle holding hands. This symbolized, we were told, the wedding ring and matrimony's holy bonds. Next, all the lights were turned off. This was our salvation, because there was after this a good deal of silent giggling. The minister's wife was not cut out for speaking on any subject, holy matrimony being near the bottom of any list of subjects she could possibly handle.

After the dark and the handholding and prayers by all who felt they had anything they wanted to say out loud to God came the singing. "Blessed Be the Tie That Binds" was the usual selection. (One year we sang "He Walks with Me and He Talks with Me and He Tells Me I Am His Own.") Refreshments followed. These never varied: cocoa and marguerites. A marguerite was a soda cracker spread with sugar, butter, and cinnamon and toasted. Pretty classy, we thought. We all needed nourishment after a ritual that made a Quaker marriage ceremony, which was to follow later, as simple as a hand clasp.

Such was the sex education of home and school before I was launched into the roaring twenties, which obviously never roared for me. I had given up my fantasies about stanchions in South America (and in any case they were not for married couples), but except that it must be something on the order of Paul's experience on the road to Damascus, which struck him temporarily blind, I had nothing with which to replace these fantasies. I didn't know what marriage was, and was determined not to find out. Such ignorance and such expectations are trying for young grooms, who are not often prepared to be the Lord God on the road to Damascus to their brides.

Sex and religion are bordering states. They use the same vocabulary, share like ecstasies, and often serve as a substitute for one another. Sex, for young Quakers in the twenties, was thought to be bad; religion, good. True, you could have too much religion. No one would have encouraged me to spend hours on my knees or to rise before dawn to pray or to fast on alternate Tuesdays. The Quakers, though considerably less so in California than elsewhere, were a sober, reticent sect. They had changed since the eighteenth century, but not a great deal. At that time, in England, a Turkish envoy come to parley about economic matters said of a Quaker delegation sent to greet him, "I like very much to talk with these Quakers. There is no religious nonsense about them."

In my home there was as little religious nonsense as among English Quakers in eighteenth-century England. I don't know where I picked up the idea, a true one, that at heart Papa and Mama loved God and tried to obey His commandments. There may have been prayers said in private. I never heard any except when Papa returned thanks, out loud, at the Thanksgiving table.

As children we were taught no prayers. No one heard us say our prayers before we went to bed. No one read the Bible aloud or required Bible reading of us. Because I liked to sing, I tried to institute singing the stanza of a hymn before we ate. The idea was rejected as ridiculous, which in truth it was.

My conclusion is that with so little formal attention paid to religious observance there must have been a good deal of informal talk about, and obvious practice of, Christian living for the impression to remain that we were the children of a God-loving household.

There was *some* religious nonsense amongst many Quakers in the early 1900s in California. The revival fever that had swept the Midwest earlier was at that time laying California Quakers low in the aisles of their spiritless little wooden buildings. I have nothing against revivals; though Lee Vernon, the best preacher I ever knew, believed them harmful, and though a great-aunt on the Indian side of the family had gone home, after having confessed at a revival to carnal knowledge of a man not her husband, and cut her throat.

The old revivals accomplished with more spontaneity what today's encounter groups and sensitivity-training sessions attempt. Hands were laid on then as now, confessions were made, tears shed, songs sung, bodies put in a weaving way. Grudges and animosities long cherished were admitted and discarded. All were bathed in the blood of the Lamb, refreshed in their faith, and renewed in their determination to live like Jesus and be a brother to man.

This is where the man purged by the old revival was ahead of the junior executive sent by his company to a sensitivity-training weekend at Aspen or Monterey. The junior executive enjoys the euphoria of an emotional group—bang. The man who has been "saved" experiences euphoria, too. But to keep it, he knows he must tread in the bloody footsteps of Jesus Christ. He has had at the revival a taste of the high that such living can bring him. It is an emancipation to be freed to be yourself; it is a dedication to find someone you want to be one with. Emancipation can be aimless; dedication is centered; "centered down," as the Quakers say.

The week before we left for Brownsville, yet to be seen, I received an invitation to attend the meeting of an encounter group. The invitation came by phone from a lady in a nearby town. The group would meet for twenty-four hours. An eminent group therapist would be present. The fee, which would include food and drink, would be fifty dollars. We were to bring our own blankets.

"What's the procedure at these meetings?" I asked the lady at the other end of the phone line.

"First of all, everyone takes off his clothes."

I was still thinking about this when she said, "You wouldn't mind that, would you?"

I didn't know whether I would.

"We shed all of our assumed labels when we do that. When clothes come off, reputations come off. We meet each other as we were born."

"Not quite. I'm afraid I might be aware of pubic hair."

"Oh," she exclaimed, "is yours scarce, too?"

The question flabbergasted me. It wasn't a matter to which I had paid any heed since the age of eleven or twelve.

"I haven't had much chance since dormitory days for comparison."

"Oh, mine is," my putative hostess continued to confess, "and I'm so self-conscious about it. But I'm determined not to let it stand between me and spiritual enlightenment."

I was sorry I had ever brought up the matter.

"After our clothes are off, what comes next?"

"There will be a full-length mirror, what used to be called a pier glass, set up in my living room. Each person stands before it, nude of course, and quite honestly tells the group what he thinks is wrong with his body."

"I don't think anything is wrong with my body."

"Well, you surely don't consider yourself a Venus, do you?"

"At my age I don't know what Venus may have looked like."

"Do you like your body?"

"Certainly I like my body. Where would I be without it? It may be the best part of me. Now, if you want me to examine my mind and soul, I can find you flaws galore. But I don't intend to stand up in front of a pier glass and run down my body. Is that what everyone does?"

"Most everyone. It does seem a little vain to approve one hundred per cent. And you do get reassurance from others."

I didn't say anything, but I imagined, Oh, it's not all *that* thin.

"What comes after the pier glass?"

"Silence. After that assessment, nothing is said. We all go into my swimming pool, which is heated to exactly ninety-three degrees Fahrenheit."

"That seems a little hot for swimming."

"Oh, there's no swimming."

"What do you do?"

"We form two lines, and each person is passed along down the line."

"Passed along?"

"We take him and swing him along from hand to hand."

"And not a word is said?"

"Not a word."

"Isn't that boring?"

"Boring? Oh, no. Usually we use words to hide behind. This is cleansing. First we shed our clothes, then by our silence we give all the hidden hurts our words have covered a chance to come out in the open and be washed away."

I declined the invitation, though I am sometimes sorry I did. What happened next I read in the paper. Somewhere between the pier-glass inspection and the 93-degree psyche-cleansing watery swing, a woman co-operating fully, doing what she was supposed to do, reached back into her past to the point where her hidden griefs and hurts were stored and found *her* particular grief: she had been raped, when thirteen, by an uncle. The memory of the violation, restored to her at the mid-point of her watery swing, caused her to begin screaming, "Rape, rape!"

She had a carrying voice, and short of drowning her, there

was no way of silencing her. The neighbors, responding to the anguished cries, called the police. The police found nine naked men and eleven naked women, one of them still screaming "Rape," in a swimming pool. It was explained to them that the rape had occurred forty years earlier. If that was the case, the cops were unable to understand the continuing uproar. It was a long time, it seemed to them, to continue grieving. On the other hand, the locale and circumstances seemed unpropitious for rape. The paper carried no more about the encounter. Hostess and guests were prominent, and further publicity was most likely not encouraged.

On the afternoon of that happening I had been quietly looking for wild burros, watching the dooryard road runner, walking in the dust to the mailbox. Had I missed something? It depended upon what I was looking for.

Of that earlier encounter group, the revival, I had had some experience. I was saved twice, which my family thought was at least once more than necessary: first at the age of seven, then again at sixteen. There was no doctrinal need for either. I was a "birthright" Quaker, since both parents were members of meeting when I was born.

I never saw my father or mother "go up front," testify, or pray aloud at a meeting. If the congregation was asked to take a stand for Jesus, they stood. It would have been seemly for me to stand with my parents, but going up front to be saved was a pleonasm.

Why did I do it? Fear, I think, was the predominant motive. Not fear of God or hellfire or of dying "unsaved," but the same kind of fear that made me test my courage by walking slowly from the house to the barn on dark nights not once turning my head or quickening my steps; the same kind of fear that made me, though convinced that the shrill cry of cicadas was the buzz of hidden rattlesnakes, continue my tramp in the foothills on hot afternoons; the same fear that made me defy the great, black, soaring buzzards of Yorba Linda, which were, I was convinced, really eagles and capable (I had read the story) of carrying off children alive to feed to their young. I was a very fearful child and for this reason had constantly to be battling my fears by doing what frightened me most.

I had reasons other than fear for going up front. I did fear making a fool of myself. That fear was probably the first reason; religion, while possibly not the last, was certainly near the end of the list of reasons. If the call had come to fight fire, volunteer to care for plague victims, or serve with the army as a sharpshooter (pacifism was not a necessary characteristic of California Quakerism), my response, motivated by fear, might have been the same: "Here I am. Take me." The coward rushes in where brave men need not tread.

Certainly there was nothing of what Andre Frossard describes in his book *I Have Met Him* as the *coup de foudre*, a total and unchanging falling in love. There was nothing of those turnabouts in life that William James writes of in his *Varieties of Religious Experience*. As a matter of fact, I'm not sure that what I had *was* a religious experience at all; though at the time, aged seven, I certainly thought so.

My great-uncle, the Reverend Lewis I. Hadley, was the revival preacher. He was an eloquent exhorter, a redhead turned white, like Mark Twain. He sang, stamped, prayed, tossed his songbook to the ceiling, tossed his great mane of white hair, sweated, reminded us that this might be our last chance to be bathed in the blood of the Lamb, reminded us that Jesus had died for us on the cross, sang solo, "Jesus is calling, calling tonight."

I liked Uncle Lewis. Once at a family reunion I stubbed an already stubbed toe. I was part of a family procession taking a walk around my grandfather's ranch, and except for falling to the end of the line of walkers for fear that the pain would make me throw up, I had made no fuss. But Uncle Lewis had seen what had happened. He came to me, put his arm around

237

my shoulders, and said, "That hurt, didn't it?" I nodded, and tears ran down my cheeks. It is so sweet to have someone pity you in your pain.

So if those two good men, Uncle Lewis and Jesus, wanted me to come to the altar and accept my Saviour, I would do so. They promised me peace if I did; and for the time being, at least, that was what I found. Kneeling at the altar, head bowed, I was a sheaf that had been harvested and was no longer torn between my fear of making that lonely trip up front and my sorrow at being a disappointment to Uncle and Jesus.

I was not treated afterward by Papa and Mama as if I had exactly had a fit in public. Getting saved was a personal and locally commendable affair, and they would never have said to me, altar-bound, "Sit down and behave yourself." But they did let me know that as far as they were concerned, I was still seven years old, wingless, and if I were truly in a state of grace, my actions would soon show it.

The revival had taken place on Saturday night. Next morning, waiting outside the church under the eucalyptus trees, between Sunday school and church, a beautiful seventeen-year-old, much admired by me, said, "Well, I hear you got saved last night." She spoke sardonically, and I, like Peter, was tempted to deny that I knew the man. It was very early for backsliding, and I found the backbone to answer her in her own words, "Yes, I was saved last night."

Getting saved at sixteen was less emotional, more like signing up for another hitch in the army. I was a member of a Sunday-school class of young people between the ages of fourteen and twenty, taught by Frank Nixon, Richard Nixon's father. Frank was an ardent and energetic teacher, and his class had outgrown one room after another until finally we were occupying the entire platform reserved, once church began, for choir, preacher, and visiting dignitaries.

I doubt that Frank Nixon could do anything halfheartedly, and this trait is appealing to young people. He was not born a Quaker (or a Republican), and temperamentally, at least, he was a Democrat and a Methodist. He was very unlike my birthright relatives, who were quiet, subdued, inclined to see both sides of every question. Frank saw one side: his; and he was not bashful about letting you know what was wrong with your side.

To offset his truculence, he had a boisterous geniality, which none of my Milhous relatives ever evidenced. He never saw my mother, a plain woman, without exclaiming, "Grace, I swear you get prettier every time I see you. How do you do it? I want your recipe. Come here and let me give you a hug."

Mama always protested afterward, "What does Frank want to embarrass me that way for?"

She may have been embarrassed, but she was also secretly pleased. No woman takes permanent offense from a man's praise, even though she recognizes its foundation in truth is shaky.

Quakers—and Frank, after his marriage to Hannah Milhous, had become a Quaker by conviction—did not believe in dancing. Frank had, apart from doctrinal precepts, his own reasons for not dancing. He did not use Dr. Johnson's language, who told his friend the actor David Garrick that he could not visit him backstage because the sight of half-clad actresses "aroused his amorous propensities"; but it was for this reason Frank told Papa that he would not dance. When his arms went around a woman, his amorous propensities were instantly aroused. Today when this kind of responsiveness is valued and whole books are written on the most effective means for males and females to induce such an arousal, Frank's scruples may seem ridiculous. But our need of such books today may bespeak our lack of understanding the strength of such propensities in an ardent man fifty years ago.

Frank was certainly ardent in his Sunday-school teaching. His cheeks flamed, and his voice trembled. He was the first person to make me understand that there was a great lack of practicing Christianity in civic affairs. Frank was, in his thinking and feeling, a political animal. He cared about what public officials did. At the age of seven, his son Richard, on the way to his second-grade class in the Yorba Linda grammar school, explained to his classmates the merits of some upcoming candidate and the issues he represented. Rusty was one of those instructed. "I didn't understand a word he said," Rusty tells me now.

"Where did a boy of seven pick up such ideas?"

"Frank, of course."

I do not remember, though he may have preached them, any partisan politics in Frank's Sunday-school classes. I was a socialist, he a Republican, and what Frank had to say about probity in politics pointed, as far as I was concerned, straight to Norman Thomas. The entire class felt somewhat as Nader's Raiders or a group of Vista Volunteers do today. Christianity was not just a matter of the blood of the Lamb, but of seeing that that blood had not been shed in vain.

So when the next revival was held in Yorba Linda, my going up front was not very emotional for me; and perhaps once again not very religious, either. All of us who had been in Frank's class had been convinced that Christians should be political, and that politics, if not Christian, should at least be ethical. Going up front was a way of making known to the church what we had already decided in Sunday school.

En route to Indiana, we ran into some evangelical appeals. They were not difficult to resist. Perhaps being engaged and in love had something to do with it. In any case, my trip to the altar when I was a Sunday-school pupil of Frank Nixon's was my last attempt at public salvation.

The sermons, none Quaker, that we happened to hear on our trip east were of a kind I had never heard before. They astonished me. Their theme was less "Be Christlike" than "Cease lusting. Stamp out concupiscence." Since, to my knowledge, I was neither lustful nor concupiscent, I felt no need for any public renouncement. There was in these Midwestern sermons an element I had never encountered in California—energetic, enthusiastic, and emotional as California preachers often were. These Midwestern preachers campaigning, in language that sometimes shocked me, against the sins of the flesh were no doubt the other side of the coin of such sins, but the coin was so thin that it was very difficult to differentiate between preaching and practicing.

# XXII

———•◆•———

When we reached Indiana, we went first of all to Indianapolis to visit Papa's relatives there. Mama removed her cold
cream, put on her switch, big hat, and Cuban heels. She looked
pale and dashing, a California rancher's wife who obviously
had never worked in the fields. Carmen and I shed our travel
pants and put on dresses. The boys wore knickerbockers. For
all that we managed, I *think,* to look like townspeople, we, the
children, entered Indianapolis with the revulsion of red Indians or Eskimos. For two weeks we had lived outdoors, with
less shelter at night than a redskin found in his tepee. In
Yorba Linda, though our lodge was permanent, we lived partially outdoors. Even when inside, wind and sand came into
our unbattened, unsteady frame house.

The only city we had ever known was Los Angeles. In 1920
Los Angeles sprawled in clean sea air over a lot of territory.
There was enough space around every bungalow for oleander
hedges and festoons of bougainvillaea. There were sunflowers,
pens of rabbits, and roaming banties in the back yards. Visitors
to Los Angeles, then and now, were put out because the residents of Los Angeles had the inhospitable idea of building a
city comfortable to live in, rather than a monument to astonish
the eye of jaded travelers.

We had never before seen a city that had to keep itself alive
during snowy winters with roaring furnaces and base-burners

loaded with coal. The soot from these wintry fires had begrimed and blackened the buildings. People cooked with gas
or coal; their homes were still lighted with gas. The city, to our
fresh-air noses, stank. Our grandfather's small home, where
cooking, heating, and lighting were done with gas, smelled
putrid to us. I had read in novels of heroes who made the
removal of "a soot" from the heroine's eye the prelude to more
intimate contact. I had never really believed in this soot emergency. I had never seen soot. I had never read of it except
when it got in a heroine's eye. I thought it the invention of
romantic novelists for purposes of furthering love-making
scenes. To my astonishment soot was real. It got in my eye—
no heroine; and no hero nearby to help get it out.

We were put to sleep at night in feather beds. They smelled
like stale feathers, and they reached up around us like energetic old hens preparing to mother us to death. Like Indians,
we preferred the floor.

I had had a water problem en route to Indianapolis. Arrived, I had a food problem. There were no dieting fads fifty
years ago. Getting fat was accepted as part of maturing and
aging. My determination to keep my weight, which at 125 was
about right for a girl of five feet seven, was a fad of my own,
akin no doubt to my daintiness kick on the way east and
abetted, I'm sure, by the sight of aunts and great-aunts who had
left 150 far behind and were forging or foraging on toward the
second hundredweight. My water obsession had done nothing
more than make my deprived parents mad. My refusal of food
did something worse: it hurt the feelings of our cook-hostesses.
It wasn't that the food didn't taste good to me. I could easily
have stored it all away. But I had Max constantly in mind. At
175 I would probably have broken his thigh bones when I sat
on his lap, if indeed at that weight I was ever again invited to
sit there.

The trouble was that all of our relatives were putting their
culinary best feet forward, which meant not only quality but

quantity. There was Southern fried chicken and gravy, baked home-cured ham, hot biscuits, mashed potatoes, candied sweet potatoes, creamed peas, corn custards, and jams, jellies, pickles, and piccalillies without number. Desserts without number, too. Coconut and devil's food cakes, hazelnut cakes. Apple-custard, lemon meringue, and sweet-potato pies. All at the same meal. I refused second helpings, a slap in the face to any cook-hostess.

"What is the matter with the gravy, Jessamyn? Is it too thick? Is the chicken a little too brown? I'm afraid the bottom crust of the pie is a little soggy."

Papa said, "There is nothing wrong with the food, Aunt Nellie. Jessamyn wants another helping."

So I had another helping, and except for Rusty, who could eat his second helpings and help me, unobserved, with mine, I *would* have gone home the size of a great-aunt.

There was nothing, beyond washing the dishes, for a girl my age to do. I located the nearest library and walked through dropping leaves of late September, past the ugly, begrimed buildings, to take out books that had been held by many soot-darkened hands. I had never seen books before so soiled, so worn. I carried my armloads back with me, depressed with city living, depressed with talk about relatives I didn't know, and with talk of local crimes that repelled me. A woman two blocks away had had her nipples chewed off by an attacking stranger. I listened with horror. Perhaps my stanchion explanations were, if anything, too idyllic.


We moved on from Indianapolis into the deep country of Southern Indiana. California-raised, I did not then see its beauty. It was, to eyes accustomed to California, unkempt, scraggly, melancholy. In Southern California land was either cleared or uncleared. When a rancher there set about preparing his ten- or twenty-acre ranch for orange trees, he did not leave patches of mesquite and sage and cactus to clutter up his orchard. There were forests in California, great stretches of barren desert and mesa, foothills covered with buckbrush; but where the land was cleared, it was cleared; where it was cultivated, it was cultivated. There was no intermingling, as in Southern Indiana, of nature's leftovers and man's planting. California was one-or-the-other country: wild or tamed. The effect in Southern Indiana was of inefficient husbandry, of men who had tried and failed, or who had given up. It made me sad: houses unpainted, rail fences collapsing, barns neglected, windmills with blades missing, upping blocks overgrown with four-o'clocks. Even the gloomy woods lots were not filled with straight-standing trees but were clogged with brush and undergrowth.

Not until I returned in 1945, after the publication of *The Friendly Persuasion,* was I able to see the beauty of the land about which my mother had talked. But I was a thoroughgoing Westerner by then, and much that was characteristic of "back East" (actually the Middle West) was still strange to me—and not appealing.

This time I came by train from Indianapolis (without any stop with relatives) to North Vernon. My eyes were on stalks, my heart in my mouth. This time I had no dream to insulate me from reality. I was coming to a countryside I had written about, with nothing but my mother's memories and my own imagination to guide me. What would I discover? That her memories were undependable and my imaginings faulty? It is one thing simply to "go home again"; it is another to return to a home you have attempted to re-create and to check your fabrication with what, while you were writing, you believed to be real. "Writers," the wife of a poet said to me, "see nothing. They have to build a world of words, otherwise they are homeless." I had built a world of words. It was perhaps a mistake to try to find its counterpart, let alone the identical countryside, which had been so real to me in my imagination.

On the train between Indianapolis and North Vernon I

scanned every face, listened to every word I could overhear. These people were Hoosiers. I had put words into their mouths, expressions on their faces. I was begging them not to make me a liar, though I was stupid to do so. A hundred years and two World Wars had gone by since "my" Hoosiers had lived. Faces and ways of speech had changed.

I had ridden from San Francisco to Chicago on a train that carried a number of recently freed prisoners of the Japanese. Would what they had experienced ever be erased from their faces?

An ex-prisoner burst into my roomette as the train neared Chicago, crying, "Let me stay here. Talk to me. Don't leave me until I have to get off. Help me. Help me to face them. For God's sake, talk to me."

What could I say? My impulse was to put my arms about him and rock him like a child. He was probably in his twenties, though he had the face of an old man who had suffered. I didn't do so for fear he would collapse completely. I was afraid to talk to him about his experiences or about why he feared those he would meet. I held his hand and talked to him, in a drowsy, singsong voice, of my own fears. I don't think he cared about or perhaps even heard what I said. "I wrote about people I didn't really know, and now I must see them, and I am afraid to see them and the land where they live. I am afraid, but I must do it."

"Afraid" was probably the only word he heard. He nodded and nodded as if I understood *him*. I didn't even understand myself. When the train pulled into the station at Chicago, he saw those he had said he feared and ran out of my roomette with a great groan of misery—or rejoicing. He was immediately surrounded by those who were not afraid to clasp him, and he stood with his head pressed into a woman's shoulder, while others embraced them both.

The ex-prisoner's face showed where he had been, but it was not open to further hurt. The faces on the train from

Indianapolis astonished me with their openness. They were round, pink and white, and—naked. The Western face is not always a Marlboro face, but it is more of a mask than the faces of small-town women of the Middle West, homeward-bound after a day of shopping in the city. The Western face, even in 1945, was sun-tanned; the make-up on it was not there for china-doll prettiness; the dark glasses were already a habit. Caucasians say that all yellow faces, all black faces, look alike. There may be some truth in that for them, though the truth lies not in the likeness of the faces but in the mask that darkness spreads over a face to eyes accustomed to the higher visibility of white. I had never seen faces so visible. I felt shy about looking at them. Much more was revealed than anything the pier glass could have reflected. Unco-ordinated, not streamlined, exposed, primitive. So good (the good faces) I felt like a peeping Tom. The faces of people who had never acquired public faces, who were wholly unaccustomed to arranging their faces for sight-seers. My mother's face.

In the late afternoon the train moved through a landscape still sorrowful to me: lone houses, rocky hillsides, streams running on, oblivious to whether the frame houses on their banks were being raised or were tumbling down, wild woods, then a patch of corn—everywhere evidence of struggle, of man's hanging on by his toenails. Or so it seemed to Western eyes. By the time the train reached North Vernon my hands were sweating as much as the ex-prisoner's; and no one to hold them, either.

I got off at the station with my multiple bags (I go prepared for *anything*), and a young black man asked me if I needed help. I said, "I need a taxi. Would you get one for me, and then help me with these bags?"

"Where are you going, ma'am?"

"To the Hotel Metropole, here in town."

"Ma'am," said he, "if you take a taxi, you'll clean overshoot the town. The Metropole's right around the corner."

I felt at home at once with him. His face was more Western than those I had watched on the train. He could also joke, which is the traveler's Esperanto.

"Can you help me carry these bags to the hotel?"

"That's what I'm here for. Looks like you're moving in, bag and baggage."

The hotel lobby was filled with spittoons and traveling salesmen. At the desk a returned soldier, drunk and maundering, was registering. He carried with him a souvenir samurai sword. There were no porters or bellboys. "Would you mind helping me up the stairs with these things?" I asked my fellow Westerner.

"You'll be all night getting up if I don't."

Every eye watched us, or me, as we went upstairs. I don't think a woman had been in that hotel, except for one purpose, for years. Once in my room, the young man immediately opened a window, which was the first thing that needed doing. As he did so, the train on which I arrived pulled out of town, Louisville-bound, a few feet under the opened window. Steam and smoke poured into the room. The young man opened the second window. "Don't let it bother you. It's what you call steam cleaning. Shoots in one window and out the other."

Next morning I wrote my father and mother.

"First, my most sincere congratulations on your early removal from this dump. This is Sunday morning, 10 A.M. I am ensconced in a 1902 chicken-wire bed (the springs are of chicken wire) in the Hotel Metropole, North Vernon, Indiana; lighted, believe it or not, by a coal-oil lamp. I got in about seven last night. A nice funny young Negro helped me get my bags from the station to the hotel, then up to my room.

"I didn't know a hotel room like this existed anywhere: dark, dirty, grimy, stinking, sordid. It looks like a dive, a joint. The wallpaper appears to be covered with crushed spiders; ex-white, ex-lace curtains are at the windows; the ugly linoleum lies on the floor in flakes like the earth at the bottom of a sinkhole in a drought; stand table and dresser, once varnished, are now scarred and chipped; the transom is held open by two rolls of toilet paper; the ceiling is twenty feet high; there are two windows, one useless, since it is two feet from another building, higher than the Metropole. Someone has taken advantage of this two feet of walled-in space to make a chicken run. Crowing roosters add a nice rural note to the sound of trains, which balked, shunted, switched, and snorted all night long. Behind a paper-thin wall the couple next door did the same thing.

"I had breakfast this morning in an establishment that couldn't be duplicated for darkness and number of flies any-place in the Western Hemisphere. The hot cakes were this thick [I drew a picture, two inches thick], the sausage cakes this big [another picture the size of a dinner plate]. Price: forty cents.

"The waitress at breakfast said that she was leaving her job and going home to New Orleans. Her brother was coming for her and her effects in a wagon. She would be vacating her room in a nice house on Jennings Street.

"P.S. After breakfast I got a taxi to drive me around so that I could see the town and a bit of the surrounding country. The taxi driver, a fat old fellow with a cane, spits tobacco juice through a two-inch slit in the window and calls me sis. I like him just fine. He said, 'Sis, the Metropole Hotel is a bad place. And all those eating places around it the same. I'd clear out of there as soon as possible or sooner, if I was you.' I was glad to hear that I wasn't just being fine-haired in thinking I'd landed in a den of iniquity, and a dirty den at that.

"For the first time in my life I am in a town where 'the wrong side of the tracks' has some visible meaning. This is a railroad town, as you know, and the Metropole is definitely on the wrong side. Down there in that section I saw for the first time in my life, outside of the *National Geographic*, two- and three-year-olds running around with nothing on but shirts to their hipbones. In the eating places there were so few teeth nothing solider than a pancake and gravy could have been chewed. At noon, I went into a grocery store to buy some milk and crackers to eat by the roadside.

" 'Do you want Clover Cream or Yellow Gold milk?' the clerk asked me.

" 'I don't know the difference,' I said.

"The girl gave me an incredulous stare. 'Where have you been all your life?' she asked.

" 'California,' I said.

"Her look then conveyed her amazement that I knew about bottled milk at all.

" 'Are there many cows in California?'

"This is a subject I'm not up on, but, a true Californian, I said, 'More than in any other state.' I hoped her next customer wasn't a Texan.

"On the right side of the tracks is another town—entirely: a Booth Tarkington town of stately elms and maples, spacious lawns, ten- and twelve-room wooden houses, with porch swings on their newly painted verandas and stained-glass windows over the window seats at the bend of the stairs, which spiral to the bedrooms. There are, in fact, two towns here—wrong side and right side, as is not possible in our little railroadless California towns. There are really three towns, I suppose, since the *Banner Plain-Dealer,* I see, has a special section devoted to news of the 'colored,' and called just that—Colored—so that no one reading of the death of Sarah Webster will be misled, thinking that a white soul instead of a black has gone home to its Maker. I haven't discovered the location of 'colored' town yet."

After some more talk with the waitress and with her friend who works in the five-and-ten, I went to see the waitress's about-to-be-vacated room. The five-and-ten clerk worked eight and a half hours five days a week, and on Saturday she worked twelve hours. For this she received seventeen dollars a week. Before the war her pay had been twelve dollars a week.

I rented the room the waitress was vacating, a large front bedroom, upstairs, with windows on two sides, for $3.50 a week. It was no palace, but after the Metropole it seemed to be. There was a feather bed, in which I learned to wallow, and an enormously enlarged picture of my landlady's son, who, like Thoreau's brother, had died of lockjaw. After I had heard the details of his final suffering, I seemed to see in the unearthly rigidity of the enlargement the onset at the age of nine of a *rigor mortis* that did not actually occur until four years later.

The upstairs was occupied by three other roomers: Mr. Bland, an ex-jockey who worked at the railway-express office; and two itinerant road workers. The road workers I never saw except when they, hunting the bathroom at night (there were no locks on the doors), would stumble into my room. They looked like ghosts in the long white underwear they slept in. A few nights of my screams of "Get out of here!" taught them the direct route to the bathroom. The ex-jockey, soothed by his bottle, slept the night through like a baby, or without at least any wandering in the hallway.

I stayed in my own room night and day, leaving it only in the late afternoon to explore the countryside on foot or with rented car. My solitude, except for the company of books, pen, paper, and the lockjaw boy, was complete—a mistake, I now think. I should have been downstairs with my landlady.

She was an extraordinary woman, aged seventy-two. She called Mr. Bland, in his mid-fifties, "that old jockey," and, compared with Mrs. Hogan, he was old. Mrs. Hogan had been born Rose McCarthy, of Nebraska, Indiana. She had also been born a Catholic, but a priest, when she was a girl, had made the mistake of giving her a kiss in the midst of her playing of "Adeste Fidelis" on the parlor organ. The kiss she might have forgiven—Rose McCarthy understood that the flesh, even of a priest, was weak—but she could not forgive the unseemly interruption of that holy hymn by a man whose vocation it was not only to profess but to protect the holy. She left the church and became a Methodist.

She went to church twice on Sunday, morning and evening. One Sunday afternoon between church services she went to a double-feature movie. Before going to church that evening she said, "I reckon I ought to go up to the mourners' bench this evening. I saw that old Costello in his drawers this afternoon. Didn't see him long, but they shot the pants clean off him, and I watched him as he ran away for as long as he was in sight. Had a good look toward the end." She was quite aware of the *double-entendre*.

Rose's sister-in-law, Emily Hogan, aged eighty-two, lived with her. One morning Rose waited impatiently for Emily at church time. Emily finally came down the stairs.

"What's been keeping you so long?" Rose asked.

Emily held out her ration book. "Mr. Bland's been explaining my points to me."

"I bet that's just your alibi."

"You watch out, Rose McCarthy. You'll be putting bad ideas in my head."

A friend of Rose's had moved to Cincinnati. Surprisingly (to me) Rose asked her, "Are there many birds over there in Cincinnati?"

"God, no," her friend answered. "Hell's no place for singing."

Of a neighbor, Rose said, "She's so spendthrifty, if she had five dollars she'd buy a bank."

I hired a driver to take me at one o'clock one day out to Graham Creek and to pick me up again at five. I was writing another book with Southern Indiana as its locale, and if any bird or flower, leaf or cloud was wrong, it wouldn't be because I hadn't looked. This driver was not my fat friend, the tobacco chewer, but a man whose blue eyes were pebbles picked up out of a glacier. He, too, called me sis. When we arrived at Graham Creek he said, "Who're you meeting out here, sis?"

I was loaded down with notebook, pens, pencils, *The Flora of Indiana,* and a bag in which to take specimens I couldn't identify home to Rose—equipment planned, I suppose, to his eyes to hide my clandestine intentions.

"Sir," I said, "I hope to meet out here whippoorwills, bobolinks, sumac, pawpaws, goldenrod, and the famous cumulus clouds for which the Midwestern states are famous." My pebble-eyed driver left immediately; thinking, I suppose, Crazy as well as loose. He picked me up at five according to our agreement, and we rode, unspeaking, back to town.

With Rose I found my tongue. "In California," I said, "I could walk from the Oregon border to the Mexican border and no one would ask me a question like that."

Rose listened calmly. "Back here," she said, "a lady goes to the woods for only one purpose."

Well, that's the way those gloomy woods lots had looked to me all right, and I flounced upstairs not bothering to leave the flowers and weeds I could not identify with Rose.

Indian summer was departing, and the winds and rains of true autumn were beginning. "What am I doing here," I asked myself, "alone under the picture of this lockjaw boy?" The wind cried around the Gothic turrets of the turn-of-the-century house. Maple leaves, pasted against my rain-streaked windows, gave me stained glass through which I could see the red-brick Methodist Church down the street. The look of the land had changed, but the wind was unchanging. It had cried to four generations of my ancestors its November warnings exactly as it was crying them to me.

Four generations! Before that visit I had known of only three. When I took *The Flora of Indiana* from the library, the librarian, concluding that I was interested in local history, put *The History of the Vawter Family* in my hands. "There's a lot about the old days in here. Vernon was founded by a Vawter." I took the book back to my room. There, sitting in the wicker rocking chair under the picture of the lockjaw boy, I turned its pages. Suddenly I saw, spelled wrong, my own name, "Jessamine West." So I was a Vawter!

Mama—so great was her regard for her father, Jesse Milhous, and his preaching mother and grandmother, all Quakers—had led me to believe that I would see their names writ large across the land. It was not so. Those Quakers had moved westward, leaving behind no sign of their occupancy except for a few inconspicuous gravestones and three white clapboard houses. The McManaman name I saw on a bridge. The Clark name was all over the state. The state itself, called Indiana, could be said in a way to have been named in honor of my Indian great-grandmother. In a graveyard outside Vernon I saw a Vawter headstone, which said, "John Vawter, Proprietor of Vernon."

All, Quaker and non-Quaker, had been on the move, always westward, for unnumbered years. The Milhouses, not yet Quakers, left Germany for England in time to fight with Cromwell against the Royalists and to be rewarded by Cromwell with land seized from defeated Royalists in Timahoe, County Laoighis, Ireland. There the Milhouses became Quaker converts of William Penn. In 1729 they set sail for Penn's colony in America. The Griffiths, with whom they were to intermarry, had come to Penn's Woods with Penn himself in 1682.

The Vawters, Church of England people, had arrived in America ahead of the Milhouses. They had a traceable European history, while my other ancestors were still engaged in their unrecorded wanderings in England, Wales, Ireland, and Germany.

The first Vawter of record was a Norman—Reginald de Vawter—who settled in Plymouth, England, in 1108. From England, a Vawter moved westward in 1685 to Culpepper County, Virginia. There he became a Baptist and a revolutionary, fighting in 1776 (was it his Norman blood?) once again against Old England. From Virginia the Vawters moved to Kentucky; from Kentucky, in 1806, to Indiana. There seemed to be a great attraction between Vawters and Wests. Vawter girls married Wests, and their descendants turned around and married Vawters again.

The Vawter pattern here was the Milhous pattern, except that they stopped short of California. I was a backtracker. Our ancestors explored the land, and we, their descendants, on the edge of the Pacific now explore our ancestors.

Philip Slater, in *The Pursuit of Loneliness,* finds in Americans the loneliness of long-distance runners. "The avoiding tendency lies at the very root of American character. This nation was settled and continuously repopulated by people who were not personally successful in confronting the social conditions obtaining in their mother country." They valued "money over relationships." We also, Slater tells us, when we behave "like good American consumers," tend "to satisfy our emotional needs with material products . . . to turn to things rather than people for gratification."

I had not read this when I lived on Jennings Street, but I think about it now, having done a bit of running away myself, here to my cabin on the river. Slater's statements can be both questioned and contradicted. The Quakers who "ran away" were not running after "things"; they discarded things by the score: fashion in clothes, a double way of talking, pictures on their walls, color in their attire, weapons, war, class distinctions, wigs, fancy buttons, musical instruments, bells, steeples, the marriage ceremony, Christmas, and names for the days of the week and the months of the year. The Quakers *did* "run away"; perhaps Slater would have run away, too, had he spent as many years in prison as had seventeenth-century Quakers in England. But once here, it is true, they kept on running. Were they after "things"? And did they lose "relationships" because they ran? "Things" may have been involved. They had settled, my Quaker ancestors, in one of the most beautiful but unfertile sections of the United States. They were nurserymen, and in California they sought and found better soil and climate for their trees and shrubs. But they moved en masse—three brothers, two sisters, with their families and their aging mother—to a Quaker community in California. They did not lose "relationships," and they did leave behind many "things": buggies and churns and sadirons and the tin-doored food safes and two-wheeled carts and crocks for "putting down" sausage.

My mother in California was lonely, honing for Indiana. The Norman Vawters, in wet and windy Plymouth, no doubt were lonesome for friends back home in France. What's so bad about loneliness? I am lonely here in my cabin on the Colorado. I was lonely on Graham Creek, Sand Creek, Rush Branch, and the Muscatatuck. Accept your loneliness. It's part of the human condition. It is a usable commodity. "Take it sadly home to yourself," Emerson said, "there is no co-operation." "It is not that we love to be alone," Thoreau wrote to his friend Blake, "but that we love to soar. . . ."

Thoreau's loneliness did not result either from running away or from accumulating things (unless you count the world itself and all its attributes a thing). And he was lonely. No man keeps a journal the length of Thoreau's who is not lonely. The person who loves solitude must write. Or pray. There is so much to tell. The lonely man, if he does not have a God, must find a reader.

My loneliness in Bigger Township in 1945 was deeply layered with people. Only one layer was "alive": Rose, Emily, Mr. Bland, the road workers in their underwear. The people in the book I was writing were coming alive to me. Each day I saw them more clearly, heard their voices more distinctly. And the voices of my ancestors (some of these voices I could remember) were thick on the winds of that autumn, liquid in the cold rains that were beginning to fall.

Two houses built by these roving ancestors still stood: Mount Glad, which John Vawter, "Proprietor of Vernon," had built in Madison; and the house built by my great-grandfather Joshua Vickers Milhous in 1854 at Sycamore Valley Nursery. Mount Glad, since my father didn't talk about his people, I hadn't known about. Sycamore Valley Nursery and its house were well known to me. Great-grandfather Joshua had died when my mother was ten years old, but she had often visited her grandfather's home and was happier there than with her own mother.

I went to visit the house of my great-grandfather. I touched the pillars that supported the front porch, for I had seen pictures of my mother, cheek against and arms around one of those pillars. I drank from the spring of cold sweet water at the back of the house. I climbed the stairs and looked out over the rolling wood-covered hillsides, which were beginning to look beautiful to me. Easterners are repelled by the bareness of Western deserts and mesas, by the brown, treeless foothills. It takes some time—and for some, eternity is not long enough —for them to see beauty in an earth without foliage. They are like persons who, accustomed to clothing, find the naked body unappealing. I was like a savage, accustomed to nakedness only, who had not yet developed a taste for the trappings of leaves and vines and trees. Looking out of Great-grandfather's upstairs bedroom, I was beginning to be able to take in and appreciate simultaneously both the swell of a hillside *and* its sassafras-red, hickory-yellow, and maple-gold raiment.

I wrote to Mama of what I was seeing, and she replied, "I always have an awful homesick feeling for the old Indiana woods of my little girlhood. Your description of it seems the most like it of anything I've heard of since leaving Indiana."

Then she went on to write of the Indiana she remembered: not the autumn by which I was surrounded or of Great-grandfather's nursery but of spring and her own home. "In the old Indiana woods the wild blackberry bushes bloomed. There

257

were wild flowers, blue Johnny-jump-ups, we called them; lamb's-tongue, a yellow flower, butter-and-eggs, white and yellow, little spring beauties, which carpeted the woods. And now the soldiers tramp all over the old farm, over the 200 acres of the strawberry patches, the red and blackcap raspberries and currants and gooseberries, tame blackberries, peaches big and sweet by the bushel, to sell and to keep; plums, apricots, the big grape arbor with red and black grapes, not to mention the apples by the hundreds of bushels. Ah, that was living! Now tramped over by the soldiers. And early death even then for the women who tried to keep up with the work—and Grandma always tried, as she said, to 'keep ahead of the work.' No electricity for power to churn and wash and even sweep and iron. Grandma's arms and body did all of that—and she died at fifty-six. Well, what a letter! Love ever, Mama."

I went out to the 200 acres over which the soldiers were tramping. The house I remembered—the Big White House—had been destroyed. But I could see where it had stood, for the ornamental trees of a nurseryman's planting towered in domes and pyramids above the scrub that had replaced the currants and gooseberries, the black and red grapes. I could not get near those domes and pyramids. A high wire fence, with metal plates saying, STAY OUT. JEFFERSON PROVING GROUND separated me from the house where I had lived a good part (perhaps the best part) of my first six years. I could see the ruts of the lane still persisting, which led to the house, and down which I had walked on the way to the Fairmont School when I was in the first grade.

But I could not climb that fence. What was being proved behind it? The efficacy of shells, of mortars, bombs, explosives? Behind that wire wall, named for Thomas Jefferson, civilized man of Monticello, was a place where the technology of killing was being tested. No H-bombs would be dropped there, but the hardware for lesser catastrophes (equally deadly if you were the target) were tried out where nursery stock once grew.

Such was the penalty visited upon my great-grandfather for his temerity in choosing beauty over utility. Acres in Iowa and Illinois, capable of introducing their bumper crops of corn and wheat, were not chosen as a proving ground for explosives. But this rolling, shallow-soiled earth, responsive to the coaxing of a skilled nurseryman but useless for bumper crops of basic cereals, was not too good for blowing up. It was as if war—which had spared all of my brothers, uncles, grandfathers, father, not because they were Quakers but because they were always too old or too young to fight (except for the Revolutionary War Vawter and the Civil War Clark)—had leveled a blow at my grandmother, Mary Frances. She was not the nurseryman; the budded peaches, the grafted apples, the Lucretia dewberries, were none of her doing. But the house, with its stenciled curtains, its ingrain carpets, its footstools covered with velvet and hand-painted with scenes of bulrushes and swans, was hers; she had died at fifty-six after furnishing it, polishing it, and keeping it running. And war had blown it up. In the Jefferson Proving Ground it had been proved that houses are truly built on sand.

When the wind blew around my windows as I sat beneath the lockjaw boy, it was to my ears not the Santa Ana of my girlhood, but the autumn gales Mary Frances listened to as she flew, tiny and black-haired, upstairs and down, "body and arms" supplying the power that ran the farmhouse. I had the strange sensation there on Jennings Street that the wind I heard was truly the wind she heard, and that I was to some degree truly Mary Frances, not Mary Jessamyn. And that may be true; both by nature, and probably even more by nurture. There was no discernible outer likeness. I had the frame of my Indian ancestors, and, like my West grandmother, could hoist a 100-pound grain sack. I had, alas, neither the coloring of the black McManamans nor that of the bronze-skinned, black-haired red men. I was sandy and freckled like the Millhouses and perhaps the Norman Vawters. But inside the unlike exterior there *was* some likeness. Mama said I was a Mac (not, as I have said, her highest praise). She said, and meant it as praise, that I had been a mother to her. But she had resented a good deal of the mothering of her own mother, and perhaps of mine, too. A daughter's mothering is slightly perverse.

I don't know how much of my first six years I spent with my grandmother. More perhaps than with my mother. What Grandma ran in addition to a farmhouse was, I understand now, a one-child head-start school. I was her first grandchild; she was a born teacher. She had taught until she was married at twenty-eight, and she had had a long vacation from the profession she enjoyed. At two days she had me drinking from a cup. At two weeks I was eating bananas. At six months I was talking. At nine months I called snow "pretty flowers." At twelve months my grandfather was paying me a nickel for every ten minutes I could keep my mouth shut, or so I am told. At two I drove a horse and buggy. At four I made biscuits and sausage gravy. There is no telling what I might have been doing at ten or twelve if my association with my grandmother had not ended when we left for California when I was six.

Alone in my boardinghouse room, gazing west toward Maple Grove Nursery (Grandma named *every*thing: when she came, dying, to California, she called her home there Sunnyside), leaning against the proving ground's wire fence, I thought not of the grandma of my first six years, but of the young Mary Frances, called Dollie by her people and Mollie by her husband's. I lived in my mind her life not as "Grandma" but as the young wife of Jesse G. Milhous, and the mother of Walter Raymond and Grace Ann. (Mama hated her name. She wanted to be called Gladys Juanita. Thank God "Jessamyn" struck her as exotic enough.)

Mary Frances was the oldest of four girls and two boys. One of her sisters died of tuberculosis. The old Celtic defenselessness against the tubercle bacilli was in the Mac blood. Her son, Walter, died of consumption. Myron lies ill with it now.

I knock on wood for myself as I write the word. Her sisters who lived had babies very soon (perhaps too soon?) after they married. There was going to be none of that for Mary Frances. The wonder is, Grandpa's being the bashful and cautious fellow he was, that there were any children at all—early or late. Mary Frances was a very pretty girl, perhaps a little formidable in her determination not to be a "wild Mac" and in her schoolmistress authoritativeness; but she must have had admirers before twenty-eight. I cannot believe that Grandpa, with his "queer turn," his freckles and sandy hair, his lopsided smile and wandering nose, stirred her hot Mac blood. More likely his piety and steadiness aroused her own pedagogic respect for these virtues. As the thinking of the time went, she was probably thought to have married up, not down. She was not, I believe, a woman who could have married any other way.

Once Mama wrote, for me, an account she called "Childhood Mornings," which begins like this: "In summertime up at 4 A.M. Papa made fire in wood cookstove. He and two or three hired hands go out to barn, throw down hay, feed horses, slop hogs, give corn to hogs and horses, milk the cows. Grandma and hired girl get breakfast, grind coffee, put it in pot with the day before's grounds, let it boil up, then settle it with an eggshell. They fry ham or shoulder or bacon *always*—perhaps eggs also. *Always* gravy, fried potatoes, and big loaves of home-made bread, a big slice of sweet yellow butter from the cellar, and jelly and jam and preserves, three or four varieties at least. A plate of doughnuts or cookies. Or a pie. A big pitcher of thick cream and a pitcher of cold milk for the children.

"After breakfast Mama fed her little chickens, 100 to 300. She fed her little turkeys with boiled egg or smearcase, as my Grandmother Milhous always called clabber cheese (cottage). Lots of little chickens died with the gaps. I learned to pull the worms out of their throats with a twisted hair from a horse's tail.

"In the spring I had to creep after the turkey hens to see

where they had hid their nests. This job of trailing an old turkey hen was counted good work for me. Mama never let me do much work inside—she said I got in her way. I enjoyed the detective work, through dew-laden high grass, clear to the edge of the woods—by an old log, maybe in a hollow stump, maybe in the orchard by an old apple tree, or in a blackberry patch.

"After Mama had fed the chickens and turkeys and the girl had the breakfast work done, if it was washday they'd pump water, carry it in buckets to fill up a boiler on the stove. They'd put a big iron pot of beans—green or dried—and a hunk of sowbelly to cook while the washing was going on. They washed the clothes on a board in a tub, then they'd boil the white clothes and rub them on the board once again. They'd maybe not be done until 3 P.M.

"Dinner was at 11:30. Men were starved by then, nothing to eat since 5:00 or 5:30. There would be cabbage slaw to go with the beans, some pies, rhubarb probably. Probably hot corn bread.

"After breakfast, washday or not, Mama would always have to skim the old crocks of milk into a big three-gallon jar to be churned. The clabber went on the back of the stove for cheese.

"The women made all of the clothes for the family then. My mother made all of our dresses, skirts, and underwear, everything except our outside winter coats, which were bought. The dresses were made with five to seven gores in the skirt, and the basque had five separate pieces in the back and fitted tight in front. Everyday dresses, even, were clear to the floor. A farm woman would not have had her ankles showing for the hired man to see for anything. Pregnant women always wore a 'Mother Hubbard' and did not appear on the streets or in their own front yards like women do now.

"When cows were all fresh in the spring, the women had to churn every day in the old dasher churns, up and down, up and down, until the cream 'broke'—then go easy and gather the little chunks of butter. Hot water would make the butter come quick, but the butter would be soft and white. Our mothers would have to watch us; hot water shortened the tiresomeness of churning. But Mama and all the mamas would say, 'No, no. No more hot water. Keep churning.' Your father says he used to tell his mother that his back ached so (and it did). But her reply was always, 'Keep churning. Stop it the way you started it.'

"There was a big washing-up job on the milk crocks, cream jars, churn lid and dasher, strainers, milk buckets. In summer everything was washed and scalded and put on a long home-made table in the sun. That 'sweetened' them, Mama said.

"We had a big garden. Most of the neighbors' gardens were made by the women. But none of the Milhous men—my father, Grandfather Milhous, or Uncle Frank—had their women make gardens.

"We washed dishes on a long kitchen table. Under the table was a shelf. On the shelf was an old pie pan, with a piece of soft brick and a pile of brick dust. The knives and forks were scoured at least once a day."

I have an entire notebook, seventy-five pages, both sides of each page filled with Mama's continuing account of the work of a woman's day in the 1890s. Soap making, cider making, apple-butter making. Drying of apples, corn, peaches. Knitting stockings, crocheting edging for pillow shams, shimmies, night-dresses, drawers. Gathering fox grapes, hickory nuts, butter-nuts, beechnuts. Making sorghum, maple syrup, yeast, twisted paper lamplighters. Pickling peaches, pears, cucumbers, corn. "Putting down" comb honey, lard, fried sausage, sauerkraut. They braided rags for rugs, then sewed the braids together. They cut rags into strips, which were then woven into "rag carpets." They raised the geese and plucked them for feather beds. They pieced the quilts in patterns fanciful, strange, and sweet; put them on frames and quilted them with tiny decorative stitches; they made and tied the comforters. They put together and embroidered the mosaic of the many-colored crazy quilts.

They did all this and more. Mary Frances did all this, "with her arms and body," with her little hands (her wedding ring goes just to the first joint of my little finger). She did it all without the joy in her husband that lightens a woman's work. This judgment is based not on words overheard, but on happenings I can myself remember.

Before we left for California, the three West children—aged six, four, and two—were seated on the lawn in front of the sweet-pea vines that climbed up a trellis to the outthrust semicircle of the parlor's bay window. There we were planted in the afternoon sun to have our pictures taken as a keepsake for Grandpa and Grandma when we were far away out West. We were dressed, if not in our best, at least in something better than everyday. Myron was in a Buster Brown short-kneed suit; Carmen and I had ribbon bows as big as our heads tied to our hair. All were barefooted in the warm weather, but the bare feet of only two can be seen. Two, with heads thrown back, are laughing. One stares straight ahead, unsmiling. All this I can check to this day in the greatly enlarged picture Grandma had made of the scene. Why was I unsmiling? Why were my bare feet not visible? Out of so many things forgotten, why does one happening stick?

As soon as we were seated in front of the sweet peas and the picture taker was stationed in front of us, Grandpa, with a couple of sheets of newspaper, began to "act up." He crowed like a rooster, with the newspaper flapping for wings; he pranced like a horse scared by the newspaper he himself held; he soared like a kite, the chances being he would never come down again. No one had to tell us to smile. Grandpa, his stringy mustache flying, was the funniest sight we had ever seen. We were laughing our heads off. Me, too, until Grandma said, "Jessamyn, pay no attention to your grandfather. Keep your eyes on me." I did so. It was one of the lessons I had learned in her head-start school. Grandma didn't think Grandpa was funny, and perhaps it *was* silly for an old man with a droopy mustache to hop around like a chicken with its head cut off. Perhaps? It was, of course, silly. I looked at Grandma in stern and complete agreement.

"Jessamyn," she said, "you're too big a girl to have your picture taken barefooted. Tuck your feet under your dress." I tucked them under.

In that picture today I can see those two invisible persons: the man dancing, the woman commanding and disapproving. What was there in her, or in him, that made it impossible for her to take pleasure in his efforts to make three children laugh? Some affront deeper than his antics on the front lawn? I was the means by which she said to him, "All, you do not control. You may make these babies laugh, but see, this older one does not find you funny. She ignores you. She gives her attention to me."

I did. I wanted to please Grandma, even at the expense of hurting Grandpa. On the evening of the day before we left for California, I sat beside Grandma at the supper table. She let me put my head in her lap and I lay there, with the tablecloth hiding me from sight. She stroked the hair behind my ear, a habit of hers and a caress I have always liked.

The head-start school was not discontinued when we left for California. Books and magazines arrived; poems clipped from papers or copied by hand were received, with instructions to memorize and recite. I don't know how this was managed. Did I go to my teacher and say, "I have memorized a poem my grandma sent me, and she wants me to recite it"? However it was accomplished, I recited them. They were, for the most part, "Let us now be up and doing" poems. "My head is bloody but unbowed" poems. "If you can keep your head when all about you" poems. Poems of strife and resistance, and finally, if nothing could be done, "When God sorts out the weather and sends rain, why, rain's my choice." I was a kind of Western outpost in that battle, perhaps against her very nature, that Grandma was waging. She sent me dresses—natural linen embroidered in red; lavender soisette smocked with white silk—to wear when I recited. She always wanted to know how I did. Did I forget? Did I speak up? Did I stand straight? When the reports were good, she must have felt that the center still held, though at the edges there were signs of fraying.

She died saying, "Hurry, hurry, hurry," not to a nurse, not to anyone at her bedside, but to herself—little Doll McManaman, who had accomplished so much less than she had planned.

Her funeral, for some reason, was held in the parlor of her East Whittier home instead of in the Friends Church a few yards down the country road; the same parlor where later Grandpa and I sat while he played his evening concert on the Victrola. Perhaps she had wanted it that way. The parlor was filled with objects of her own making. She was not born a Quaker. The Quaker meetinghouses may have looked as desolate to her as they did to Thoreau; perhaps she preferred for her last appearance above ground something more homey than those wooden sheds where the Quakers in silence sought God.

She died in early February, the time of year in California when the narcissuses called Chinese lilies are at the height of their blooming. They are more heavily scented than any other flowers, except perhaps honeysuckle, tuberoses, regal lilies, night-blooming jasmine, and gardenias. The parlor was banked with them the day of Grandma's funeral, and I still cannot smell them without thinking of her.

To understand the nature of the relationship between Grandpa and Grandma, I have thought that it would help if I knew what he called her. Did he go along with his family and change her name to Mollie? There is now no one I can ask. When I stayed with him after her death, he spoke of her to me as "your grandmother." But even as I have been writing, I remember that once when visiting him to avoid a trip, I went into the sitting room to tell him that supper was ready. He was sitting at his desk in the warm gloom of a summer twilight—the desk where he kept his accounts: how many boxes of lemons and oranges picked, how much paid out for fumigating and fertilizer. He faced the west windows, so that I could see the tears on his cheeks. In his hands he had a penwiper made by Grandma, a half-dozen heart-shaped pieces of absorbent material covered with red flannel, with a ribbon bow at the top and embroidery around the edges. Grandpa was turning the penwiper around and around in his hands; as he did so, he said, "Doll. Doll."

The dissatisfaction, if there was any, in the marriage was mostly on Doll's part. She did the waiting. The one who is waited for, even if he is berated on his tardy arrival, can take it as a sign of how much he has been missed and wanted.

All that I saw in 1945 and more I could have seen in 1920 (though the Jefferson Proving Ground had not yet been established, Grandpa's house still stood). I didn't, because I was living in the future. In 1945 I lived perhaps too much in the past. I was Vawter and Clark and West and Milhous and McManaman. And every one of them dead. I had their ears for hearing, their noses for smelling, and almost their tongues for talking. Added to this handicap for true recognition of the countryside about me were my Western eyes, accustomed to the spare and the ordered, the one-or-the-other land—mountain or plain, orchard or desert. I couldn't accustom myself to what rain does to a land. I was like a woman who had never seen a man with a beard: I wanted more face and less hair.

My eyes since then have had more training in landscapes. I have moved further from (though in some ways closer to) the dead. The wind that blows around my cheekbones when I walk back there now is not so loaded with the past. The intermingling of fields and woods is not now the fracture of some

267

universal law. I see *it* now and its own beauty; not as Mama's remembered dreamland of fairy-tale snow and play party songs of "weevily wheat to bake a cake for Charlie" or as anti-California, a land gone mad with vines and trees and shrubs and bushes.

A land's beauty lies not in what is remembered about it, or in what coincides with the known. Its beauty exists in itself for eyes clear enough to see it.

It is full spring now on the Colorado, and because I have been away, though only in remembering and writing, I seem to have returned from a long journey and am surprised to find the season so far advanced. The bees have harvested all of the nectar from the cottonwood blossoms and are off elsewhere making honey. The cottonwood domes are quiet and melancholy without that frenzy of buzzing: abandoned apartment houses.

What would Grandma have made of this cabin on wheels? I think she would not have liked it. When she, in the last months of her life, lived in California at Sunnyside, Mama invited her to ride in the foothills in back of Grandpa's ranch. Grandma rejected that offer with the spirit she never lost. "Ride in the hills? What do I want to ride in the hills for? Take me to town. I want to see people."

Hills were nothing but mounds of earth, and earth was where she was bound. People were what she was leaving. Mama felt the scorn in Grandma's voice, a scorn she never forgot. Take a dying woman to look at the hills? It was stupid to have suggested such a trip. Mama, all of her life, felt the edge of her mother's scorn. Would Grandma scorn me now for my hermit life? It would be difficult for her to understand. She wanted to see people, and there are not many people here.

Like it or not, a life away from the farm would have been impossible for her. There are Mom and Pop grocery stores now. The farms then were Mom and Pop farms. Who would

cook for the hired hands, feed the poultry, dry and can the
fruit, if she left? Apart from that, sitting under a half-dozen cottonwoods, in the midst of a desert cut through by a river, would
not have appealed to her. The idea of wilderness then was of
a landscape that needed changing. The wilderness was a place
to be improved. It was a potential food factory, which, when
cleared and planted, would start producing. A hundred years
ago in the United States, a world so occupied with people that
wilderness would be valued in and for itself could not be
imagined. The mountains of Switzerland, until the romantic
poets came along, were simply land too perpendicular to be
productive. Perpendicularity plus snow has now become valued
in itself: a sight to see and an angle to use.

Apart from what would probably be her low regard for
unproductive ground, Grandma wouldn't have appreciated the
loneliness. Son would not have crossed her threshold twice.
That first "ass-hole" would have sent him flying, with a pail of
cleansing mop water in his face.

Thoreau wrote, "I feel the necessity of deepening the stream
of my life. I must cultivate privacy. . . . I cannot spare my
moonlight and my mountains for the best of man I am likely
to get in exchange."

Grandma would take a human being, particularly a young
human being, instead of moonlight and mountains any day.
She saw the young of her day accomplishing for America the
equivalent of today's young—but in reverse, that is, the de-
greening of clearing and plowing.

Mama didn't feel the need of "deepening the stream of [her]
life" with privacy, either. She wanted no privacy that excluded
Eldo. She could not have gone anywhere without him; though
a Walden on Wheels the size of a nutshell, with plenty of room
for cooking and not too many square feet to clean, would, with
him, have suited her to a T.

# *XXIII*

———◆———

S. B., the editor of *The Whole Earth Catalog*, says, "I have lived in a 22′ Airstream with wife and two cats for most of three years now. It's the only high-tech home I've found which is at all lovable, indeed comparable to the way some ocean-going boat owners feel about living on board. The Airstream is an elegant honest design-job. It makes us conscious (and parsimonious) about using water, gas, power. It frees us from owning land and encourages us to live in wilder places. It is proof from fire, earthquake, floods (drive away), and mice, except what the cats bring in and lose. It's one of the few domes I know that doesn't leak. When we travel with it wherever we go we're going home. One more month of production and we're hauling ass out of here to the desert."

Loren Eiseley might have been speaking of all Cancerians—Thoreau was one, and I also—in *The Invisible Pyramid:* "There is a certain virtue in the sidelong retreat of the crab. He never runs, he never ceases to face what menaces him, and he always keeps his pincers well to the fore. He is a creature adapted by nature for rearguard action and withdrawal, but never rout.

"The true poet is just such a fortunate creation as the elusive crab. He is born wary and is frequently in retreat because he is a protector of the human spirit. . . .

"One of the most perceptive minds in American literature,

Ralph Waldo Emerson, once maintained stubbornly: 'The soul is no traveller.' Emerson spoke in an era when it was a passion with American writers to go abroad, just as today many people yearn for the experience of space. He was not engaged in deriding the benefits of travel. The wary poet merely persisted in the recognition that the soul in its creative expression is genuinely *not* a traveler, that the great writer is peculiarly a product of his native environment."

But if you are able to take a considerable part of your native environment with you? I understand S. B.'s appreciation of his trailer because "wherever we go we're going home." What I don't understand is his choice of home. It is true that the Airstream, a cigar-shaped aluminum Zeppelin with wheels, is lighter to pull and has less wind resistance than more conventional trailers, but I myself do not care for a home shaped like an air-raid shelter. I do not care for the curved wall inside or, outside, the look of a tin can waiting recycling.

In our twenty-five-foot Traveleze, the dining and sleeping ends are both almost wholly glass. One end of S. B.'s Airstream is occupied by the bathroom, tub-shower, wash basin, and monomatic toilet. This room, quite naturally, is not all glass. No one employed in a bathroom has much time for or interest in the outside world, and even less in being an object of interest to passers-by. The Airstream bedroom is placed in the middle of the trailer—where the Traveleze bathroom is placed. A bed is useful for a number of purposes, not the least of which for a reader and writer is reading and writing. And while doing this, I don't want, when I lift my eyes, to see, as S. B. must in his Airstream, the kitchen sink. I want to be able to see, as I can this very minute, two hawks, one road runner, and my cobblestone mountains, with a strange band of cobalt blue separating them from the mass of thunderheads higher in the sky. What's the point of "hauling ass" in an Airstream to the desert if, once there, the Airstream seals you away from what you came to see?

I have asked myself if what I want in a trailer is comparable to what early auto owners wanted in a car; that is, something that looked like a buggy. Do I want a trailer that looks like a house? If I'm going to use it as a house, why not? When I'm outside I don't need to fence the outside farther out. But I'm enough like S. B. to enjoy the feeling of going home. No matter how far you go, home is always where you're going with a trailer.

This is the time of the spring winds. They come from the desert, but they blow across the unmelted snow of mountains and are not yet hot. The trailer is a boat. It rides the wind waves. I wish I had an anchor to throw out. The wind hits us end-on, not sideways. Otherwise, with Yorba Linda memories, I could hunt me the equivalent of a weir box. I watch two, three tumbleweeds running a ghost race: ghost because they're dead; nothing but skeletons. But these skeletons carry seeds. There's a generation gap between old and young in the tumbleweed family, too. Two rotund old heavyweights are unable to make it over a cairn of stone, but a lightweight youngster bounds across and is on his way to sow his wild oats.

After lunch I went into Mesquite. The supermarket there carries everything, including crutches. I could spend a day in the Market Basket listening to people talk—and almost did.

"All of my life," one woman said, "I have wanted a hand-cultured pearl."

A large fat Indian boy carefully touches a set of plastic chessmen. He is joined by his still larger father and mother.

"Look at this, Mama," the boy says.

"That's just for boys," the mother says. Are they looking for a gift for Sister?

"Oh, no, Mama," the boy tells her. "Girls play it, too." They buy the set.

At the paperback-book rack a woman says to the elderly clerk, "Oh, you old goat, you! You have found me that book by my darling. And in big print, and cheap. Robert W. Service. Oh, my lost world. Save it for me, will you? I can't buy it till payday."

"She's got a wonderful head on her shoulders," one man tells another. "She saved two hundred dollars on the drapes alone."

"Before the war," a lady tells the checker, "I used to enjoy the forbidden." The checker seems to understand what she's talking about, but there, with groceries paid for, the conversation ends.

"The forbidden?" I repeat to the checker, but she is a trustworthy confidante. "Yes," she answers, and begins counting aloud the price of my purchases as she rings them up on the cash register.

In spite of the wind, spring has brought more boats and water skiers to the river. Rivers have always been used for commerce and pleasure, and I shouldn't be so affronted by these speeding water bugs and whooping skiers.

The noise made by most machines is ugly. We are an eye-centered race. Manufacturers concentrate on producing articles that will be attractive, they hope, to our eyes. No one advertises a car or a boat by saying, "It sounds good." Not much about smell good, either. Look good, feel good. Sound good? Forget it.

The Colorado is too elegant, elderly, and wise a stream to be made into a playground of this kind. But it is the noise I resent most.

I am annoyed only by insects that are noisy. A quiet bite from a flea would not be resented, I think. But then fleas don't bite me; mosquitoes find me unappetizing; wasps explore and smell without stinging. I can endure the promenade of a quiet fly. Live and let live is my motto, until the noise starts. First I shoo and herd. Then, if they refuse to go out of opened doors and window, I swat. Except for bees, wasps, hornets, yellow jackets, and bumblebees. These I cannot kill. But noisy mosquitoes and flies that will not shoo or herd die. The only kind of sniping I could understand (though never approve) would be a double-barreled-shotgun blast at an outboard motor.

At dusk the wind died down; the skiers went home; the boats were docked. I lit the coal-oil lamps for their scent, not for their light. I sat at the table, where the view is of the Colorado, the river, and of Arizona, the state. Down the hall I can see in the lighted bedroom the shelf of books above the windows there. The votive light burning on the table under the windows illuminates the books and sends a little star beam onto the water. The mud hens rolled up the sunset sheen off the river long ago. I have books to read, paper to write on, beside me on the table. I gaze at a picture that Papa, aged eighty-seven, painted. It is a scene of his own imagining: one of Oregon's snow-covered peaks reflected in water. An old Chinese might have painted it. Now and then a small stray wind, lost from the day's blowing, hurrying to catch up, whistles by the corner of the trailer. I can hear the occasional rustle of the cottonwood leaves. Slowly my eyes open wider, my mouth loosens, my fingers separate. I do not think anything. I know that I am in the midst of perhaps not beauty but of delight. The room opens as do lilies in those motion pictures that show the process of their blooming from tight bud to opulent blossom. That is it. The room blooms, grows quieter, brighter, and I am part of the room and partake of its qualities.

There was a knock at the door, and the room shrank, darkened, became the kitchen end of a trailer. It was Son at the door, with a donation of Lily's chocolate gingerbread. Also to check the refrigerator. Also to say to me, "I never told you the bad part yet."

"No, you never did."

"You said, 'Come over and have a drink and tell me the bad part.' "

I didn't remember the "have a drink" part, but I may have said it. "Okay. What do you drink?"

274

"Everything."

"I'm not going to bring out everything. Settle on something."

"Vodka. I'll have a Salty Dog."

I'd never heard of a Salty Dog. As Son made it, it was vodka with a couple of teaspoons of water. Son sat across from me at the table.

"If I'd said, 'I'll tell you the story of my success,' you wouldn't have been interested, would you?" he asked.

It would have been harder to believe, but I didn't tell Son that.

"But the 'bad part.' That grabs you, doesn't it?"

It didn't exacty grab me, but it would perhaps explain some things.

"Don't feel ashamed of liking the bad part. That's what all women like to hear about men. The bad part. Then they can help them. At least feel superior. That's what women need. They need something to make them feel superior. 'Tell me the bad part,' they say. Once they've heard it, they say, 'Shit, he was nothing but a worn-out prick, anyway.' "

From here on, that is, two-thirds of the way through the first Salty Dog, Son's language became the language I have read and understand but cannot write or speak. You do not write French by putting a couple of French words in every sentence. Obscenity has its own rhythm and construction. You do not use an obscenity as a substitute for another word. As in all foreign tongues, you do not really use it well until you think in it. Son thought obscene and about subjects for which his vocabulary was suited. Obscenity was his language as another man's might be Swahili. It was no more personal than that. Telling him to use another language would be like telling a Chinese that you found the Chinese language repulsive.

While I was thinking about these things, Son finished Salty Dog number one and mixed—it didn't take much mixing—Salty Dog number two.

"Are your teeth false?" he asked as he sat down.

"No," I said, surprised to be asked. "They might look better if they were."

"No, no," he said. "Better none at all than false. False is a lie," he said. "If there's one thing I can't stand, it's a woman with false teeth."

"Men, too?"

"Men, too. Falsies are okay. I don't care if a man wears a corset. But what's inside your mouth ought to be your own."

"I would prefer that myself."

"You're waiting for the bad part, aren't you?"

"Maybe there isn't any. Maybe that's just in your mind."

"If it is, I'd be crazy. That'd be bad, wouldn't it?"

"Yes."

"That's what my wife had me committed for."

I didn't ask him which wife. I hadn't been able to sort them out—and I didn't think it mattered, anyway.

"Committed to an insane asylum?"

"The bughouse."

"What for?"

"Not a thing. I was celebrating a little. I got a little noisy."

"Can that be done? If you get drunk and noisy, can somebody put you in an asylum?"

"I told you she did it, didn't I?"

"Did they come and get you?"

"Did they come and get me? Came and got me and put me in a strait jacket."

"A strait jacket?"

"You don't think I went willingly, do you?"

"What next?"

"What next? I went to bed drunk and woke up sober. So then they come in with all sorts of tests. What day was it? What month? Can I touch my nose? Do my knees jerk when hammered? What does an ink blot look like? I told them that. I gave them some new ideas about ink blots. Ideas that had never entered their heads before. They say one word, I say what it reminds me of. I gave them some new ideas there, too. Then they gave me an IQ test. Know what my score was?"

"No."

"Know what's average?"

"Around one hundred."

"Know what's high average?"

"One twenty-five or so."

"Know what's a genius?"

"By IQ test?"

"What're we talking about?"

"One forty and above."

"I was one fifty-seven. A genius. And in the nuthouse! That's all my wife knew to do with a genius. Send him to the nuthouse! They loved me there. They really loved me. They wanted me to stay and work there. The head psychiatrist, he wanted me to stay. 'I've got nuts in here,' he said, 'working for me. And guys like you roaming the streets. It don't make sense.' "

"You weren't roaming the streets, were you?"

"When they picked me up, yes. Hell, yes. I was drunk. What do you expect?"

"But at the . . ."

"Nuthouse."

"You sobered up?"

"Hell, yes. The place ain't a bar. I got soberer and soberer. The more sober I got, the better grades I got on the tests they gave me. My answers were so good I ran right off the chart. I was asking the shrink questions now. I tell you, that man loved me. He said, 'There is one thing I will say for you. I've never known anyone like you.' That's what he said. Would you agree with him? Have you ever known anyone like me?"

"No," I said, "I never have."

"I knew it. I knew that would be your answer. I knew it before you opened your mouth."

"What happened next?"

"At the nuthouse?"

"Where else?"

"They set me free. What else could they do? Sober as a judge and smarter than they were. 'Get gone,' is what they said. So I did. With a friend I had made there. He was loaded."

"Drunk?"

"No. Money. Drunk came next. Did we get drunk! Best drunk I ever had. Best friend. He wouldn't let me pay for a thing. That's the way I am, too. If I have money, it's yours. That man loved me. There wasn't a bar in town we didn't stop at. Or a drink we didn't try. You don't get sprung from a nut-house every day. Then I went home to tell my wife she'd had a genius locked up."

"How did she take the news?"

"She had the house locked. Tighter than a drum. Didn't forget a window. But she did forget the garage. I got a pick out of there and broke down the front door. Hacked it down."

"Wouldn't the back door have been easier?"

"It's my own house. I don't have to creep around to the back door like some delivery boy. I didn't ask what was easy. I did what as a home owner it was my right to do. I went in my own front door."

"Was your wife there?"

"Yes, sirree, Bob. She was there. On the phone. Screaming her head off to the police to come and get me. I'd broken out of the nuthouse. And here I was *graduated* from the nuthouse—with honors—and come home to celebrate. What kind of a wife is that?"

Normal, was what I thought. What I said was, "Did the police come?"

"They did. Lady screaming like she was being raped. They wasted no time. They burned rubber."

"What did they do this time?"

"Back to the nuthouse with me."

"Didn't you have dismissal papers—or something of that kind?"

278

"What do you think? I go around carrying a certificate of sanity? 'Hear ye, hear ye, this man is no nut'? I tore up those damn papers the minute they gave them to me. I didn't want to go around with papers saying, 'This man is a released nut.' I may be a released nut, but I'm not that crazy."

"So back you went."

"Not so fast, not so fast. The police can't arrest a man for breaking into his own home. He can burn it down if he wants to. He can't claim insurance, but he can burn it down. I know that. They know that. They don't have a warrant. I'm in my own house, with my own wife, talking with a bunch of guys with an average ninety-seven IQ. Counting in a high one or two to pull up the average. Who's going to swear out a warrant? Not the neighbors. I'm not disturbing anyone's peace."

"Smashing down that door must have disturbed the peace a little."

"That was no fault of mine. My preference, if I'd been given it, would've been to walk in by turning the doorknob."

"What was your wife doing all this time?"

"Keeping her mouth shut like I told her to. But she got out one squeak: 'He's broke out of the nuthouse.' That gave me an idea. So I said, 'That's right, boys, I did. She's telling the truth. And she sure ought to know. She's the one had me put there. Take me back to where I belong, boys.' So I walk out into the lights, hands up, because I don't want to get shot by any of those trigger-happy morons, and they take me back to the nuthouse."

Son now began laughing. Actually he had been laughing, and me with him, during much of this story. I don't know why. He had his Salty Dog to make him merry; I had nothing. But the story, which wasn't actually very merry, made us laugh. It wasn't the "bad part," as I had imagined it might be, though being drunk and disorderly and having your wife commit you to a madhouse isn't what can be called really good. But the really bad part was whatever had in the past—perhaps forgotten—occasioned that drunk, was setting the stage now for another, and was using me both as audience for a recital of the past drunk and as witness to the one that was developing. *That* was the bad part: the drunkenness itself and what had caused it. Perhaps he had thought he could tell it. He had decided, or the Salty Dog had decided, or my laughter had decided him, to be entertaining; not to go down to where the awfulness lay.

The recital was becoming less brisk. The second Salty Dog was finished, and the third was in hand. "That will be the last," I told myself. "There's no nuthouse near here."

"Did they welcome you with open arms back at the nuthouse?"

"Welcome me? You've never stayed in one of those places, have you?"

"No, I never have."

"Well, you don't just walk in the door of a nuthouse, hand the bellboy your bags, and say, 'Show me to the bridal suite.' You got to be certified."

"I thought you were certified."

"Well, I was decertified. I told you that this is a complicated story. Don't let your mind wander. You're a writer. Writers have the idea that they're the only ones whose words they need to pay heed to. Let anyone else start a story and their minds wander."

"I'm paying heed."

"Okay. Back to the nuthouse. The cops say, 'We got an escapee.' Well, the guy at the door isn't the vice-president in charge of escapees. He can't tell an escapee from a cop. So he calls the vice-president in charge of escapees. The vice-president has just come on duty, and he don't have a list of escapees at hand. While he is going to get this, the head shrink comes by, the one who knows I know more about blots than he does. He throws his arm around my shoulders and says, 'Son, we'll kill the fatted calf.' The cops now think they have two escapees. The head shrink sees this, and he says, 'I am Doctor Walcott, in charge here. What are you doing with this man?'

" 'He's an escapee,' the cops say. 'We're returning him.'

"The doctor looks at them like they're a herd of monkeys strayed to a human habitation. 'This man,' he says, 'has an IQ all of yours added up together and multiplied by two couldn't equal. He was dismissed from here several hours ago. He was put here from spite. Take him away.' The shrink gives me another hug. That man loves me.

" 'What'll we do with him?' the cops ask.

" 'That's your problem, not mine. You picked him up. I didn't. Good-bye, Son.' "

"What *did* they do with you?"

"Took me home. No door. No wife. No nothing. She'd packed all the silver, packed all the blankets, packed all the Corning ware."

"She's a fast packer."

"She is. But she'd missed a bottle I had hid. Hid it in the bottom of the flour bin. She didn't ever cook, so the flour bin was a sanctuary. I could've hid a sidewinder there, and she'd never have been bit."

"So what did you do then?"

"Nobody but a writer would ask a question like that. It don't take any imagination to know what I did next, and you're trying to imagine something. Here I was, no door, the wind whistling through the house, my Corning ware gone, and too smart for my own good. What would you do under those conditions if you found a bottle at the bottom of the flour bin?"

"Find a better place for it."

"Shit. It wasn't vodka. I don't like vodka. It was pink Chablis. A half-gallon jug."

"You had a big flour bin."

"I live big. I told you that, didn't I? There's nothing small about me. I've got my failings, but that's not one of them. I shut the kitchen door, turned up the oven. For heat. Got me a sofa pillow she'd somehow missed and made myself comfortable and had a drink."

281

Son reached for the vodka bottle, which he had brought to the table.

"Time, Son," I said.

His reaching hand paused.

"What do you mean, 'Time'?"

"I mean, bar's closed. Bar closes at ten. I'm going to bed."

Son, who had been truculent, turned pleading: "Don't cut me off. Don't do that. One more drink. That's all I need. Don't cut me off. One more and I'll go home."

"I'm a working woman. I have to work tomorrow. This is my bedtime."

"You go. I'll be quiet as a mouse. One more drink and I'll creep out. I'll lock the door behind me. Don't cut me off."

I could say no, grab the bottle, and run for Lily's. I could say no and run into that truculence again. I had never encountered drunkenness before. Refusing Son "one more glass" made me feel like a hostess telling a guest one slice of bread was enough. Selfish.

I said, "Okay. I'm going to bed. The bottle is yours."

I locked the door between kitchen and bedroom, though the act seemed melodramatic. Son was going to stay where the bottle was. I put on my pajamas, put my wax earplugs in my ears, and went sound asleep.

At three o'clock I awakened, cold. The coldness awakened me, but once awake, I held my breath trying to identify a strange sound. Spry, who ordinarily sleeps on one of the divans in the kitchen, had been sleeping in the bedroom. He was at the door trying to listen or smell or see under the door into the other room. The sound was scarcely human; I had never heard such a sound before, but I knew at once what it was. It was Son, drunk. When I opened the door to the kitchen, I saw also why it was cold. Son was lying on the floor, the outside door open, his legs hanging outside. Had he started home and collapsed? My first idea was to get him completely outside, then get Lily. The noise Son made was a combination of snore, bark, and strangling. It is bad enough to have an uninvited man spend the night on your kitchen floor. That's the end of solitude. But an uninvited, noisy man kills something else as well: quiet. And it isn't the noise of a speedboat or hornet, a normal noise. Son sounded as if he might be dying. Then I remembered what Mama had said about Old Silver and decided that what I was hearing had nothing to do with death.

Thoroughly alive, Son was, nevertheless, a dead weight. I could not pull him out the door. I could surely have pulled a 180-pound sack of potatoes through the door. But human flesh, though unconscious, seems to have a will of its own. Where it falls it is determined to stay. I gave up trying to get Son outside the door and tried to get him inside. Finally, using Son's buttocks as ball bearings, I was able to swivel him so that he lay parallel to the doorway and wholly inside the trailer. I closed the door and lit the stove burners for warmth. I put a blanket over Son and let Spry, enormously interested in the sounds Son was making, stay in the kitchen.

At seven Son was exactly as I had left him at three, asleep or unconscious and still making the same sounds. I took Spry with me and started for Lily's, mad. By the time I got to her place, I wasn't mad. I was fifteen years older than Son and fifteen years younger than Lily. As these things go, I felt that Son and I were more or less of the same age, while Lily was an old lady vastly my senior and deserving my sympathy and help. She was standing outside her house, holding a feather up between her eyes and the light. I didn't know whether she was absorbed in seeing how the sun looked through a feather or was simply examining a feather. She was small, something the shape and color of an acorn. But she had burst her shell. Son may have been a sorry, even a fallen, oak, but Mother was still productive. She hadn't given up.

"Son is over at my place," I said. "Drunk."

"Bad?" she asked.

At first I didn't understand her; then I did. "Bad" meant

breaking down doors, in need of a strait jacket, disturbing the peace.

"No."

"Did you take your keys?"

"Keys?"

"To your car."

"No. He passed out. He's been passed out on my kitchen floor all night."

"You shouldn't have given him a drink."

"You should have told me not to."

"I should have. I didn't think you'd have liquor. I thought he'd be safe talking to you."

"I'm sorry."

"We don't even have coffee at our place. We never have had liquor. It's nothing he picked up at home."

I wondered how it would have been if Son had been brought up in a society where being unable to hold your liquor was thought messy; not a society where getting drunk was thought to be manly or defiant. Getting drunk was one of the ways you showed you weren't a mama's boy. And who were the boys who needed to demonstrate this? Mamas' boys.

"I used to pray," Lily said, "that Son wouldn't be in an accident. Now I pray that he'll be in an accident and have to have both arms in those metal cradles for six months."

Lily was stroking her feather to pieces. "People say I never gave Son a chance to stand on his own feet. Well, I'd get a telegram from his wife saying that the children were starving to death. What could I do? Let them starve in order to teach Son to stand on his own feet? I'd send for them, of course. I'd take care of them. So Son came to depend on me. Did that make him a drunkard?"

I didn't know. I don't know what makes a drunkard. I knew that it didn't take much drink to make Son drunk. The one more drink he'd had after I went to bed had finished him off. The vodka bottle was about as full when I came out at seven as when I went to bed at ten. Vodka's potency explained the pink Chablis. Son knew he didn't have much tolerance for alcohol. This intolerance also explained why Son looked so healthy. His liver had never had to cope with much alcohol. I don't understand the effect alcohol has on some people. I am unable to imagine the alteration it makes in their world—an alteration so great and so desirable that they never want to return to the nonalcoholic world; so superior that they give up that world entirely in order to live wherever it is that alcohol takes them.

Thinking of this, I asked Lily what I had no business to ask: "Was Son a preacher at one time?"

Lily didn't seem offended, though the question was personal and prying.

"Son was never ordained. And he was in the army for a long time. But what Son was, and is, is a faith healer. He did preach and sing songs. But what brought people to him was his healing."

"How did Son think he did this?"

"Think? He knew. Through God, of course. It wasn't any power Son had in himself. Son knew that. Didn't you ever hear of Sonny McCurdy and his healing service?"

"No, I never did."

"He was on radio."

"I never heard him."

"There are people alive today who wouldn't be alive except for Son."

"Why did he stop?"

"He lost the power."

"Was the drinking before or after?"

"All the time. I think God made a bargain with Son. He said to Son, 'Stop drinking and I'll restore the power.' But Son's bullheaded. He's sweet, but he's bullheaded. He said, 'Restore the power and I'll stop drinking.' So it's a standoff."

"Did Son tell you all this?"

285

"He doesn't have to tell me. A mother has intuitions about her own flesh and blood."

"Where did he pick up all of his bad words?"

"I have never heard Son use an indecent word. To those he respects, Son's language is pure."

"Son doesn't respect me, then."

Lily answered this in a different, matter-of-fact tone. "He was in the army for ten years. Seventeen to twenty-seven. Then faith healing was kind of like show business, you know. People flock around you to see you perform. Son wore elevator shoes, a white suit, a white hat, and a tie made of rattlesnake skin. People thought he was Alan Ladd."

"Son told me."

"He was better-looking than Alan Ladd. He didn't tell you that, did he?"

"No."

"It's hard to keep your mind on God with people thinking you're Alan Ladd. Especially the women."

"So he lost the power?"

"I don't know. He won't try any more. He sure can't help anybody lying over there on your kitchen floor, senseless."

"Does this happen often?"

"Worse, sometimes. The easy times are when he goes under. When Son heals, he's possessed of God. When he drinks, he's possessed of the devil."

"Then he hacks doors down with an ax?"

"Did he tell you about that?"

"Didn't he tell you?"

"I was there. They sent for me. I sat inside with him while the cops played their lights on us. I talked him out of having a shoot-out. Reason was on his side, you know. Law, too. A man can enter his own house. He gave up finally because he saw that to get him they'd have to kill me, too. He was too tender-hearted for that."

"How am I going to get him off the kitchen floor?"

"You can't till he wakes up."

"Comes to" seemed the more likely word to me.

"When he wakes up, give him black coffee. He'll want liquor. Don't let him have any."

This rubbed me the wrong way. Son might be a faith healer, but I was no Florence Nightingale. I had something else to do besides wait for him to come to, serve him black coffee, and keep the liquor away from him. Then I looked at Lily. Well, I could do a little for her, anyway. She had had a quarter of a century of this at least, and this morning she had a feather she wanted to paint.

On the way back to the trailer I wondered what Thoreau would have done if Margaret Fuller, in some transcendental frenzy, had passed out on his cabin floor. One thing was certain. Two things, in fact. First, he wouldn't have liked it, and second, there would have been no liquor to trigger her into unconsciousness. I also thought on the way back to the trailer, You keep saying to yourself, "What would Thoreau have done?" I remembered that there was a man by the name of Sheldon who had written a book called *In His Footsteps*. Meaning Christ's, of course. "Is it your idea to write a book called *In His Footsteps,* meaning Thoreau's?" The answer is no.

I was infected then, as always, with the blight of the two-seeing eye. Though Blake says, "May God us keep/From single vision and Newton's Sleep," single vision and Newton's sleep are treasures I would like. As it was, I marched toward the trailer happy neither in my role of good Samaritan to the fallen nor in my desire to be alone.

Son was just where and as I had left him: unconscious and apparently strangling. I stepped over and around him in order to make coffee for myself, which I took to my room to drink. There I tried to read. I had not read long when there was a cessation of sound in the kitchen. When I opened the bedroom door, Son opened his eyes: clear, forget-me-not blue, the eyes of a man whose life is blameless and whose sleep has been

287

sound. (Was that the world to which liquor transported Son?)

"What time is it?" Son asked.

"Eleven. In the morning."

"That was quite a nap."

"It was. About twelve hours too long."

"What're you mad about?" Son asked blandly.

"I'm not accustomed to uninvited guests."

"Accustom yourself," Son said. "You may be missing a lot."

"That's obvious. I like what I've missed."

"Knock it off," Son said. "What harm did I do you? Did I burn down your trailer? Wreck your furniture? Rape you?"

"You disturbed the peace. You sounded like you were dying. You let the door open, and the wind blew out the furnace. You vomited."

This last piece of information interested Son. "Did I? I haven't done that in twenty years." He sounded as pleased as a man who has discovered the fountain of youth.

He got up from the cold vinyl floor like a man off a Beauty Rest mattress. "Did you put this blanket over me?"

"I did. I thought it might shut you up."

"Why didn't you put me outside?"

"I tried."

I gave him a cup of coffee. "This is what your mother said to give you."

"Did she mention a Bloody Mary?"

"She did. She said to see that you didn't get one."

"What did she think of my spending the night over here?"

"She appeared used to such outings."

I refilled his cup. I wondered that he didn't want to go to the bathroom—to wash or to empty his bladder. He looked remarkably tidy, pink, and euphoric. I felt as if I had been through a long sickness—with whom? Not with Son. He hadn't been sick. Just away.

Lily came to the door as he finished his second cup. "Son," she said, "I've made hot soda biscuits and scrambled eggs for you."

288

I thought Son might blanch. Not at all. He put his cup down, said, "Thanks for the coffee," and followed his mother down the path toward their house.

That evening I went for a walk along the riverbank, something I don't usually do. I see the river all day. In the evening I walk back into the threatening desert canyons. A half mile upstream I found Son sitting on a beaver-gnawed stump and gazing across the water. This surprised me. I had never seen Son looking at the landscape before.

I said, "Hello," and intended to keep on going.

Son said, "You in a hurry?"

"Yes."

"There's something you don't understand."

"There's a lot."

"Okay, smart aleck. I'm leveling with you. You want to be a writer, don't you?"

"Yes."

"Try to understand people, then. You're nowhere if you don't."

"I'm trying."

"You think I drink for fun? You think I like that stuff? I don't even like the taste of it."

"You didn't sign a contract, did you?"

"Maybe. Maybe I did and didn't know it. What I wanted to say was if I don't drink, I don't have any personality. A couple of drinks and I've got personality. What would you do if you were in that fix?"

There was no very easy answer to that question; or, rather, there were three or four easy answers but none that I thought both true and suitable. I didn't want to get into a discussion of what constituted "personality." I didn't know. Son had maybe been a "radio personality," and having lost "the power," thought that he had lost his personality as well. I was pretty sure that personality didn't come out of a bottle, and if it did, Son was a lot better off with the personality he had before he took a drink. God knows what wit and wisdom Son had believed he was displaying during his "nap," or before, when he told how he was loved at the nuthouse and was a problem for the police.

While I was wondering about what answer to make, Son said, "I suppose you think you have personality?"

"I'm a person, so I suppose I do. It may not be very attractive or appealing, but I suppose I have some."

"Don't you want to improve it?"

"I've thought about being a better person. I never thought about improving my personality."

"Think about it," Son said.

"Okay. I will."

I was glad for the dismissal. I was over my head: the effects of liquor, the nature of personality, the loss of power. Son's calico cat, the one he calls Lonely, who had been there all the time but invisible because it is the color of sand and pebbles and weeds, jumped up onto Son's lap. Spry wanted to chew it up, but I had him on a leash, and I pulled him behind me along the riverbank.

# XXIV

---

The last trailer Papa and Mama owned is parked under a kumquat tree at the bottom of the slope below Rusty's house. I don't know how many they owned before it. This one isn't entirely outmoded. It could probably still be put into running order. Possessing it is not the same as owning the covered wagon your great-grandparents used in crossing the plains. It's not even the same as having a wheel from your grandfather's farm wagon to serve as a gate. It is not in a class with Grandpa's 1915 Hupmobile in the garage or Grandma's frames for knotting comforters in the attic. Nevertheless, for me, for whom trailers became real only a year ago, it is an antique, far older than its age; older to my mind than the van of the 1930s into which Papa and Mama stepped and didn't stop traveling until they had covered 11,000 miles. The van wasn't a trailer. It was a peculiar vehicle, but like the chariot, the stagecoach, the convertible, it had its own horsepower; though, come to think of it, chariot and stagecoach were in their own way "trailers": the horsepower was separate and up front.

The trailer that is now parked at Rusty's was parked more than once in our driveway. The last time was in 1958, when Papa was seventy-nine, Mama seventy-six. They arrived after a drive of 450 miles. Papa, briskly and without resting, uncoupled car and trailer, placed his wooden blocks against trailer wheels and under the trailer hitch.

Mama was a Gypsy who hated to leave her caravan for more conventional, though less convenient, lodgings. In the trailer everything needed was at hand. In her daughter's home the bathrooms were down a hall, bedroom and kitchen were not adjacent, and the light switches were God-knew-where. I didn't understand then her reluctance to give up the known for the unknown. The trailer as home was an idea that I had not yet entertained. It was a conveyance, smaller than a truck or a train, to be sure, but on the same order; a disinclination to disembark was just as peculiar. I had sat in, ate in, chatted in, that trailer. I was not blind. I could see that it contained all the conveniences needed for housekeeping. But I had never occupied it imaginatively as a home. It was thus that Mama lived in it when traveling, and she was reluctant to leave it for a guest room even in her daughter's home.

Trailers apart, this reluctance was characteristic of her. She was always more comfortable as a hostess than as a guest. If someone had to be displaced, she preferred it to be you, which doesn't mean that she wasn't mad about travel. Thoreau was a man she would have found mighty unappealing. She thought my early journals, which she made no bones about looking into, uninteresting. "There's nothing in them but scenery and sunsets," she said. One characteristic she shared with Thoreau: she didn't care to be beholden. In the trailer she served her own food and put her knees under her own table. There was nothing Thoreau liked better—except scenery and sunsets.

This month, April, is spring by name but summer by climate. Spring, if you forget names, came in December after the first rains and faded in February sunshine. Now in April it is summer, though there is not yet that blast of dry heat off the desert, exhilarating as a blizzard, testing your ability to take it. There are skylights at each end of the trailer. The glass can be and at this moment is opened, so that, as I recline here on my couch, I watch the sky go by.

Max sent me another carton of books. No more Thoreau. I acquired the journals, both of Thoreau and of Emerson, in a strange way. Fated, even. In a secondhand book store on Sixth Street in Los Angeles I first bought, for one dollar each, volumes three, four, and five of the 1906 Walden Edition of Thoreau's journals, edited by Bradford Torrey; beautiful books, with green leather spines and green marbleized backs. Some years later at Deplcr's great secondhand store on Geary in San Francisco, I found in the same binding and in the same 1906 edition (though at $2.50 now) the rest of the set—with the exception of volume seven. I am still looking for volume seven. When I find it, I'll be happy—and fearful. It's been a long search. Endings are ominous.

Emerson's journals I likewise acquired piecemeal in matching volumes in various cities—as if they, too, waited for me.

In the carton of new books I find two people agreeing with Thoreau about travel, homekeeping, simplicity, writing. Two are French; and Thoreau was only a couple of generations removed from France. The French writers are Colette and Georges Simenon.

On first thought Thoreau and Colette are very unlike: the French hedonist and the Yankee transcendentalist. On second thought they are very alike. You might even say that Colette was a Thoreau with sex. Colette had his love of the earth and its products. She loved animals more than he did. She was a family woman as he was a family man. She was as much a lover of, though perhaps not quite as skillful a user of, words as he. (This will be contradicted.) And she, like Thoreau, I discover, was a great reader of travel books. "But on the whole," her biographer Margaret Crossland says, "she might well have agreed that travel narrows the mind. For her the contemplation of her own room, or another woman's face, could be a journey long enough."

Thoreau agreed completely. "We need only travel enough to give our intellects an airing. In spite of Malthus and the rest, there will be plenty of room in the world if every man will mind his own business."

Malthus, not Thoreau, was right. What Thoreau considered a man's "own business" can't be ascertained exactly; but it certainly included staying at home instead of traveling, and there is very little proof that the stay-at-home is less procreative than the traveler. Tourism is not the cause of the population explosion and may even, when conducted by auto, help, through traffic accidents, to control it.

Thoreau was unable to anticipate another condition of modern life. He spent "forty years learning the language of these fields," and at the end of forty years the fields about Walden and Concord had not changed. I may still speak the language of the foothills of Yorba Linda, but if so, it is a language foreign to those hills. The wild mustard, the yellow violets, the Mariposa lilies, are gone. The hills are no longer blue with lupine or scarlet with Indian paintbrush. Sage, cactus, buckbrush, greasewood, toyon, wild tobacco, have been scraped away. The orange trees my father planted have been bulldozed, root and branch, from the land. If I want to find something like the fields whose language I speak, I must leave those early fields—and travel. One of the reasons I am so happy here is that I am able to re-enter the landscape of childhood. This is my Concord. Here are fields whose language I know: wind and dust and tawny colors and spring after the first rain.

Simenon, the Belgian-born French novelist, writes, "The place where I would like to live if I had the courage, or if I had no responsibilities, would be a home, a cabin as real as those stores." The stores Simenon refers to are trading posts or general stores, which he had encountered thirty years earlier. "Essential furniture of pine, partitions of fir, a stove, a pump in the corner, maybe a shelf for books." Simenon longs for what he calls the real, and defines the real as "that which relates directly to the life of human beings. That is, what makes it possible." But he can't have it because of "responsibilities."

He has a wife and four children. He can't, as can S. B., the editor of *The Whole Earth Catalog,* who has only a wife and two cats, "haul ass" in an Airstream and head for the desert.

Nor can he, as I can, who also have responsibilities (though not on Simenon's scale), live alone for a while in a cabin, with only essential furniture and a shelf for books. Wives, when their husbands leave them, even if only for "the real," customarily feel abandoned. Husbands, on the other hand, tend to feel liberated. Max, who has also been away from home a good deal while I have been here, on school business, cattle business, or hunting, has been happy to have me here, doing at last what I have so long talked of doing.

Tub, piano box, a room of my own, here a little house of my own—what have I been seeking? Womb remembered, tomb anticipated? The edifice isn't the answer. It's what the edifice, tub, or trailer provide: solitude. It is the universe, its inward flow unendangered by human distraction. There is a pattern of light and shadow on my floor, columns of light, pillars of dark, in which I can live as they shift and change. There is a whisper of wind around the lifted front shutter. There is the smell of deep, running water. With none of these riches—alone in a tar-paper shack, one spray of feverfew in the emptied tomato can, a pallet on the floor—there is an incandescence not found elsewhere. Is it perhaps a disease—this desire and this pleasure? The pursuit of loneliness? I have not pursued it hard enough. I have never found it in its painful form.

> *The state called solitude*
> *is filled with throngs;*
> *a silent place*
> *of winds and songs.*
>
> *It is a world that holds*
> *me solitary, seeing*
> *lamplight unfold*
> *in rings of endless being*

*until the clock, the lamp*
*are sunk in time*
*too deep for this hour's burning,*
*too deep for this room's chime.*

In the river below the bank on which the trailer is parked is a floating dock, used by summer visitors as a diving platform, and perhaps as boat dock, too. It is two or three feet wide and seven or eight feet long; there are steps that lead down to it. It rises and falls with the flow of the water, and since it is not much wider than I am, it frightens me to lie on it. But I do lie on it, head on a cushion, half Lily Maid of Astolat, half swinger in a watery hammock.

I always take a book or two with me, though I don't get much reading done down there, and when not reading, I have to be the bookshelf. I am with books, I think, as persons who have had too little to eat in childhood are with food: a hoarder, a glutton. I cannot take the shortest ride without taking a book with me. It is my security blanket. I say I want to be alone. But not without books. Perhaps that is to say I want people—for a book is a person—but people I can control: put down, take up, listen to, ignore.

As I walked down the steps this afternoon to my water bed, I had three books in my arms, and their feel and the descent of the stairs reminded me of one of my last visits at home in Whittier. I came down the stairs there from my bedroom with an armload of books. Mama, watching me, said, "You remind me of Jessamyn. That's just what she used to do." Then, shamefacedly, she said, "You *are* Jessamyn, aren't you?"

I don't know of any disease more cruel than the stroke, or of any series of strokes more cruel in their attack on a person than those Mama suffered. First, a stroke robbed her of her great but not her greatest glory: her use of words. She could still speak, but she could not call up the word she needed; she who had been able in the past not only to use all existing words but

296

to add to the store of those extant could not now determine whether "buy" or "sell" was the right word for the sentence she was framing.

When words came back to her, a treasure greater than words was taken: memory. She who had remembered the texture of a dress she wore in a swing at the age of four, and the words repeated from generation to generation of a great-great-grandfather, was unable to remember her own name. "Who am I?" she asked each morning at breakfast. "You are Grace Ann Milhous. You married Eldo West. You have four children. I am your eldest."

She kept a suitcase packed in her room. "I am ready to go home at any time." This was spoken in her own home. Where was "home" to her? Thirty or forty years had fallen out of her memory. Her voice became lighter, more girlish. Piano pieces she had not played for fifty years she played again. The husband she remembered was not this gray-haired old fellow who lived with her, but a strapping, black-haired, bronze-skinned heartbreaker. The old man, though a stranger, was gentlemanly, modest, and clean. The situation was perplexing. "He seems to think he belongs here. He says he has no other place to go. He showed me a book with his name in it."

"How did you know it was his name?"

"It's the same name as his mail. That comes here, too."

"Do you wish he would move out?"

"No. He's homeless except for this house. If he were a young fellow, I wouldn't put up with him for a minute. But he's old and homeless. Let him stay until Eldo comes back."

Mama had a weakness for the elderly, as her mother had (and I have) for the young. An old lady who believed she had gas in her head was a frequent week-long visitor at Mama's. An old man who thought of Mama as a daughter (she thought) wanted his back rubbed with arnica daily. The old lady whose husband had been the jailer of Pretty Boy Floyd and who had obviously lost her heart to Pretty Boy was a frequent visitor.

Those who want the young in their homes are nostalgic; they want to restore what has been lost in their own lives. Those who cherish the elderly are forward-looking; they hope that as they have done, they will be done by.

Mama was not sentimental about babies. I never heard her cluck or purr over a baby. Nor did she want, as producer of babies, any designating of days in her honor. She saved her tenderness for the old. Carmen said, "If only we could have been born old, Mama would have had a lot more sympathy for us." So though the old man who lived in the house with her was not her Eldo, he was old and hence deserving of care. He sometimes reminded her of a younger Eldo, as I had reminded her of a younger Jessamyn. This old man liked crossword puzzles and baseball and politics. He liked to read aloud. He wrote letters to editors. He could make biscuits—soda or baking-powder—better than any woman. All reminiscent of Eldo.

For whom was this five years more hellish? The woman who did not know who she was? Or the man who knew who he was and who his wife was, but could not gain from her a spark of recognition or remembrance?

I rocked on my watery couch thinking of those years and of how little of the burden of those times we, the four children, bore or even recognized. Mama, to those who did not know of her loss of memory, did not guess it. They were strangers to her, as we all were. In conversation that did not require her to recall anything beyond the past hour's sayings and happenings, she appeared not only normal but witty and alert. She observed a teen-aged grandson talking with evident pleasure to his sister. "You two should marry," she said. "You're both tall. You'd make a nice-looking couple."

"Grandma," said the grandson, clasping his grandmother and laughing, "you have made a boo-boo. I can't marry my sister."

Mama laughed, too. "Marrying your sister is worse than a

298

boo-boo. It's incest." She had regained words, but who was the sister whom she didn't know? Even so, trying to pair off a brother and sister was certainly laughable.

Most of our sympathy went to Mama. She was the obviously stricken one, though perhaps it is better to be able to pack your suitcase for a home you believe exists elsewhere than to live accepted as an intruder in the home you know is the only one you possess.

A favorite saying of Papa's was, "As a man marries, so is he." Papa had no inferiority complex. I asked a West cousin from Indiana who knew Wests as I didn't, "What would you say was the trait most common to the West family?" He didn't hesitate for a minute. "They all think well of themselves." Papa thought well of himself by nature. Nevertheless he gave the credit for whatever he had become or achieved to Mama.

When he was in his mid-thirties he wrote to his wife, who was visiting in Indiana with her father:

"You ask, do I *miss you?* Grace, I can scarcely bear to think of it. If I meditate on that subject a moment, my heart comes up in my throat and chokes me. I want you so much sometimes I think I can't live without you another minute. I can't sleep. I lay awake for hours thinking of you.

"Grace, do you know that you are my sweetheart, my love, my pet, my everything that's good and pure, sweet and lovable? Your love is worth more to me than all else. I care nothing for money, fame, or power. You are all in all to me. How I long to hold you in my arms and love you, to kiss your rosy lips and feel the touch of your velvety cheek against mine. I can't stand to live without you much longer. You must come home soon."

It's a pity that I, then thirteen, couldn't have read this letter. Rosy lips? Velvety cheeks? I who thought my mother plain, who saw the freckles instead of the velvet and roses; I who didn't care about pure, sweet, good, and lovable but wanted decorum, order, and grandmotherliness might have had my eyes opened; though the chances are that what I saw would have been what I regarded as my father's silliness, rather than my mother's virtues.

Papa continued to write Mama after she died. He sent the letters to me—rough drafts followed by polished, condensed versions, as if postal rates to heaven might be heavy and literary standards there high.

He speculated about their meeting in heaven but, on the whole, feared it might be disappointing. "Bodies don't go to heaven," he wrote her, "and some of our happiest times have been physical." He toned this down a bit in his second version, whether out of regard for heavenly sensibilities or for literary reason. The second version read, "I long to meet you in heaven, though neither of us will ever forget, I know, our hours on earth." Spirits long departed might not understand these earthly references, but Grace, so lately departed, would understand.

I did what I almost never do: went to sleep without planning to, afloat on my watery raft. I had rested quietly; the books were still stacked neatly on my stomach when I awakened. I had never before been down on the raft so late. This is the hour for walking, not napping. But lying there, I saw what I had never before seen: the mud hens, eyeball to eyeball, passing by. They gave me the feeling I have lying in my berth on a train when the cars of another train pass by: the feeling that it is I who am moving.

The mud hens, who from trailer-view appear to move on the water as legless as Chinese court ladies, have, plain to see at water level, salmon-colored feet working underwater like stately paddles. Many looked me directly in the eye, a black beady gaze, as they passed. They did not pause or turn their heads. One look was enough. I was flotsam or jetsam to them. They were, I knew, rolling up the afterglow; but down in the afterglow myself, I could not see the operation. I was a soldier too deep in the conflict to have any notion of how the battle was going.

After I awakened, I saw a man on the other side of the river, coat over his shoulder, carrying a small bag, followed by a man carrying a suitcase. The man with a coat over his shoulder looked like Max. For a minute or two I was convinced that it was Max. What he was doing on that side of the river I didn't know. Then I thought, He flew to the airport, hired a car, the car broke down, and now he is coming, with the driver carrying his suitcase, to shout to me to take the car across the bridge to the other side, where I can pick them up. It was a foolish idea. I could not possibly have heard a word from the other side, even though shouted into a bull horn. But it was an idea that permitted me to believe for a minute or two that the hurrying man was Max. He hurried right on into a house on the Arizona side. After that I lay there for a while, companioned by mud hens, filled with disappointment. The disappointment was followed by decision. Go home. Who did I think I was? Huck Finn on his raft?

I remembered Max's and my arrival. We had come down the Owens Valley on the eastern side of the Sierra Nevada, with strong gusty winds hitting us broadside all the way to Victorville. As we passed Victorville, we saw at the foot of the next range of mountains a wall of dust, half the height of the mountains themselves. Yet why should there be so much more dust over there than where we were? Was the land more cultivated there, hence more loose topsoil? A heavier wind? Finally Max said, "There is a forest fire. That is smoke."

All conjectures were wrong. We were running into smog. We had arrived in Southern California. If the smog hadn't told us so, the increase in number of roadside eating places and service stations, and signs advertising both, would have. As the nervous system becomes more calloused with the variety and strength of the lights, the weirdness of the wording increases; stronger lights flash more often; buildings become more eccentric; names more outlandish are devised. A kind of mad abstract novel of merchandising unfolds. The roadside looks like one of the *New Yorker*'s recent illustrated stories. You can't read the signs exactly, but we knew, at least, what the message was: buy. There were combinations of words, syllables we had never heard or seen, singly or combined, before.

"Have you been to the Hokamatatutu?" the sign read.

"Hokamatatutu? What does that mean?" I asked.

"Damned if I know," said Max. "Let's find out."

What it meant was a building put together of old cars, steamship fittings, smokestacks, old toilet-bowl flowerpots, transparent gasoline tanks for fish bowls. Behind the bar was a large fish tank inhabited by an enormous, gray, sinuous fish, scarcely fish-shaped, more like a piece of the large intestine of an elephant kept alive as brains in science fiction are kept alive outside the body; except that this intestine had large, predatory red eyes. In the tank with the intestine were four goldfish, who kept to the corners of the tank. Each day the intestine engulfs five. Sometimes one at a time and at long intervals. Sometimes, in a frenzy of goldfish hunger, it snaps up four or five at a single eating. The intestine swims very near the surface of the water; the goldfish stay at the lowest possible level, scurrying from artificial flower to artificial flower. If you remain at the bar long enough, you may enjoy the sight of cannibalism. Many evidently do. The bar was crowded, and the barkeeper took bets on the time between meals and the number of courses. It was almost Roman.

Through this we must backtrack if we head homeward. But we are old Southern Californians ourselves and more inured to Hokamatatutus (or -tui?) than most.

Max will be here in five days. He had business near Boise, cattle on a cattle ranch, the dream of his life. He takes great pleasure in walking among those square-headed, stiff-legged, rollicking Black Angus calves. I can't do it myself. I may not eat *them,* but I will eat their brothers. Is it sentimental to refuse to enjoy the life of those whose death you plan and whose flesh you will ingest? If I think flesh eating wrong, why not give it up? Would I be able to touch those velvet muzzles then? I doubt it. Little Black Angus, I know where you are going. I am one of those sending you there. For this reason I don't often go out with Max to look at the cattle. Perhaps it is a hangover from my stanchion complex. Perhaps I should go to India and be a cow worshiper.

In any case, Max will fly from Boise to Las Vegas; from Las Vegas to the airport at Mesquite, where I will pick him up. Then we'll decide what to do next.

Now that I am leaving, everything else takes on for me the farewell, sorrowful, abandoned look of places and people from whom I am departing.

People can walk away from me and do, and they thus save me the pain I feel when I do the parting. This is worse than sentimental. It is egocentric. I am like the thief in Papa's song who leaped onto the train singing, "Don't you, don't you, grieve after me." Do I think rivers and hills—and people— will grieve after me? It would be easier, though, if the river dried up; if Iron Mountain collapsed and the wild burros who won't come near me anyway galloped off into the Borego Desert. I am equipped to stand loss, but not to inflict it.

That is one reason travel is difficult. You must constantly leave what you love. For a long time I was afflicted with the need of pronouncing a benediction of departure. From any room I had occupied—a room in my parents' home, in a motel or hotel, alone or companioned—I could not, bags packed, last drawer inspected once again for forgotten possessions, take my leave without a prayer (prayer is, I suppose, the name for it). The words were not pronounced aloud. Nevertheless I said them with all my being. "O room, bless and keep you." Not thanks for any comfort or happiness I had known there, not supplications for the well-being of future tenants, though some of both was implied in my parting benediction. Mostly, it seems to me, I said farewell to what I was leaving behind: a roomful of solitude. I looked back into the room before I left, so filled with its own emptiness, and wondered, as a man sneaking away from a sweet wife wonders (I suppose) how he can do it. Where will I find anything else as good? I ask myself this question as I look back into that empty, humming silence.

So, with the days here numbered, I gaze about me with increasing tenderness. The temperament that values most what it is about to lose is not a happy one. I love the departing guest as I do not the guest who is arriving. "Leave me and I will love you"? No, it is not that bad. And that temperament, though it has its shortcomings, has its merits. What happens is usually better than anything anticipated, and what is remembered is usually better than either. Expect nothing and you are frequently happily surprised. The grass never looks greener to me on the other side of the fence. It often is, of course. The name for the person with this kind of eyesight is "stick-in-the-mud."

I said to Spry last night, "Do you want to go home?" I don't know whether it was the word "home" or the tone of my voice that roused him from his doze. He sat up, ears uplifted. "Do you want to see Lobo? Spec? One-Eye? Two-Eye? Fat Cat? Little Mama?" He became more and more excited as he heard the names he knows. He jumped down from my bed and went to the door as if to welcome them.

In my early days of reading Thoreau, before I understood that what he wrote about himself was in no way factually autobiographical, I searched *Walden* and the journals for some mention of Christmas pleasure. He was as mum about that subject as about the pencils he made; which may mean, since we know the pencils were made, that he hung up his sock regularly every December twenty-fourth but didn't care to record the fact. I searched his writing for mention of pets. Except for the cats he fondled after he was housebound, Thoreau was evidently petless.

Henry Beetle Hough, in *Tuesday Will Be Different*, says that the Thoreau Society made a mistake when it reported that Thoreau "kept a dog to stir up the dead air in a room." This is as wild a notion as I ever heard, and I was happy to have Hough refute it. Thoreau said in his journal, August 11, 1852, writes Hough, that his friend Channing kept a dog "to stir up the air of a room when dead." I wish Thoreau had said what *he* thought of that idea of Channing's. Spry breaks wind now and then, but whether this can be considered stirring up the dead air of a room, I don't know. Better, it seems to me, let sleeping dogs lie, and leave dead air unstirred.

In the night a sentence came to me. I thought it truly described Thoreau. I told myself to remember it, but feared as I went to sleep that I probably wouldn't. I did. The sentence was in my mind as I awakened. "He bore witness." My God, how he bore witness! Many have done this; the value of the undertaking lies in what was witnessed and how the report is made. What Thoreau wanted to bear witness to, he said, was the joy he had known. Men, he said, lead lives of quiet desperation, and there was undoubtedly desperation in his life; but what he wanted to bear witness to was the joy he had known. And this he did. "Joy" was the word I remembered, but checking through the Thoreau quotations in my journal, I find that Thoreau also said, "I wish to communicate those parts of my life which I would gladly live again myself." And again, "I am eager to report the glory of the universe." "Joy" is my word, as well as Thoreau's, for communicating "those parts of my life which I would gladly live again," and for reporting "the glory of the universe."

All life is a leave-taking. The Muscatatuck near where I was born still flows. The Santa Ana, where once I lay on my back like an otter, is no more. Soon its very bed will be lost to sight, as the Los Angeles river bed has disappeared between walls of cement. The Colorado, too big to be completely manhandled, still winds snakelike but with fangs pulled. Water from these

rivers had made the desert bloom, though "bloom" is a eu-
phemism. The desert has been made to house tycoons and
produce artichokes. The mountains still stand. We are the
earth eaters, but so far we have not been able to gulp down
Whitney or the Marysville Buttes or Old Saddleback, though
we alter them with our roads and casinos and ski lifts. The
foothills have become platforms for tract houses. There are
more flowery names for subdivisions today than there were
sonnets in Elizabethan times, the object of composition being
the same: to gain possession of what is desired.

With the time I'll be here growing shorter, I revisit the
places I have known. Another person might be intent, in the
little time left, on seeing what he had thus far missed. Not I. I
revisit those places encrusted with my feeling about them.
Three months has changed— I started to say "them." They, I
suppose, are unchanged; what has changed is my feeling about
them. One is capable of only so much emotion about an event
anticipated but never occurring. In flash-flood canyon I ran out
of my fear of a flash flood. It is then, when fear disappears,
that the flash flood claims its victims. First it makes us trustful;
then it strikes. Nevertheless Spry and I now clamber over the
loose boulders and through the tortured inhuman crevasses
like visitors to a harmless man-made wonder. Familiarity has
not bred contempt but carelessness. Today two boys on mini-
bikes roared past us, bouncing like bellowing mountain goats
from boulder to boulder. Who can feel fear where mini-bikes,
straddled by twelve-year-olds, penetrate?

Spry and I waited, far up in the canyon, for the boys to leave.
I wanted what might be my last walk there unmarred by mini-
bike roar. The boys ascended and descended, again and again
hypnotized by the rocketing difficulty. Spry and I had both to
be spry, to keep out of their way. For the irony of it, I was almost willing to be struck down in a canyon where I had feared
nature by something as unnatural as a mini-bike. "Death by
mini-bike." I who had so much feeling for what might have

306

happened here in the past would at last, in death, be with it—also dead, but part of the living present.

It was twilight before the boys left, and darker than twilight at the bottom of the canyon, which the sun enters only at midday. Spry and I went along cautiously. It would be one thing to die by mini-bike; quite another to crack your skull through an awkward step on an untimely evening ramble.

By the time we reached the highway, though it seemed bright to me after leaving the canyon's dark tunnel, some cars had already turned on their headlights. I picked up Spry, though I had him on a leash, as I always do when near the road, opened the gate and closed it, and there paused. Son, stumbling a bit, was coming down from the riverbank toward his and Lily's cabin on the other side of the road. I didn't want to encounter Son in a stumbling state, so I waited, Spry in my arms, inside the gate, until Son should be in his own home.

He never made it there. His dear, trained-to-kiss Blackie ran out to meet him. (Lily, who had gone out to sketch for the day, was still, with her Scout, absent.) In the semidarkness I wasn't absolutely sure what happened next. Did the bitch entangle herself with Son's legs? Did he stumble and fall onto her? In any case he fell; she yelped. Son raised himself slowly and stood, his long-time obedient servant by his side. Now Son, upright though weaving, gave the dog he had trained to kiss him a tremendous kick broadside. Son, carried forward by the energy of his kick, fell down on all fours. I don't know how Son looked to the dog. Would she have bitten him if he had been standing upright? Perhaps so. Perhaps the bite she gave him now was less for the kick she had just received than for the compulsory kisses of months past. Blackie was an animal; she had her own ways of expressing affection, and kissing wasn't one of them. Kiss, kiss, kiss. Especially if visitors were around. Then the bitch (I then imagined myself to be) said to herself, "I'll give you a kiss with some teeth in it." It was Son's turn to yelp.

What followed was very strange. I do not know whether Son could not get to his feet or whether out of bravado he said to *himself,* "I'll beat you at your own game, on all fours." In any case the fight, for such it had become, proceeded not *mano a mano* but *animo a animo;* a fight with the teeth and on all fours for both.

I did not know what I could do, or whom to help, if I did anything. Surely I was for the man, against the animal? For man against nature? I wouldn't stand still while a dog tore Son to shreds? But I was equally sure I wouldn't stand still while Son tore this good animal to shreds. My sympathies were with the animal. She had been humiliated, made for no good reason to deny her animality and serve Son's vanity.

Son was evidently not being torn to shreds. Blackie was motionless and howling. Son was also motionless; his face pressed against his dog, and his teeth, I supposed, clamped on some tender part of her anatomy. Suddenly Son, who had been on all fours, toppled forward, face down, and lay still. The bitch stood unmoving beside him.

Then I went forward. Though Son's cause in the fight was not just, I did not for that reason feel justified in condemning him to bleed to death. I found him in no danger of bleeding to death. He had one bite, not deep or bleeding much, in the calf; one gash, Blackie's last kiss, low on his left cheek. He was unconscious, but not from his wounds, and suffering no pain. The night was warm, and Lily would soon be home. I left Son where he had fallen.

I tried to persuade Blackie to come home with me. She had a torn and bleeding ear. But she was Son's bitch in peace as in war, and she wouldn't leave his side. She settled down beside him, as she had many a night before.

In ten or fifteen minutes I heard Lily's Scout and Blackie barking. I didn't leave the trailer to go down to help Lily. I thought she would rather I didn't.

Spry slept. The river flowed past, silent as always. The leaves of the cottonwood trees sang their papery song in the night breeze. I hoped the coyotes would give me one last farewell concert. They did not open their mouths. I wished for a sound, but any human voice seemed too loud. I wished I had, as the Chinese do, a cricket in a cage to chirp. Chirping was about the only song I felt up to.

Always, when I walked in the canyon, I experienced the frustration of not being a geologist. There, I was like a man with a book, who cannot read, but who is convinced that on the pages he cannot decipher are hidden messages of utmost importance to him. That night in my cabin the whole world, as well as the canyon, took on the appearance of a book I was too illiterate to read.

Up the lane lay a man with the faith to heal; shut from himself, even; destructive; so that one he had loved and misused had turned on him with teeth bared. The wounded river flowed past. For the sake of cottonwoods the beavers had been ousted from their territory. The burros had made a break for it; they had found a reverse gear and had shifted from tame to wild. The road runner was still his own man. The coyotes sang their own song. The mud hens toiled—it was their nature, it seemed —like factory workers: out in the morning, home in the evening. There was some message in all of this. Even my presence was part of the message. I did not know what it was. I could trace the inscription, describe it, but not decode it.

Watching Max's plane come in—the Cessna, in which he had departed, with Bruce again at the controls—I had the feeling that I was seeing, as in a movie, a film run backward. This was his leave-taking run in reverse. The three months had been dreamed. Nothing had changed. Even Hazel's husband (I never learned *his* name) was there, with his truckload of gasoline. The plane, for some reason, came in low, lifted, and circled once more. When it finally settled, I ran toward it, waving.

As I did so, I yelled back to Hazel's husband, "Look, I'm waving!" He stared at me in astonishment. He had forgotten that I was the nonwaver to whom he had given advice in January. Max still remembered *me*. He waved back. Lucky for me.

LEARNING RESOURCES

CENTER

East Peoria, Illinois